ALL KINDS OF MAGIC

PIERS MOORE EDE has worked as a farmer, boat driver, surfing instructor, poetry teacher and baker. He has travelled widely, and contributed to many literary, travel and environmental publications including the *Daily Telegraph*, the *Times Literary Supplement*, *Ecologist*, *Traveller* and *Earth Island Journal*. He is the author of *Honey and Dust*, winner of a D.H. Lawrence Prize for Travel Writing.

ALL KINDS OF MAGIC

A Quest for Meaning in a Material World

Piers Moore Ede

BLOOMSBURY

LONDON · BERLIN · NEW YORK · SYDNEY

First published in Great Britain 2010
This paperback edition published 2011

Copyright © 2010 by Piers Moore Ede

The moral right of the author has been asserted

Bloomsbury Publishing, London, Berlin, New York and Sydney

36 Soho Square, London WID 3QY

A CIP catalogue record for this book is available from the British Library

ISBN 978 1 4088 0962 4
10 9 8 7 6 5 4 3 2 1

Typeset by Hewer Text UK Ltd, Edinburgh

Printed in Great Britain by Clays Ltd, St Ives plc

MIX
Paper from
responsible sources
FSC® C018072

www.bloomsbury.com/piersmooreede

LOTTERY FUNDED

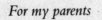

For my parents

All kinds of magic are out of date and done away with, except in India, where nothing changes in spite of the shiny, top-scum stuff that people call 'civilization'.

(Rudyard Kipling, *Plain Tales from the Hills*)

Prologue

From the parapet, I looked down on to a vast plain, ringed at its far edge by mountains. There were no animals, only a few stunted trees. In this low-oxygen world, there wasn't even enough moisture in the air for snow to fall. Sheltered from the rain-bearing clouds of the Indian monsoon by the Great Himalaya, only a portion of Ladakh receives snowfall. Today it was minus fifteen, so cold it burned.

On the edge of the plain, a lone monk ascended the zigzag path. He walked methodically, hands clasped behind his back. I imagined him chanting, as monks are trained to do, a mantra to keep his mind empty. *Om Mane Padme Hum. Om Mane Padme Hum. Om Mane Padme Hum.*

Behind me, the long rumbling blast of the *zangstung*, an eight-foot-long copper horn, told me something was happening. Turning, I saw that the crowd – hundreds of villagers who had flocked here for this winter festival – had fallen still, and were looking fretfully up at the highest parapet of the monastery. They wore long homespun robes of maroon and ochre, some of the women sporting turquoise and coral headdresses known as *peraks*. Eyes blinked fast in the Himalayan light. Dark skin, deeply wrinkled from altitude, faces frowning in apprehension.

'Soon, the oracles will come,' whispered a Ladakhi child to her mother in front of me. She crouched fearfully in her mother's skirts, pink cheeks sucking in air.

These oracles were the reason I was here. For hundreds of years, monks that live in this remote Shangri-La have maintained a practice which may come from shamanism, the tradition of *lhabas*: oracles who enter trance states to commune with spirits and demons. There are many oracles in Ladakh, both villagers and monks, but none are considered as powerful as the ones I was about to see. For the previous three months, the two monks who provide the vehicle for the spirits had meditated silently in a remote cave. Once a day a meal was left outside the cave mouth and, for a time, the monks uncrossed their legs to eat and perform ablutions. Then they began again. Any less discipline than this, it is claimed, and they may lack the strength to carry the spirits. Failure can result in madness or physical collapse, perhaps even death.

But in these states, the Ladakhis believe, great knowledge and wisdom can be found. The oracles come into contact with the *chos skyong*, a group of deities assigned to protect Tibetan Buddhists against adversaries. They can be wrathful and assume a terrifying disposition. But if the medium is able to placate the deity, and the right offerings are made, he may learn things outside the human order entirely: the method to win battles and triumph over enemies, the ability to cure the most serious diseases, even knowledge of the future.

Much of this information came to me through a young monk, Khedup, who'd approached me that morning, beaming behind his hand-cut John Lennon glasses. He was studying to be an *amchi*, a traditional Tibetan doctor, but said that in order to gain entrance to the famous medical college in Darjeeling, he must first practise his English. It was good

2

fortune for both of us, for without Khedup I would have understood little of all this. Tibetan Buddhism is, at best, a highly esoteric religion. But of its oracles, even less is known. Like the miraculous saints of the Catholic tradition, opinions about them remain divided, the modernists embarrassed by this link to a mystic past.

'Why are the villagers so nervous?' I asked Khedup.

'Oracles are very powerful,' he said, scanning the monastery parapet again, as more *zangstung* lowed their eerie notes. 'They are like wild animals, but with the strength of ten men. No one can control them. But there is one more thing people fear,' he added. 'When the oracles first appear today, if they are wearing a red ribbon on their heads it will mean something very bad for us in the coming year. A warning.'

'What kind of thing?'

'Famine or war. Perhaps some natural disaster. The oracles see things beyond our own sight.'

Above us, the final horn blast died out. In a second, the entire courtyard of Matho monastery had fallen silent; not a single cough. Hundreds of villagers peered upwards, some of them shielding their eyes with weathered hands.

The oracles had arrived.

At the Back of the Wardrobe

As a child, I was fascinated by magic. Wardrobes whose backs invited access to Narnia. Arabian carpets which flew. Magi who could summon storms with a gesture of their hands. In old houses I would knock, occasionally, upon the backs of old wardrobes, anxious for the crunch of snow under my feet.

Aged seven, all of that changed. 'Knowledge,' as Francis Bacon once said, 'is power' – or at least that was the way my mother had intended it. She'd told me about Father Christmas in case I found out inadvertently at school, believing that the truth would come better from her than in the schoolyard. In my case, however, the overwhelming feeling was one of disempowerment, loss of possibility, a kind of grave disappointment. It wasn't the deception that bothered me so much as the fact that, without magic, the world was suddenly intensely mundane. Behind the curtain, the Wizard of Oz was just a man moving levers, and it made me feel – for want of a better metaphor – like a priest disillusioned of his faith.

By my twenties, I'd come to accept the muted normality of things. In the wake of magic there were job ladders to climb, health insurance forms, the myriad distractions of city life. I put my shoulder to the wheel like everyone else, and yet even as I went through the motions, something was whispering in the back of my mind: a gnawing hunger for more. There was nothing I could put my *faith* in amongst all this. Nothing that provided significance and meaning. I was part of a generation sated by more material wealth than any before us in history, yet I felt a starving of the spirit.

For a long time I disregarded this feeling, or merely tried to blot it out through ever more elaborate mechanisms of escape. I travelled as much as possible, always convinced that the truly unique place was around the corner. I was that quintessential late-twentieth-century vagrant: arriving on one tiny atoll after another, looking for the lost Eden that would match the one I had in my head.

Music was another distraction. I collected records obsessively, and spent a good portion of my time in private communion with the recordings of long-dead jazz musicians. Somehow, the notes had the capacity to lift me up beyond the ordinary world, to a place where I was no longer hungry. Books and films also had this power and I sucked them in voraciously, finding temporary reprieve from my restlessness in one kind of narrative or another. But when the book ended, or the song, there was my mind again, never satisfied with the moment.

After I survived a major hit-and-run accident at the age of twenty-five, the restlessness became something more serious. Having stared death in the face, I found the futility of my daily existence unbearable. Unable to find purpose in anything, I spiralled into a depression that left me cut off from friends and family, unable to enjoy the tastes of food or to feel any hope for the future. For months I scarcely left the house, numbing reality with whatever tools I had available. I felt like a spectre trapped in a human body: a ray of sunlight could pass right through me.

Finally, it was a strange series of events that set me on the path to recovery. I went to work on a farm in Italy, and spent several months learning how to keep bees. This experience had a profound effect on me. As well as quietening a troubled mind, it allowed a renewed sense of wonder to take root. Peering into the teeming ecosystems of the hive, I found myself falling in love with life again. Back in England, I conceived of the journey that I would later record in a book entitled *Honey and Dust*: a search for wild honey and the tribes who still hunted it. For a year I travelled in search of sweetness, finding, in each spoonful, a new lease of life.

But if *Honey and Dust* began with a search for the simple product of the honey bee, it ended with a different question in mind. As my mind began to heal itself and I weaned myself off the deadening antidepressants, I wondered what it was that had brought me so close to the edge. The accident provided a convenient excuse but it seemed clear that all of this had been building for a long time. Neither did I suppose that I was alone in my existential dilemmas. Amongst my friends in London, a huge proportion seemed to be battling demons of one kind or another, taking pills to bring them up or down, for sleep or wakefulness. With the Office for National Statistics now suggesting one in four British adults will experience a mental health problem in any given year, it seems that many of us are leading lives of quiet desperation.

But why *are* so many of us struggling to lead happy, fulfilled lives? Despite all the advances of our civilisation, something elemental seems to have fallen through the cracks: a simple contentment. Environmental writer Gregg

Easterbrook phrased it perfectly when he wrote: 'capitalism renders its chosen covetous, insecure, unfulfilled, constantly twitching . . . Materialist obsession has performed the amazing feat of making unprecedented abundance unsatisfactory to its beneficiaries.'

It was in India – a country that has yet to reap many of the benefits of twenty-first-century materialism – that I was struck by a revelation of sorts. En route for the Annapurna foothills, I had my first experience of a country which seemed, to use an unavoidable word, 'magical'. Despite enormous poverty and social problems, the Indians seemed to have an awareness of their place in the scheme of things very different from our own. Although anxious neither to idealise the East nor demonise the West, I couldn't help but see a thread of *meaning* in Indian life, long since exorcised from my own culture. It was the meaning provided by religion, and it was evident in a thousand sparkling details on any given day: a rickshaw wallah touching his statue of Ganesh before a journey, a smouldering incense stick or the Muslim call to prayer, echoing through the dawn. Despite having been an atheist for as long as I can remember, I found this intensely moving.

Clearly, when one describes India as 'magical', it means something other than any reference to the supernatural. Perhaps closer to what was meant by German theologian Rudolf Otto when he coined the word 'numinous'. For Otto, the word suggested divine majesty, the intense feeling of unknowingly knowing that there is something which cannot be seen; it alludes to the holy and the transcendent. More than any specific religious connotation, it was *this* which made me feel so alive in India. Inside my rational, empirically driven culture nothing was allowed a significance beyond itself. But in India, the opposite felt true.

Everything, both animate and inanimate, was filled with a living spirit.

When I returned to London, this memory of the numinous stayed with me. Like nowhere I'd ever been, India seemed to shine in my mind's eye as somewhere alive with possibility. It was, in many ways, the very feeling I'd had as a child, believing in a more literal kind of magic. It was what I felt peering into the seamless unity of the beehive, or in the long wailing tones of a jazz solo. It was what I felt standing on the banks of the Ganges, the water lit up by devotional oil lamps, each one of them glinting with light.

That feeling, it seemed clear, was one of the richest, most compelling in all human experience. And yet to actively seek it out seemed close to impossible. Was it magic I was interested in finding, or mystical experience? What was it about these moments of heightened awareness which seemed to give my life a significance beyond itself?

Despite these uncertainties, a journey was already plotting itself on the maps within me. I would return to India, to seek out in its burning ghats (cremation grounds) and mountain villages, some understanding of what the numinous really was. I would look for mystics, who hold there to be a fundamental unity beneath the surface of day-to-day phenomena. I would find oracles, shamans and the itinerant *sadhus* for whom the material world is nothing more than an illusion. Perhaps I would even find the supernatural itself, that most ancient lure for Westerners heading East. Despite the much vaunted economic miracles of the new India, could it be possible that a different kind of magic remained?

This rather unconventional journey, I was forced to admit, was as much in revolt against something as in search of something else. I wished to leave behind me the reductive materialism that now governs Western life. For Francis Crick, the molecular biologist who co-discovered the DNA molecule, ' "You", your joys and your sorrows, your memories and your ambitions, your sense of personal identity and free will, are in fact no more than the behaviour of a vast assembly of nerve cells and their associated molecules.' This seemed to me to be the kind of notion that was not only pushing our society to the brink but was sending so many others, like myself, to yoga classes and t'ai chi centres, in the hope of uncovering some essential meaning.

Perhaps, too, it was pushing others elsewhere: towards fundamentalism, with its own remedies against the fear and uncertainty of the modern world; towards the cult of personality in which we idealise 'celebrities' whose lives seem to have some importance denied our own. At the heart of our alienation lurks a deep yearning for fulfilment, a basic human need for coherence. In my own life that coherence had generally eluded me, but now I was going out to find it.

It was approaching autumn when I packed my small bag for departure. Sodden ochre leaves clogged the gutters along the Caledonian Road. En route for the train, I passed two women carrying yoga bags beneath their arms and I wondered how many other people, even now, were stretched out on yoga mats across Britain, and whether, if enough of us reached for these states of consciousness, we might begin to turn the tide against the spiritual vacuum which seemed to lie at the heart of Western life.

My own small journey would be to follow this river to its source. It would be a journey concerned less with facts than with feelings, less with proof than wonder. I would follow the clues wherever they took me, seek out anyone who might help me draw the veil aside. But for now I was at the journey's beginning: standing outside the old wardrobe, a child again, willing it to let me in.

The Miracle of the Buddha Tree

Just after dawn, the first passengers on the train began to wake. Beneath me, Mr Gulparna, retired auditor, stretched out first one pyjama-covered leg from his lower bunk, then a second. I watched him blearily through a half-closed eye as he enacted five half-hearted attempts to touch his toes, then five slightly more spirited knee bends. Stretches completed, and just a little out of breath, he gathered his metal beaker, Neem powder for the gums, an enormous crimson comb and a tall bottle of cologne. Tucking all this beneath his arms, he pushed the curtain aside and went to queue for the bathroom.

I drifted back into sleep, coming awake again as the familiar refrain 'Chai, chai' echoed down the corridor. The morning's first tea seller had boarded the train, and grateful passengers were sitting up in their bunks, reaching into trouser pockets for three rupees, then tilting back the first important chai to jostle away the cobwebs of sleep.

Someone opened a window and a blast of cold air testified that we had come north.

I was on my way to Darjeeling, where, so the rumour had it, a miracle was under way. On the top of a blustery hill a tree had assumed the perfect form of Siddhartha Gautama, the Buddha himself. As if from the pages of some dime-store novel, a drunk had been sleeping it off in the bushes when he opened his eyes, stared in disbelief at the form of the pine tree in front of him, then ran into town proclaiming that he had witnessed a true miracle. Whether he had thrown away his grog wasn't mentioned but it had, in any case, reached the pages of several newspapers.

Like the thousands of seekers before me, a miracle seemed to me entirely in keeping with my expectations of India. Even now, as the country reached the height of an economic boom begun in the early 1990s, we arrived in our droves seeking some antidote to the pressures of Western life. Despite the protests of a slew of Orientalist scholars who claim that we have fashioned the East to our own liking, the image seemed impossible to shrug off. Even the latest slogan of the tourist board, 'Incredible India', seemed designed to emphasise the notion that here we would find things too extraordinary and improbable to be believed.

Last night, during a round of gin rummy, I'd discussed my own motives with Mr Gulparna. With the night gathering around us, we were drinking Bagpiper whisky and whiling away the journey with a round of cards. The third hand was taken up by the man in bunk 12c, who merely referred to himself as 'Wing Commander', former helicopter pilot for the Indian navy.

'Miracles,' said Mr Gulparna wistfully. 'They do not happen like they used to. When I was a boy they occurred weekly. For us they were nothing special.'

'Do you remember the Ganesh Milk Miracle?' said the Wing Commander in his plummy voice, dealing the cards. 'It was 1994, when all over India, icons of the elephant god began accepting offerings of milk. I myself took a saucer of milk to my local temple and Ganapati reached out his trunk and slurped it up. I am not making this up, dear fellow. It was clear as day.'

'I also saw this,' said Mr Gulparna. 'I am a rational man, not inclined to believe in such things. But my wife's Ganesh was drinking milk *thirstily*. Scientists tried to claim it was capillary action, the natural absorbent properties of stone, but I don't believe it. This was a true miracle! My wife's Ganesh is made of bronze. How could it absorb milk?'

As the night progressed, I wondered whether my interest in the miraculous would have been received so lightly by someone of the younger generation. Many young people I spoke to seemed to resent the continual string of Western seekers following the well-trodden path to the East. And who could blame them? They were lifting themselves up by the bootstraps, finding economic freedom their parents could never have dreamed of. That all these Westerners should come here asserting the need to leave the material world behind was both patronising and faintly hilarious. They wanted what we had, we wanted what they had. The twain, it was now undeniable, were meeting head on and sparks were flying.

Mr Gulparna's generation, however, seemed receptive to my questions. For them faith was the mortar which held India together, and the miraculous merely evidence of what was already known. As we played cards, grew mildly drunk and munched piquant samosas from a Tupperware box, he told me of great saints who could fly through the air, how the distinctly polluted seawater outside Mahim Creek in Mumbai had recently turned sweet, thousands coming to drink it. Outside, the train rocked and lurched over the tracks in 4/4 time.

'Only a few months back,' said the Wing Commander, flicking a morsel of pastry from his RAF-style moustache, 'a Hindu family was cooking their morning chapatti when they turned it over in the pan to receive a nasty shock.'

'What was it?' Mr Gulparna and I asked.

The Wing Commander looked grave. 'In block capitals, the world ALLAH was written on the chapatti!'

Almost two days later, 500 rupees down and with a sawdust taste in the mouth, I departed at Siliguri, the largest city in north Bengal and the jump-off for the Himalayan foothills. The seasons had changed overnight; the palm trees replaced by cold-weather pines. After a few rounds of haggling, I found a shared Tata jeep heading north to Darjeeling, checked that the tyre treads were at least vaguely in evidence and crammed myself in with a family of eight for the winding route upwards. It was mid-morning by this stage, on a misty, inclement Sunday. The sky was patterned with grey-tipped clouds.

The eldest member of our retinue, a snowy-haired matriarch in a resplendent purple sari, was the first to prepare me for the weather ahead. '*Tanda lege jabey*,' she said in nasal Bengali: 'You'll catch cold.' This was accurate, for as the jeep ascended, the mercury seemed to go into freefall. By the time we'd made it halfway, at about 4,000 feet, a brittle sleet was drumming the windscreen. Outside, amidst the chest-high bushes of emerald tea, plantation workers drew their shawls more tightly around their shoulders, plumes of cold breath issuing from their mouths.

Despite the weather, I felt a surge of excitement as we travelled up into the hills. As the road steepened, the villages grew further apart, the hillsides a deeper shade of green, and the air so pure it smarted in the nostrils. In the shadow of a tea bush I saw a pheasant – strangely reminiscent of home – and later the famous 'toy train', one of the last working steam locomotives in India, chugging past us, its 'coal wallah' offering a sooty thumbs up.

By early evening I was in Darjeeling. It was sub-zero, a dense mist obscuring the valley floor, the town all but boarded up for the winter. Straggled along the ridge, the shops and cafés were silent and forlorn, the faded grandeur of the Raj disappearing beneath a patina of orange rust. Globalisation has not been kind to the tea industry here, with plummeting commodity prices causing unemployment and social unrest in these hills. In the winter, tourism dwindles to almost nothing, and the streets return again to a mixture of tea merchants, Tibetan refugees and the red-robed monks drawing worn prayer beads through their hands. I was glad I'd come.

That night the temperature dropped so low I couldn't sleep. Cocooned in musty blankets in one of the few guesthouses still open for winter trade, I sat and read by candlelight, frost vapour pooling in the glow. My room was an ice-box of unpainted concrete, its window permanently glued shut. Shivering, I finally ventured downstairs to persuade the caretaker to fill my hiking flask with boiling water. Wrapped in a wool sock, this impromptu source of warmth has allowed me a few hours' sleep on a number of occasions. Outside, the great mountain cold seemed to crush the valley in its hands. Lines from Mary Oliver's poem, which seems to speak of cold so emotively, ran over and over in my dreams.

> Cold now.
> Close to the edge. Almost
> unbearable. Clouds
> bunch up and boil down
> from the north of the white bear.

Bone-weary, I arose next morning. There was a thin film of ice on the water glass beside my bed, which I cracked, spitefully, with my fingertip. Nevertheless, despite my exhaustion, I reminded myself that I was in the Himalayas, after all, and the day was ice-clear, exposing a line of jagged mountains on the horizon. Things could be worse indeed.

As I stepped out into the street I took a deep, life-affirming breath. Everything was pristine. Beyond the perimeter of the town, I could see Kanchenjunga, the third highest peak in the world. From Darjeeling, one gains the finest view of it anywhere, and I had long wanted to see this legendary mountain, literally, 'the five treasures of snows'. According to the indigenous Kirant religion, the treasures represent the five repositories of God, which are gold, silver, gems, grain and holy books. It was first climbed on May 25, 1955 by Joe Brown and George Band, on a British expedition, who honoured the beliefs of the Sikkimese by stopping a few feet short of the actual summit.

Down at the Mall, once home to the social clubs and villas of the nineteenth-century British, I found a more bustling atmosphere. Bundled up in scarves and puffer jackets, the citizens of Darjeeling took the air, shopped, gossiped and waited for the spring thaws. I stopped for a while to watch a street magician who had a huge crowd enthralled. From within a small reed basket, but covered beneath a strip of canvas, he was taunting what looked like the head of a cobra. It bobbed to and fro, raising the canopy aggressively, and then dropping in retreat. What was most peculiar about the snake was that it seemed to respond to his every command, rising then falling as if it were preternaturally attuned to the sound of its master's voice. The *jaduwala* (magician) was a seasoned professional, keeping up a running commentary in his gravelled though surprisingly musical voice, goading the crowd to new heights of wonder and anticipation, and invoking the gods of multiple faiths to strike him down if he was deceiving anyone with simply trickery.

The pièce de résistance came when the magician threw a live chicken beneath the canopy, then stood back while a veritable thrashing took place beneath. When all went silent, the magician peered furtively underneath, tilted his head gravely and then held up the bloodied, still twitching, body of a headless fowl. The crowd wailed in horror and delight, only quietening down when the magician, by dint of a *bansuri* (bamboo flute), stilled the snake and sealed the lid with a padlock. To a round of applause, he passed round a copper bowl which rattled with falling rupees like a tin roof in a hailstorm.

Out of curiosity, and because the role of street magic in India seemed to bear a good deal of relevance to my own reasons for being here, I sequestered myself in a doorway to watch the magician clearing up once the trick was complete. Slowly, the crowds dispersed, the money was poured into a spotless handkerchief and tied with a firm knot, and the magician began to collect his belongings together. Finally, after a glance to either side to check that no one was watching, he gave a double click with his tongue, and unlocked the basket. A small boy – of perhaps no more than six or seven – climbed out. His string vest was stained crimson with the blood of the chicken, but he was grinning broadly. Patting his assistant on the back, the magician hefted the basket on to his shoulders and the two performers walked off down the street, no doubt for a celebratory breakfast.

In a Raj-era tea room, I ordered steaming porridge and honey against the cold, and a pot of golden flowery orange pekoe, one of the highest grades of Darjeeling tea. It came in a silver-plated teapot that I fancied might once have served army officers and their wives 150 years before. As I sipped the delicate brew, I asked one of the Tibetan waiters, Sonu, if he'd heard of the miracle. I was sitting before a glass window, views of rolling hills speckled with snow in the distance. Behind me an elderly German couple riffled through their Lonely Planet guide, occasionally circling things in red ink.

'Hindu miracles are happening often,' Sonu explained, clearly amused by my interest in such things. 'But this is the first Buddhist miracle I can remember. People have been coming from miles away to see it, and even some lamas from Sikkim.'

'What did the lamas think?'

He shrugged. 'They had tea in here afterwards, so I heard them talking about it. They were laughing very hard, actually. I don't think they took it very seriously.'

Had he seen it himself?

'I am not having much time for miracles,' Sonu scoffed. 'I want to get out of Darjeeling as soon as possible and move to Delhi. This place is too small – I want to live the city life. So I'm working double shifts right now to save up for a motorbike. Do you know the Bajaj Pulsar? – that's the one I want. Man, that's a cool bike.'

'What if it's a real miracle?' I said. 'You'll have missed your chance.'

He thought for a time. 'Perhaps you're right, bro. It will make my grandmother happy at least. If you come back at six, we can go up there together.'

I spent the day wandering the hills and terraces, glad to be alone. I visited Sampten Choling, a Buddhist monastery of the Yellow Hat sect, where I watched a monk making prostrations before the fifteen-foot statue of the Maitreya Buddha. 'He will do 100,000 of these,' whispered a young, large-eared monk, standing beside me. 'We call this *ngondro*.'

I asked him why they did it. Was it merely devotion?

'It is a method of purifying karma more quickly,' the monk told me. 'All of us are burdened by the actions of past lives. With *ngondro* we are letting go of what has been, and embracing Buddha-nature.' He grinned. 'Actually, it is a good practice but it is making the back too sore.'

'Have you done it?'

'Oh yes. Before I had some problems with pride. *Ngondro* helped me quite a lot in this respect. All my family have done these prostrations. My grandfather actually did them from our home in Eastern Tibet all the way to the statue of Jowo Rinpoche in Lhasa.'

'I'm on something of a pilgrimage myself,' I said. 'But I'm not sure I have the strength for that.'

The young monk smiled. 'Towards the end of the practice, your body is becoming very light. Mind is quiet. Great love is there for all beings.'

As evening fell, I returned to meet Sonu, who led me briskly up the steep path towards the miracle site. Within a few minutes we could see the town lit up below us, dotted with light. My heartbeat was racing now, partly from the climb, but partly from the fact of being here, high in the Shiwalik hills, en route for a glimpse of something that fell through the cracks in everything I'd held true until now. Already I was beginning to break free of the familiar, with a new vitality coursing through me.

Sonu, like many young Tibetans in Darjeeling, had been born in north India yet retained a longing for his homeland. Tibet was the country of his heart, he said, and his only dream in life was to return. No matter how often conversation strayed to other things – rock music, the movies of Jean-Claude van Damme – it always returned to Tibet. The struggle defined him.

'We will organise a huge protest when the Olympics come,' he told me, his face a mask of resolve. 'Our aim is to shame people into an economic boycott. We will say "every product you buy from the Chinese is tainted with Tibetan blood. If you support president Hu Jintao, then your hands, too, are red."'

It was fighting talk. Sonu, like many young Tibetans, revered the Dalai Lama above all others, but also felt frustrated with his Holiness's refusal to take a more combative stance. The Dalai Lama's 'middle way', essentially a conciliatory approach in which he accepts the possibility of a Tibetan autonomous zone (rather than total independence), has saddened a great many of his followers. For Sonu, and the thousands like him, the past thirty years of struggle have achieved nothing. As the possibility of ever seeing their country free becomes narrower, their frustrations – and their willingness to commit to armed struggle – become greater.

For tonight, however, the mood was very much one of piety and respect for the great wheel of Buddhism. Reaching the top of the hill, we gathered with several hundred pink-cheeked Tibetans to view the miracle. People of all ages were present, swathed in woolly hats and scarves, some of the women wearing the distinctive striped aprons called *bangdians*. It was a bleak and lonely place, far above Chowrasta hill, and surrounded by the enveloping ridges of the Himalayas. From here the overdevelopment of the town gave way to a forest of evergreen pines. I could smell the resin in their needles, and for a second was transported back to the forest where I'd played as a child.

Above us, the moon hung fatly in the sky. As it broke through the clouds, we knelt down and prayed to the Enlightened one, while others merely set their mobile phones to camera mode in preparation for the event. (Miracles, as everything else in the new India, seem to link the most ancient needs of the human spirit with the vanguard of technology.)

'Watch that tree on the end of the ridge,' advised Sonu, after conferring with one of his friends. 'You will see the Buddha only when the moon shines.'

We watched and waited, and then, as the clouds parted, we saw it! Whether a trick of the eye or a play of shadows, the tree – it was suddenly very clear – began to look like a Buddha. More precisely, it looked like a seated Buddha, the tiny leaves forming an uncanny silhouette of a figure in the lotus position, complete with the pointed head, visible in a series of swirls rising sharply to the crown. It was pointillism at its most bizarre, as if some preternaturally skilled topiarist had enacted a masterpiece.

An old woman to my left began to chant as we saw it: '*Om Mani Peme Hung, Om Mani Peme Hung,*' her voice worn and smooth and resounding over the hills. Soon even the most sceptical youngsters put down their mobile phones to view the spectacle. One man prostrated himself, his face buried in the dust.

I stared at it confusedly. If it was a trick it was superbly done. And yet, as a miracle it was almost too random to be credible. What an unlikely way for the divine to become manifest! Why this? Why now? What could possibly be the point of it all? Coincidence seemed equally unlikely, however – how could a tree form itself, so perfectly, into such a shape?

'What do you think?' I asked Sonu, when people began to disperse at last. 'Is it a miracle or coincidence? It certainly *looks* real enough.'

He grinned. 'For me, Mr Piers, it is a strange-looking tree. But' – he pointed to the old lady chanting – 'for her it is a message from Lord Buddha. I suppose both are true.'

'The Buddha didn't believe in miracles,' I pointed out. 'He said that we should find our way to the truth.'

'Then for you it is also a tree,' said Sonu. 'But for the old people, these things are important. For me, a real miracle would be if the Chinese announced immediate withdrawal from our country.' He shrugged. 'But one cannot expect such a thing. In the meantime we will work at the problem ourselves, as the Buddha taught.'

So saying he clicked a picture on his Nokia phone and began the descent back down into town. He had a shift to begin in the restaurant and, miracle or not, there were practical concerns to attend to. For myself, I wished to stay a while and observe. In the sky, the moon was almost full and its yellow light washed the tree with a pale fire. On the hilltop, the crowd had dwindled to a small group of the most ardent believers, none of whom – it seemed – were ready to give up on the belief that the great Shakyamuni had entered their lives with a palpable message. With the placid chanting still softly filling the night air, I leaned against a tree and looked down at the scene. In my mind sang a phrase I'd once read: 'He who believes all these tales is a fool, but anyone who cannot believe them is a heretic.'

Several days after the miracle, I boarded the Darjeeling Mail for Calcutta. Truthfully, I hadn't learned much. I'd seen something quirky here, but with nothing like the power to convince me of anything. What remained, though, was the view I'd gained of the generational split that was widening in India, the young more interested in economic development than the traditional faiths of the past. As in any small community in winter, I had quickly found myself greeted by familiar faces as I walked through town. In the stories which unfolded I saw the changing face of India: the bookshop assistant whose daughter yearned for New York, the momo cook who boasted to me about his activity in the Gurkha separatist movement: 'It's a question of identity,' he told me gravely. 'Our people have been working these landscapes for generations, but bad management has kept everyone poor. We want change now! If they don't give it to us, we will simply take it by force.'

As the train whistled south, I reflected on the enormous challenges facing India. It was modernising at breakneck speed, that was undeniable. But could the rich, intricate belief systems at its heart – largely unbroken for 3,000 years – survive the process? Could modernity ever truly arrive without secularisation? Perhaps the Indians could find a middle path, between materialism and spirituality, that we had not.

Certainly, this 'middle path' was not the goal of the man I was next to meet. I was going to see Prabir Ghosh, India's leading rationalist, for whom the country's future depended on scouring away all traces of its spiritual past. Established in 1985, the Science and Rationalists' Association of India works to oppose superstition, blind faith, the caste-system, spiritualism and other obscurantist beliefs. In plain terms this means coming up hard against some of India's most respected gurus and holy men, and risking enormous antagonism in the process. Having just witnessed a miracle of sorts, I felt it was important to allow for the other point of view.

But before then, there was Calcutta to investigate. To arrive from a hill station in winter to the world's fourteenth largest metropolitan area is a shock, by any standards, and yet it was a city I loved from the first. Frenetic, certainly, and not entirely undeserving of the sobriquet 'Hustlefussabad' given it by Edward Lear: But also intensely poetic, shot through by visual haikus: a barge loaded with flowers poling down the indolent Hooghly, tiny fishes fried in front of you at street stalls, dusted in primary-coloured spices.

For a few days I wandered its chaotic thoroughfares, taking in both the relics of empire and this new world bursting from the ashes. If Darjeeling had been teeth-chatteringly cold, this sea-level city sweated under a constant sunlight. Taking refuge from the elements, I found a covered vegetable market, which seemed a miniature universe in its own right. From raised platforms, cross-legged vendors traded fistfuls of *brinjal* and jackfruit and broke wagonloads of garlic bulbs into individual cloves to entice the more thrifty customer. Noticing me sneaking a photograph of him as he offered his takings to a faded print of the goddess Lakshmi, one old vendor quoted Tagore to me: 'Faith is the bird that sings when the dawn is dark!', before casually lapsing back into trade.

On the appointed day, I ventured to Park Street (recently renamed Mother Teresa Sarani) to meet Prabir Ghosh and his assistant Sumitra. Wearing dark sunglasses and a red peaked cap, Prabir strolled into Flury's on the dot of twelve. He seemed, possibly with good reason considering his minor celebrity, like a rock star afraid of being noticed. Sitting down before me, he effected a cursory handshake, left his sunglasses on and began to drum the linen tablecloth with his sausage fingers.

Flury's is something of an institution in Calcutta. It was founded in 1927 by a Swiss expatriate and quickly became the tea venue of choice for both well-to-do British and Indians. A recent refurbishment, however, has scoured away all remnants of this illustrious past. Electric tea machines roared in the background; gleaming refrigerated cabinets brought the food to any icy crunch point. Mirrors and gold trim dazzled the tea drinkers. I found myself longing for a roadside chai stall.

'I will lay it out for you quite simply, sir,' Prabir began at last, 'and perhaps save you some trouble in your quest. There is no such thing as the supernatural. There is no levitation, no yogic powers, no Reiki, no telekinesis, no astrology, no fortune telling. I could go on. They are relics of the past.'

'You don't believe in any of them?' I asked. 'Or you're saying they can't be proven?'

'Both. I have personally offered twenty Lakh rupees (50,000 US dollars) to anyone in the world who can prove me otherwise. No one has even come close.' He held his palms up, tilted his head quickly from side to side, intoxicated by his own logic.

I asked him about his background. How had he come to make it his life's mission to expose miracle workers? It seemed an unusual vocation.

He sipped his Coke thirstily. 'My life's mission is to eradicate the superstition which has held our country back for so long,' he said. 'I grew up in the 1950s in small railway towns like Kharagpur. My parents were devout believers in God. And so very early on I had the opportunity to be around holy men and to observe the way they worked. And what I learned very quickly was that these so-called *siddhas* – or yogic powers – were little more than cheap conjuring tricks. I began to practise these tricks myself, so that when I saw a yogi or a *fakir* hoodwinking people out of their money, I could step forward and demonstrate exactly the same trick, to make them think twice. I did not like seeing my parents giving their money away to these people.

'But as I grew older, I began to see that actually I could do some real good for our India. Faith healing, in particular, is responsible for many deaths. Most doctors move to towns, so in rural places, faith healers do excellent business. In those places, miles from civilisation, quacks pose as gods in human form and take thousands of rupees from our farmers and peasants. I set out to stop this, and to date we have exposed literally hundreds of people as pure charlatans. We are helping India change.'

'I have to ask about Sai Baba,' I said, mentioning India's most famous guru, a frizzy-haired 'messiah' whose devotees number tens of millions, many of them leading politicians. 'If he's a charlatan, he must be one of the most successful in human history. People believe him to be a living god.'

'Sathya Sai Baba is a complete fraud,' said Prabir, his voice growing strident. 'It is all cheap conjuring. Sleight of hand. Tricks. How can India expect to become a great economic power while we continue to worship such people? Your BBC has made a documentary confirming this. And we have made our own videos. Unfortunately, though – for reasons, I think, of cultural conditioning – many of our leading politicians take their religion quite seriously and believe Sai Baba to be the real thing. It is a kind of brainwashing. It will take generations to really eradicate all this.'

'What about the Christian saints?' I said. 'Mother Teresa, for example.'

'Also a fraud,' he answered, 'in that she performed no miracles. Certainly she was a very great woman – but she cured no one by divine miracle. Those claims are false. I offered to shut down my entire organisation and turn over two million rupees to the Catholic order if the sisters put the medallion with which one woman claims Mother Teresa cured her of a tumour to the test. Of course they refused. This was also reported in many papers worldwide. But the myths remain – people *want* to believe.'

'And the Ganesh Milk Miracle?'

'Oh no!' he snorted. 'One of the worst. I can demonstrate

that trick to you with any statue, at any time. Stone has absorbent properties. Capillary action, we are calling this.'

'*Sadhus* who walk on coals?'

He sighed impatiently, already tired of my line of thinking. 'You could do that yourself. In fact, we show villagers how to do it as a method of exposing the god men. The soles of our feet are thick and conduct heat poorly. Similarly, the ash on top of the hot coals is a slow conductor of heat. So if you walk at a good pace, you will not be burned. Sometimes, however, the god men throw sugar or glass on to the fires, so that during our demonstrations we get hurt. We are now *very* careful when we set up our demonstrations to make sure that no one comes near the fire while it is heating. This rationalism is a risky business.'

I sipped my tea, aware of Prabir Ghosh's steely gaze affixed on me from behind his lenses. It wasn't that I didn't agree with most of his reasoning, so much as that his tone was so contemptuous of anyone who would even consider the possibility of a miracle that I found myself recoiling – as much as I might have from a fundamentalist of the other sort. Certainly, many of the people he exposed – if not all of them – were probably frauds – but could it be that every *single* miracle worker in all of human history was also fraudulent? Prabir Ghosh would have us believe that humanity, since the dawn of time, has been hoodwinked by a slew of stage magicians, for whom the manipulation of water into wine is no more than clever chicanery.

'You must understand the *influence* of these people in India,' he continued. 'Perhaps you cannot? By exposing these god men we are shaking the very foundations of power. Many of them have political affiliations and entreat their devotees to vote one way or the other. Many crores change hands. Since I have been doing this, I have survived *many* attempts on my life. We instruct all our young rationalists, in fact, in the martial arts, for this reason.'

'This is true,' concurred Sumitra, gazing protectively at her employer. 'Many people try to kill him. Most recently a *goondar* on a motorcycle tried to do a hit and run – and Prabir got four broken ribs. But there have been others. Prabir is fortunately a very tough cookie.'

'Just now we are engaged in a big debate with Ramdev,' continued Ghosh, pulling his peaked cap down tightly over his brow. 'He claims to cure any illness through the use of *mudrās* [symbolic, ritual gestures] – even serious problems, I should tell you. For example, for a cardiac problem, you press a special point on your big toe.' He chuckled. 'This man has millions and millions of devotees. He is on television every day. And he is recommending to press the big toe!'

'Is he hostile towards you?'

'Certainly. He is getting very angry with me. I said, Mr Ramdev, if you are such a powerful yogi, why do you not cure your own eye problem? After that he became absolutely furious, shaking his fists and so on. So I said, Mr Ramdev, if you are an enlightened man, why are you so angry with me? Where is your equanimity?'

After Prabir Ghosh and his assistant left, I watched them as they got into their car and sputtered away through the smog. At the lights, a young man on a motorbike pulled up alongside them. He wore mirrored sunglasses, had a mobile phone strapped to his waist in a vinyl pouch, and wore his hair tied back in a ponytail. On the far side of Mr Ghosh's car, I saw the opposite end of the economic spectrum, a *tana* or hand-pulled rickshaw, now quite rare in India and pulled by an ivory-haired man in a simple checked *lungi*. He wore no shoes and was probably a daily wage labourer from Bihar or Jharkhand, who pulled a rickshaw during the summer, then returned to his land for the winter farming. His skin was pitch-dark; his face had a watchful dignity.

Like Janus, the new India has two faces, both looking in opposite directions. For the young man in the leather jacket, religion was perhaps less important than it had been for any of his forefathers; a cultural backdrop but with scant relevance to the struggle for prosperity. For the rickshaw wallah it was everything: a refuge and a code. The land was his 'mother' and the rains that swelled the rice paddies the gentle manifestation of God's presence.

These issues – it was becoming increasingly clear – were not merely for the believers and the atheists or consigned to theological debate. They were impacting on all our lives for ever, changing the world in very concrete ways. For my part, I felt trapped between the same rejection of a miraculous God that I'd always had and a profound unease about the consequences of our post-enlightenment divorce from spiritual life. I understood that 'reason', by itself, could never provide me with the means to understand and appreciate my life on earth. And yet, at least not yet, neither could I turn away from a third possibility: that the holy men, the mystics, even the magicians, had something to teach us . . .

In search of such characters, I was unlikely to find anywhere much better than my next destination, one of the great Mela festivals. Occurring every four years, with the largest and mother of all every dozen, the Melas are essentially mammoth religious fairs, in which tens of millions of pilgrims descend upon one of four sacred Indian cities. In only a few weeks, the Ardh Kumbh Mela was to begin in Allahabad, drawing *sadhus*, holy men and mystics from all over the subcontinent in one of the most colourful, bewildering spectacles of Hinduism.

'You are *too* lucky to have this opportunity,' said Uday,

the doorman at my hotel in Calcutta, for whom a visit to one of the great Mela festivals was a constantly nurtured dream. 'It is my belief that at this Mela you will see *genuine* wonders.' He grinned. 'In such a spiritual place, all wishes will be granted.'

Sadhus: the Sky-clad Ones

Ash-smeared, dreadlocked, possibly naked, the *sadhu* is both one of our most archetypal images of India and the one most at odds with Western civilisation. Our culture grows ever more obsessed with material wealth and the body beautiful. For *sadhus* the body is a mere vessel and the world an illusion. The starting point of their quest is to leave our world behind.

Alexander the Great, crossing the River Indus in the spring of 326 BC, saw a group of such holy men and called them 'gymnosophists' or 'naked philosophers'. It is likely that the holy men he saw were not that different, either in appearance or customs, from those that still wander modern India today. As the story goes, Alexander was so impressed by their feats of endurance that he had the idea of adding one of them to his entourage. Dandamis, one of the oldest of the *sadhus*, refused at once, saying that 'he was as much a son of Zeus as Alexander, and that he had no need of anything Alexander could give, since he was contented with what he had'.

Even for Hindus, *sadhus* can be enigmatic figures. Some of them claim supernatural powers and all of them, to some degree, are believed to be conductors of divine energy. For myself, it was impossible not to be fascinated. They lived life on their own terms. Their obsession with their inner journey was such that they'd given up everything to pursue it. They were romantic figures without the burden of possessions, worldly ambition, money of any kind. I had often seen them sitting peacefully by the roadside all across the subcontinent. Perhaps I even envied them a little. They weren't trying to 'be' anything, unlike the rest of us. They were interested in absolute freedom and that suggested a sort of evolution to me.

No better opportunity exists to see the full pantheon of *sadhus* than at Mela festivals, gatherings which celebrate the creation myth of Hinduism. It is said that during the creation of the universe four drops of *amrit*, the nectar of immortality, were spilt on earth. Every four years, the festival is held at one of these points, with the most important in Allahabad, at the confluence of the three sacred rivers: Ganga, Yamuna and the mythical Saraswati. For Hindus, to visit a Mela is the equivalent of making the *haj* to Mecca, and the festivals are amongst the largest human gatherings in the world.

Allahabad is in north-east India, in the state of Uttar Pradesh. As I travelled north, the talk of my fellow passengers began to fill me with trepidation. Twenty million people would be there, said some; fifty million, said another. I would see wondrous feats of asceticism. I would see the most austere meditators, who leave their caves only twice in a decade. There would be stampedes during the auspicious bathing days. And the greatest gurus of the *sadhu* ranks would move through the crowds on sacred chariots.

All of it sounded most daunting, and, as my rickshaw trundled away from Allahabad station, my concerns only magnified. From the railway bridge, a scene reminiscent of a medieval battleground came into view. Across the river plain, an ocean of old-fashioned tents stretched away on the horizon. I had never seen, nor even imagined, such multitudes. In the early morning the campground looked serene. But even in its silence, the size of this gathering beggared belief. Here was the very heart of the Hindu faith. A belief in the governing influences of planets and in the sanctity of rivers, so that to bathe at the confluence at the auspicious moment was to cleanse away earthly sins. Its presence, in the early years of the twenty-first century, was an unforgettable reminder of the world of the spirit.

A complete confidence in the spiritual realm is all well and good, but the navigation of the material world remains to try us. With the polluted lanes of Allahabad crammed to bursting, traffic sat bumper to buffalo. Carts overloaded with holy men. Maruti people-carriers bringing high-ranking civil servants behind tinted windows. Whole families on single wheezing scooters. Bus drivers leaning from the windows to spit great Jackson Pollock spurts of *paan*. Matriarchs clasping woeful hands to their brows. From the bullock cart, the holy men smiled and looked down on the scene with detached amusement.

Conducting all this, a scrawny traffic policeman clamped his lips around a penny whistle and waved his stick as if this were the defining battle of his life. Perhaps it was? He looked too young for the job. His moustache hung limply from his upper lip. Around him, the world spun past, disregarding his instructions. Horns blared derisively. Abuse rained down on him in several different dialects. His white gloves grew black with dust.

Next morning, as the sun rose weakly over the Mela ground, I entered the *kumbhnagar*, the tented city. I was dressed simply, with a brown *khadi* shawl around my shoulders, but nevertheless felt remarkably out of place as I walked amongst the colourful throng. Everywhere, long bearded sages wearing orange or white strode purposefully about. Tired-looking pilgrims, many of whom had travelled hundreds of miles to get here, moved towards the *sangam*, the confluence of rivers. Uniformed police, street sweepers, electricians and sanitation experts went about their business, keeping this makeshift spiritual metropolis running smoothly. In the air, the smell of cooking fires and sweet incense. Beneath my feet, an ochre carpet of dust.

Stretching over thirty-five kilometres, the Mela ground is the largest campground in the world. More than 25,000 tents had been erected, their tent poles fluttering with flags and banners. Building had started the previous July, as soon as the rivers started drying up after the monsoon. Some 20,000 workers had laid water pipes, sanitary facilities and electrical cable. The irrigation department, the public works department, the bridge corporation, the waterworks department and the Ganga Pollution Control Board had sent delegates to lay the ground for the impending onslaught. Devotees had begun to decorate their makeshift temples with garlands of flashing lights and devotional images, some of them hand-painted in primary colours, others lit up in electric neon.

Two months later, the first holy men began to arrive. A ragtag army, clad in robes, some carrying archaic tridents or broadswords, on foot, by jeep, bus and sacred elephant. One of the *sadhus'* rights in India is to receive a pass that guarantees free travel on public transport. Despite their minimal worldly possessions, this *sadhu* ID card is a valuable part of their livelihood, legitimising their way of life. While police may harass beggars, they leave the *sadhus* be, allowing them an almost free rein to move through society at will.

Early morning still and an air of calm over the Mela ground. I moved gently through the throng, my eyes boggling at every turn. Spindly old men stretched out in contortionist yoga positions. Barrows of fresh flowers. One *sadhu* walked past me dressed in a leopard skin, another wearing nothing at all, but with a heavy stone strung from his genitals. Much of India is now as modern as anywhere else but, save the odd detail, this was to step back a thousand years.

Several passers-by, stained with crimson and yellow powders, stopped and welcomed me. Others merely raised their hands in a friendly *namaste*, both surprised and pleased to see a foreign pilgrim. Already the night chill was lifting and a mellow sun casting pools of light over the ground. Swarthy crows jostled each other on their tent poles. Above me, a vast lambswool sky.

In the seventh century, the indomitable Buddhist monk Hiuen Tsang, apparently following the call of a dream, made a journey to India and back that would take him seventeen years. As the guest of Harshvardhana, the last of the Hindu emperors, he attended a Mela in just this spot, and remarked upon its 'ageless' bathing tradition. Even in his day, the festival was an ancient one, whose origins stretched right back to Vedic times.

In my mind, as I picked my way carefully through the sea of tents, was the notion of the Mela as the living embodiment of Hindu *dharma*, or universal law. In the East, religion has always been more about practice and experience than dogma, and nothing so illustrated the fact as this gigantic confluence of humanity. What was important for these pilgrims was not so much the written scriptures or the canon of any specific tradition. It was the idea of religion as practice, as lived experience bringing one closer to God. Perhaps no Hindu saint so expressed this concept as Ramakrishna, the Bengali saint of the nineteenth century. For him the scriptures were 'a mixture of sand and sugar' and science 'mere dirt and straw after the realisation of God'. Learned people, to him, were like wanderers in an orchard, who count the leaves and fruit and argue over their value instead of plucking and relishing the crop. These people here were the living embodiment of this belief, intent only on the fruit, and indeed racing in their millions through the dust to taste it.

At one particularly busy crossroads I noticed a crowd of people who seemed to be arguing furiously. Were they fighting? They were huddled together in a scrum like conspirators. Curious, I went over to investigate, when suddenly, as if from nowhere, a cup of something warm and sticky was hurled across my back. It hit me hard and exploded. Instantly, I spun round to find two men sprinting towards me, their hands stretched out, seemingly about to attack.

Holding my ground as tightly as I could, I prepared for a fight. But just as they came within grabbing distance, a tall *sadhu* leaped out from one of the tents, holding a wooden staff. With his pale, angular face bearing a ferocious expression, he looked like one of the Tibetan demons. The two assailants stopped in their tracks, shot each other a look of abject horror and then broke for the cover of the tents. Behind them the *sadhu* roared a terrible stream of obscenities in their wake.

'What the hell just happened?' I fumed, catching my breath 'Those bastards!'

'They're thieves,' said the *sadhu* in English. 'They throw food on to you and while you're disorientated, steal your bags.'

As I turned to look at the *sadhu* who'd helped me, I realised that beneath the matted beard and dreadlocks, he wasn't Indian at all, but a Westerner.

'You're not Indian?' I said, still panting.

He walked behind me to examine my back, which was dripping with the sticky condensed milk ice cream known as *kulfi*. I felt like killing someone.

'I'm an Aussie,' he said. 'Or I was once. Wow, they really covered you. Did you lose anything?'

I shook my head. *Kulfi* was in my hair, running down my back and all over the back of my trousers, but I seemed to have all my possessions. I hoped there were no swarms of bees around, or I might be diving into the *sangam* somewhat sooner than expected.

'I'm sorry you've experienced that kind of behaviour here,' he said. 'Pilgrims make rich pickings, I guess. Anyway, I'm Ram. Why don't you come to the *Juna Akhara* camp with me and clean yourself off. It's not far.'

I thanked him and we walked, side by side, through the maze of tents. Despite the annoyance of what had happened, I realised that this might actually be a stroke of good luck. The *Juna Akhara* are amongst the most feared and respected of the *sadhus*. Also known as the *Naga Babas*, the warrior ascetics, they subject themselves to more austerities (with many of them forgoing clothes entirely) than any other of the *dasnami*, the ten Saivite sects (the oldest of the sects of Hinduism, whose followers revere Shiva as the Divine Being). Perhaps meeting Ram might be a means of introduction.

As we walked he told me about himself. He was indeed Australian but had been a *sadhu* for some ten years. He came from a middle-class background; his parents owned a garden centre. On a trip to India in his mid-twenties, he had met some *sadhus* and had a profound spiritual experience. It changed his life for ever.

'I liked the way they lived,' said Ram, whose accent was now a strange mixture of Strine and Hindi, 'and how peaceful they seemed. But it was really when I met this one *baba* that the most shattering realisation came. He seemed like an incarnation of God to me. I was this typical Westerner with all these deep questions that I wanted to ask him but when I stood in front of him they disappeared. There were no questions left. He was simply a living manifestation of the divine. So I went home and got my affairs in order, and told my parents I was moving here. I never gave it a second thought.'

I found his tale extraordinary. To see him now, with his long dishevelled hair, sun–dark face and only a small pouch of possessions, was to see a *fakir* from story books, albeit one born in a suburb of Cairns. I envied him the certainty with which he'd left the past behind. Now he wore a long string of *mala* beads, and his possessions were only his clothes, a begging bowl and a small chillum pipe. I wondered how many Westerners like him had chosen such an unlikely path for themselves. Perhaps, had things gone differently, Ram might be sitting in an Australian boardroom, even now, brokering some million–dollar deal.

'I appreciate your finding a valid path to God,' I said, 'but why such a difficult one, with so many hardships and austerities?'

'How much of the stuff you own do you actually *need* anyway?' said Ram lightly. 'Besides, I really felt so disgusted with the world I came from. I wanted no more to do with it.'

'In what way?'

'Almost every way.' Ram stopped walking suddenly, his bony face lit up by an almost messianic fervour. 'The West has become obsessed with trying to seek fulfilment through the external world. We think if we get *that* car, *that* house, *that* stupid electronic gadget then we'll be happy. But each time the bar raises. Even with ten houses we're still not happy. And yet we don't come to our senses. We idolise those people most in our culture who are the most deluded.' He grinned. 'You know what I'm talking about,' he said. 'You're here, aren't you?'

I nodded. I understood well enough, but nevertheless I was a very long way from wishing to join him. Renunciation, frankly, seemed a little selfish.

'What I found here was an incredibly ancient method of self-exploration and, ultimately, for finding happiness. India is changing fast, of course, but the *sadhus* aren't.' He cackled. 'That said, they *are* beginning to get mobile phones. One of the phone companies is here at the Mela, offering free talk time for *sadhus*. They see it as good marketing to have *babas* using their brands. Never thought I'd see such a thing.'

I asked Ram if he felt that he was accepted here: a white man dressed as a renunciate.

'By the *Juna Akhara*?' He paused, and his brown watchful eyes softened. 'I believe so, yes. They accept anyone, providing you jump through the right hoops. That's one of the greatest things about the *sadhus*, actually. But then conversely there are many rituals, initiations; money must change hands in some circumstances. Actually, there are many pecking orders, you'd be surprised.'

'Why is that surprising?' I asked.

'Well, I was surprised,' said Ram. 'I mean, it seemed ironic to me that although *sadhus* have renounced the world, they have recreated so many of its barriers within their own organisation.'

We came to the camp at last. A line of open tents revealed about twenty different *sadhus*, of various ages. Before each tent, an open fire smouldered, fed only with wood from dead trees, or wood that had fallen naturally. Several enormous chillum pipes were being passed round, glowing red with *charras* – black marijuana resin. A cluster of wizened but seemingly contented faces peered up at me. Some of them had long dreadlocks in imitation of Shiva, from whose matted hair it is said the Ganges first flowed.

Most of them were smeared in sacred ash, so that their skin glowed as white as Greek statues.

Ram greeted his comrades and told them, in guttural Hindi, what had happened to me. Several greybeards tutted at the story, while one of the younger *sadhus* – his pupils dilated to soup bowls – let out a shriek of wild laughter. They were sitting cross-legged on the ground, on Kashmiri rugs or folded wool blankets. Strings of crimson, yellow and orange marigolds hung from above, while from the ashes of the fire a great iron trident pointed to the heavens. Everything was carefully swept and cleaned. Smells of *nag champa* incense in the air.

An old greybeard, noticing my attention, spoke out in broken English.

'Trident is weapon of Shiva! With it he destroys enemies. But also he is destroying attachment to the world. He is cutting us free.' He patted the ground beside him in invitation.

While Ram went to get me some water to clean myself off, I removed my shoes and sat down on the edge of the circle. For *sadhus* (and Hindus in general) purity is everything. One must always remove one's shoes when sitting before them, as well as avoid pointing one's feet directly towards anyone. For them the world is alive with unseen forces and it is a part of their *sadhana*, or practice, to keep these forces at bay. On one level that means dirt, and they will always begin their day with a ritual bath – usually in a sacred river or pool – but on another level this means more insidious forces: energies, and negative influences of all types.

Their fireplace – the *dhuni* – is another integral part of this belief system. Its origins are unclear, save that on some level it is a relic of an earth goddess cult. The *dhuni* itself is not the fire but the hollow in which it sits, representative of the *yoni* or female vulva. Into this, a flame is kindled, on to which suitable objects are fed and consumed. This is a symbol of the world itself: a process of continual change and transformation. It is also a reminder of the possibility of evolution from the physical to the spiritual level, and to offer ghee or other objects to the flames is to honour this notion.

Some months later, a Swedish Indologist added another interpretation to my understanding of the sacred fireplace. 'The opening up of the self to the mystical realms of consciousness can be very dangerous,' he said, 'because it leaves the practitioner open to all kinds of influences. That's why the *sadhus* are always drawing boundaries around themselves. They do it with their lines drawn in the earth, by sprinkling water and by sitting before fire. This protects and grounds them. It purifies everything it touches.'

As Ram returned with a metal tin of water and a rag, several of the *sadhus* helped me to clean my shawl free of *kulfi*. I was touched by their kindness, their attentiveness to putting this foreigner at his ease. My awkwardness at suddenly being thrust into the heart of the *sadhu* encampment began to recede. I felt entirely welcome.

Meanwhile, one of the older *babas* – a man of indeterminable although certainly advanced age, with furrowed bronze skin and matchstick limbs – proceeded to load himself a chillum pipe. In the popular Western imagination, all *sadhus* smoke vast quantities of marijuana. But it is actually only the Saivite sects, and of these mainly the *Juna Akhara*, who smoke. (For most *sadhus* smoking is as off limits as all the other worldly pleasures.) Certainly, for the *Juna Akhara*, marijuana is a sacred plant. In scripture, Shiva is permanently intoxicated by it, in a state of divine bliss, and it is believed that to smoke the plant allows the devotee to share in this, a momentary journey beyond the veil. *Sadhus* who smoke will generally honour Lord Shiva before an inhalation, chanting a chillum mantra, such as: *Bum Shiva!*, or *Bam Bam Bholanath!*

To my right, the old-timer did just this, wrapping a scrap of muslin around the end, raising the heavy clay pipe to the sky and uttering a forceful chillum mantra, before sucking on the end, then exhaling a great pungent cloud that momentarily obscured everything around us. Instantly, I could see his pupils expand, a beatific smile play about his lips and his whole bony torso slacken. Refusing my own turn, I passed the pipe to the *sadhu* on my left. These days, marijuana affects me poorly, and the last thing I wanted in this sprawling and highly disorientating environment – where I'd already been attacked once – was to lose my senses. Nevertheless, it was pleasing to watch the *sadhus* smoke, and to observe the effects of the intoxicant. Recalling the notion of anthropologist David Abrams that magic is merely an expansion of the senses, I could well imagine how marijuana might facilitate such a process. One's ears tune in with delight and appreciation to previously unnoticed sounds. The wandering nature of the mind is temporarily stilled, and a sense of equanimity comes over the user. To be in nature is to find oneself overcome with the wonder of being.

Drug use as a means of reaching God is, of course, as old as man himself. Of the over 1,000 hymns in the Rig Veda, 120 are devoted to a substance called *soma* – a sacred drink with the power to transport the user to the heights of ecstasy. Several thousand years later, the exact identity of *soma* is unclear, but many Vedic scholars have their theories. Some believe it was made from *Amanita muscaria* – a mushroom favoured by Siberian shamans. Others contest this, suggesting instead the psychoactive plant *Peganum harmala*, or, according to Terence McKenna's theory, the fungus *Stropharia cubensis*. Perhaps most convincingly, Paul Devereux, in his classic book *The Long Trip*, has suggested that *soma* may not have been one plant but 'a sort of archetypal concept that stands for the psychoactive, sacred experience that can be found in the plant kingdom'. If that is indeed true, then perhaps the *sadhus*, even as I sat besides them, were imbibing *soma* to join Shiva in his sacred realms.

'We have drunk the soma, we have become immortal . . . we have found the gods. What can hatred and the malice of a mortal do to us now? . . . the drop that we have drunk has entered our hearts, an immortal inside mortals.' (O'Flaherty)

Ram was certainly doing his best to find the gods. Now in the middle of the *sadhu* circle, he seemed to be smoking his way to oblivion. His head swayed faintly to the pulse of a small drum; his long fingers tamped great plugs of *charras* (handmade hashish) into his clay pipe. As the latest chillum touched Ram's lips he let out a hacking series of coughs, prompting one of his comrades to reach into his bag for a sticky brown bottle. I caught a glimpse of the label as he did so, and had trouble suppressing a chuckle. 'Bhati's Cough Elixir,' it said, 'tasty and effective.'

Later, once the smoking session had ended, Ram led me around the Mela ground to meet some of the other *sadhus*. Above us the sun was a burning disc, and those who had tents were retreating into the shade to sit out the worst of the heat. Cooking fires brewed tea and heated wheat chapattis, while those pilgrims with no camp to sit in made their way to the riverside in the hope of a cool breeze. To walk through the Mela as the guest of this respected ascetic was to gain a glimpse of the veneration these men are accorded in India. Everywhere, people bowed respectfully to Ram, their eyes cast courteously downward. I realised that the Indians made no distinction between a foreign *sadhu* like Ram and any of the others. The *sadhu* was outside caste, quite literally a 'god man'.

First on our list was Amrabati, one of the oldest and most

celebrated of the *Juna Akhara* ascetics. Since the *sadhu* life-style with its rituals and austerities is intended to speed up the process of burning off negative karma, certain *sadhus* take this one step further still. Mortifications, such as holding limbs in the air, or tying heavy weights to their genitals as I'd seen that morning, are methods of cultivating *tapas* or inner heat. This *tapas* is a form of spiritual energy as well as the source of the *sadhu*'s magical power.

Amrabati has been holding his arm vertically in the air, without a break, for more than twenty years. Denied proper movement and blood flow, his hand has withered like a plant without water. It hangs in a sort of noose, the fingernails curving into obscene brown ringlets. It's hard to tell Amrabati's age – he might be forty-five or seventy-five – but what is evident from looking into his deep-set, smouldering eyes is that here is someone who has tested himself beyond the limit of most of our imaginings. Now he looks out with a curiously empty gaze, no longer as interested in the machinations of the world about him as in his own internal battle. By any reckoning, he is a powerful presence to behold.

I greeted the great *baba* and sat down quietly while Ram paid his respects. Amrabati, his skeletal arm trussed up as if in some medieval hospital brace, nonchalantly packed himself a pipe with his free hand. In his case, I sensed the marijuana might have made his extraordinary ordeal a good deal more bearable. For the other *sadhus*, too, his mortification has raised him in high esteem; while we sat there a string of visitors came to pay their respects. Amrabati received them with little more than a regal nod, occasionally speaking a few gruff words. He seemed hardly of this world any more.

About an hour later, finding myself once more ensconced in the *sadhu* circle, an appalling vision lumbered into view.

More than anything I'd yet seen either at the Mela or in India at large, this sight was truly bizarre. He looked scarcely human – an amorphous monstrosity of deformed and elongated flesh. Ram turned and whispered to me: 'It's Ganesh.'

Struggling to pick my jaw off the ground, I tried to face the sight with equanimity. Ganesh was a man with elephantiasis – that much was clear. His head was double or perhaps triple that of a normal man, with a great elongated trunk of flesh protruding from the front that made the sobriquet an obvious choice.

'He was thrown out of his village,' explained Ram. 'But for the *sadhus* he's a living incarnation of the Elephant God. They revere him.'

Poor Ganesh, two black eyes peering out from behind these disturbing folds of flesh, seemed to be facing a difficult future. And yet at the same time, I couldn't disregard the positive effects of the *sadhu* culture. Whereas conventional society had rejected Ganesh, another had welcomed him in. Whereas mainstream society saw him a monster, another saw him as a god. Since the *sadhus* spent their lives trying to detach themselves from any sense of 'being' anything or anyone, they took Ganesh as he was, and even celebrated him as a facet of the divine. With this in mind, I turned to look at Ganesh again, this time finding his misshapen face less disturbing and more a manifestation of the infinite variety of creation. Around me, the *sadhus* carried on their discussions, none treating Ganesh any differently from anyone else. Somehow the sight of this was intensely moving, and the brotherhood of their community seemed an immensely positive force.

'What about magic?' I asked Ram, when the opportunity presented itself. 'Do you believe the *sadhus* can perform it?'

He looked thoughtful, and a slender hand drew itself through his beard. He moved closer, perhaps not wishing to have his comments overheard.

'*Jadoo* is certainly there,' he said. 'But you'll never see it outright. Not even I could see it. It's seen as a display of ego to show off one's powers. The only real reason people do it is to nudge the common man from his dream, get him thinking that there's something else going on in the universe.'

'Surely you've seen something?'

'Nothing blatant. But there have been occasions, yes, when I have felt myself subtly manipulated, moved in various directions. There's no doubt in my mind that powerful forces are at work. We call them *siddhas*, actually – the power to control, through yoga, the subtle energies.'

'I've heard of such things,' I said. 'And I've heard that here, at the Mela, one can see *sadhus* making stones float on water, or lying on thorny branches, or casting out demons and throwing them into the fire.'

Ram grinned, exposing stumps of teeth. It was a peaceful grin, and one at ease with the path he had chosen.

'You might be lucky,' he said. 'But if it's the real stuff you're after, you'll have to become a holy man yourself, then dedicate yourself to the most rigid austerities under the tutelage of a guru. And the irony will be that when you finally gain the ability to perform these feats, you'll realise how irrelevant they are.'

'What *is* important then?' I asked.

'Merging with the Absolute,' said Ram. 'Nothing else.'

As the festival progressed, the crowds continued to pour in. At the end of the day it would take me two hours to travel from the Mela ground to my hotel in the town centre. Arriving back in my tiny airless room – all I'd been able

to find given the onslaught – I'd wash my face to find the
flannel black with dirt.

'Population of India may be two billion by next century,'
said the Sikh concierge, when I remarked upon the multitudes that seemed to be stretching the town at the seams.
Guruchuran was studying sociology in an open university
course and was a font of useful information. I took to talking
with him from the battered leather sofa in reception, glad to
be out of my room.

'Surely that's not possible,' I replied.

Guruchuran held a finger aloft. 'Worst states will be Bihar,
Madhya Pradesh, Rajasthan and Uttar Pradesh, accounting
for almost *half* the country's population. If I am fortunate
enough to be married soon, we will go north to Ladakh.' He
grinned nervously. 'Winters will be inclement certainly, but
population will be minimal!'

'You're a thinking man,' I said. 'I suppose that's exactly
the kind of forethought the future's going to require.'

Guruchuran adjusted his pink turban reflectively, uneasy
with compliments. 'Quiet life is best, sir. City life is too
competitive. Spiritual things are quickly forgotten.'

I pointed to the hordes of pilgrims, even now milling past
the hotel door. Surely they seemed evidence that the spiritual
was hardly on the wane in India.

'Certainly, piety is there, sir,' acknowledged Guruchuran
in his sing-song voice. 'But for how long! After Gandhi-ji was
killed, the spiritual heart of our country went into decline.
Great industrialisation process began. Nehru himself said that
religion was a barrier to progress. Secularisation is inevitable.'

I was impressed by Guruchuran. At only twenty-four, his
grasp of the developmental issues was remarkable, but more
than that it was his clear-sighted vision of the future that
set him apart. All his friends were taking call-centre jobs, he

told me. Two hundred US dollars a month was good money for any graduate, and yet where did it get them? Punishing hours, little or no prospect of promotion. They spent their income frivolously to make the whole thing worthwhile.

'But how will you use your sociology degree in Ladakh?' I asked. 'All this late night study you're doing will be for nothing.'

He shrugged, part uncertain, part happy to let the future unfold. 'Journalism may be there. Teaching may be there. Failing these things I will open a restaurant like my father. We have two *dhabas* in Amritsar. Family tradition is there. Whatever I do, I think I will learn to enjoy.'

I stepped out into the street, which was lit up with the roar of trade, the orange glow of *tandoor* ovens. Certainly, there would be room for thinkers like him in the years ahead. He had the quiet optimism of many of his countrymen, and the strict moral code of his Sikh faith. He wasn't a saint, of course – he loved Punjabi cinema, the odd drink of 'country wine'. But his ideas cut a path into the future. Hard work would help him get there.

Further down the street I found a suitable-looking restaurant, ordered two stuffed *paratha* and ensconced myself on a plastic chair. The night had grown cool, and I pulled the blanket more tightly around myself. Before the *tandoor*, an elderly bald man slapped breads on to a sort of cushion, then pressed them against the clay oven wall. Steam poured from the oven into the night air. '*Naan, kulcha, paratha,*' he called out in his lilting voice. '*Tandoori roti, bhatura, puri.*'

Across the road a loudspeaker system started up, pumping tinny Bollywood fare into the night. Two rickshaw drivers swerved to avoid each other, that most salient Indian insult '*bhenchod*' (sister-fucker) ringing in their wake. How many people were in my line of sight, I wondered. Five thousand, ten thousand; it was impossible to assess. It was like watching an ants' nest through a magnifying glass: ever-present streams of life. All of them working, despite the odds, to reach the next rung of the ladder, and beyond that a moment of transcendence: secular, mystical or profane.

A few days later I ran into Ram again, just leaving the *Juna Akhara* camp. The Mela was now well under way, and I moved through the tents with both eyes open lest my attackers should reappear. After a friendly greeting, Ram invited me to follow him down to the *triveni sangam*, the confluence of holy rivers, where the second sacred bathing day would commence the following morning. I'd been heading that way myself, anxious to scout out a place to stand before the impending madness.

The sun was dipping over the Mela ground as Ram and I approached the water. A plethora of boatmen stepped forward to tout for trade, but whereas even my heartiest protestations wouldn't have quietened them, a single head tilt from a *sadhu* left us in peace. Ram pointed out the muddy pale-yellow waters of the Ganges, meeting the bluer waters of the Yamuna in mid-stream. 'Third river is invisible,' he explained. 'Some say the Saraswati is a myth, others that it springs from deep in the earth. She is mentioned in the Rig Veda as being a source of great purity and regeneration.' He closed his eyes in reverence.

Within a few hours this very spot would host the largest gathering of humanity on the planet; it would be visible from space. How long would the Melas be able to continue in this fashion, I wondered. Pollution levels in the river were now so high that several holy men had threatened ritual suicide unless it was remedied. Thousands of police with metal detectors spent their days scanning for potential terrorist threats, an almost impossible task amidst so many millions.

I asked Ram how he felt about it all. For now, India remained the best place in the world to follow a mystical path, but wasn't that all changing? *Sadhus* lived off alms, but what if Indian society became like the West: atheistic, more interested in the material than the spiritual?

Ram stared at me gravely, removing his glasses to reveal bloodshot eyes.

'Even in the years I've been here,' he said, 'it's altered beyond all measure. Traditionally, Indians from all castes have shown the *sadhus* great respect, even if they're not particularly pious themselves. But these days some of the young Indians have no respect at all for us. They'd rather watch television than hear the old stories. And the Mela, too, is a reflection of what's going on.' Ram stretched out a bony finger to point west. 'You know what I found over there the other day? Luxury tented accommodation for Indian tourists! I mean they're not even here to *participate*. They're part of a culture that's splitting in two, one side embracing the West without any regard for their own belief systems.'

Ram was getting increasingly worked up now, and he clicked *mala* beads through his fingers at lightning speed. 'Pepsi have put up *billboards*,' he continued. 'Honda has taken over an area displaying its latest tractors to tempt visiting farmers. What's happening here is just the beginning, let me tell you. It'll be like what's happened to Christmas in the West – commerce will rob it of even the most basic meaning.'

'What do the other *sadhus* think about all this?' I asked.

Ram shrugged. 'The real ones carry on with their spiritual practice. The other ones, and there are many, become embroiled in a battle for status and power. Time was this festival was the largest single gathering of the faithful on the planet! Pretty soon it'll be a fairground like any other, a giant market for consumer goods.'

'There's always a Himalayan cave,' I said, trying to make light of it.

'No way, mate,' said Ram. 'The way I see it we have two choices in life. We can live in a cave and hide from the world. Or we can strive to be *in* the world, but not of it. I'll be here as long as I'm standing. But that doesn't mean I'm going to keep quiet. Any phone rep comes up to me, I'll tell him right where he can stick it!'

After Ram had left, I stood on the river-bank for some time, staring at the multitudes who, even now, were wading into the holy waters. The *sadhus* I'd met were charismatic, certainly, but it was hard to ascertain just *what* it was they were seeking in their spiritual quest, let alone discern if any of them had found it. Rather, it was these simple acts of faith, such as villagers touching their foreheads to the *sangam* at the end of a long pilgrimage, which made me feel connected and just where I wanted to be.

Mark Twain came to a Mela once, during the journey which he would later recount in *Following the Equator*. 'It is wonderful,' he wrote, 'the power of a faith like that, that can make multitudes upon multitudes of the old and weak and the young and frail enter without hesitation or complaint upon such incredible journeys . . . It is done in love, or it is done in fear; I do not know which it is. No matter what the impulse is, the act born of it is beyond imagination.'

In my own way, I too was on such a journey, born beyond the imagination. And yet, unlike these Hindu pilgrims, I had some way to go yet. For the time being at least, I remained on the water's edge, unable to wade in.

Varanasi: the Fortune Teller of the Ghats

After the Mela I made my way, like most of the *sadhus*, to Varanasi: India's holiest city, and only a few hours from Allahabad. Here, along the primeval stone ghats of the river, makeshift tents housed a growing number who had come to pay their respects to Mother Ganga now that the festival was over. It was here, too, that I would meet another type of *sadhu*, a female recluse who would show me, as if by opening a box of delights, a glimpse of the ineffable.

On the day of my arrival, for what would turn out to be a three-month stay, the city was at its finest − a clear, lustrous January day, the air pleasantly chill, the River Ganges serene, and what seemed like all the children in the city upon their rooftops, flying kites. Ahead of the Makar Sankranti festival, an auspicious day on the Hindu astrological calendar and also the date of the great annual kite festival, keen practice was going on. On every narrow rooftop, tiny children gathered beneath their kite strings. The skies above the holy city were dotted with thousands of *patang* or fighting kites, their lines sparkling with glass fibre to cut opponents from the sky.

Kites have been flown here for more than 1,500 years; it is believed they were brought to India by the Chinese traveller Fa Hien, a Buddhist monk who visited India around AD 400.

They're the simplest of designs: tailless diamonds made from tissue paper and bamboo, and when they fly the paper rustles in the wind. No sound so typifies Varanasi in my mind as that rustling of scores of brightly coloured shapes, some decorated with gods and goddesses, dancing above the ancient dwellings, an orchestra of rustling paper.

Some time later, I found myself installed on the fifth floor of an archaic guesthouse, one of the highest buildings in the city, not far from the Manikarnika Ghat. By some stroke of luck, I was given a room overlooking the river, so that through the large panes I could see a whole stretch of the Ganges, with spires of dark smoke rising from the cremation ground and ancient river craft poling the currents. Numerous rooftops also lay within my view, so that I could see *dhobi wallahs* hanging out their washing, flame-red chillies spread out to dry in the sun, and women picking the husks from the mounds of silk-white basmati. Many city dwellers covered their roofs with wire mesh to protect themselves from the monkeys, and it was easy to see why as I caught my first sight of an entire tribe, leaping at full speed from parapet to parapet, shrieking mischievously. Monkeys, although sometimes bothersome, are considered avatars of Hanuman the monkey god, and, in Varanasi of all cities, it is forbidden to interfere with them in any way. Consequently, the city dwellers have to put up with all manner of roguish pranks: the theft of food, clothes and shiny ornaments; the destruction of property; fighting and mating rituals noisily enacted on thin corrugated roofs; or in the case of certain hapless tourists naively holding bananas, fully fledged assault.

Nonetheless, for a time at least, it is a pleasure to see them on one's windowsill. Until now, India has yet to impose those strict barriers between the animal and human worlds that render Western cities so particularly sterile. To see a cow garlanded and sleeping between rows of traffic, a temple monkey receiving *prasad* or vultures descending upon the Towers of Silence, is to feel connected still to a larger web of life. The Indian gods, too, in all their animal forms, remind us that the natural world is one of the most obvious manifestations of the divine we have.

As the dusk fell, I ventured out on to the ghats for a look at the city. I'd been here some years before and felt immediately at home on the bustling waterfront, with its plethora of pilgrims, boatmen, swamis both real and fraudulent, awe-struck Japanese tourists, tick-ridden mutts, portable barbers' shops, knuckle-cracking masseurs, beggars, musicians, goats, corpses and a million other forms of God.

Along the waterfront there are massive flights of stone steps, stone piers and platforms that jut out into the Ganges, and on each of these a Brahmin priest sitting under a palm leaf umbrella awaiting the customer; behind this, the sharp spires of Hindu temples. Amid the clanking of bells, the buzz of innumerable voices raised in prayer, salutation or commerce, male and female bathers proceed in endless streams to the water, clutching their brass vessels to save some of the Hindu world's most sacred water for future use.

What at first seems like perhaps the most anarchic place one has ever seen soon begins to reveal a complex system of order. According to scripture, each of the eighty-four ghats of Varanasi represents I lakh (100,000) of the species described in Hindu mythology. Of these, five ghats – known as the *pana jala tirthas* – have a special importance. Each represents one of the five natural elements, and to do any form of spiritual practice here is to see a far quicker return on one's investment. In the same way that for certain Catholics, walking the road to Compostella guarantees, if not the key to heaven, then a bit of oil for the lock, the Hindu who reaches Kashi (the ancient name for Varanasi) feels that what he has to say will be heard here that much more easily. For those fortunate pilgrims, to stand on one of the five *tirthas* is to arrive – as close as one may in this earthly realm – within earshot of God.

It was on the edge of one of these *tirthas*, just as the moon was rising above the river, that I first saw an intriguing character who would open the door for me, over the weeks ahead, to the tightly knit subculture of the *sadhus* who seemed to line the banks of the river. He was French, entering middle age, although a ten-year heroin addiction made it difficult to tell precisely how old he was. When I laid eyes on him he was playing chess on one of the stone piers which overlook the river, his face quietly rapt, seemingly oblivious to the gathering crowd of Indians who were following the game's every move.

Walking past at right angles, I saw only a dishevelled foreigner, pasty-faced and wrapped in a russet blanket, sitting across from a prosperous-looking Indian, clad in immaculate *dhoti* and waistcoat. The contrast struck me as amusing, for it is all too often the case that despite our comparative wealth by Indian standards, we travellers are invariably dirtier and less well presented than even the poorest peasant. Backpackers, myself included, seem anxious to quickly shrug off the expectations of conventional life, as we enter that nether world of 'the road'. Our scruffiness and sheer disarray never fail to baffle the spotlessly clean Indians, whose very religion equates worldly cleanliness with spiritual purity. By that reckoning – amongst so many others – we travellers have a long way to go.

The Frenchman, despite his dishevelment, was at any rate thrashing the Indian chess player with apparent ease. Neither was the Indian doing his own credibility any favours by making constant references to a colossal tome laid out on the stone in front of him. Nudging closer, I managed to sneak a look at its cover. *62 Masterpieces of Chess Strategy*, it was called, by one Irving Chernev.

As the moon swung out over the Ganges, *diyas* (devotional lamps) were laid out beside the players to ensure their view of the board. A chai seller trundled over with his metal canister to cater to the ever-present Indian need for a sweet decoction of *Camellia sinensis*. I struck up conversation with another spectator, who was able to give me the low-down on how this extraordinary match had come about.

'That *feringhee* [foreigner] is from France,' Amir explained excitedly. 'And he is coming here every year to Benares [another name for Varanasi]. Each evening many people are playing chess out here besides Ganga, and one day this Frenchman is asking for a match. Foreigner is *thrashing* his first opponent!'

'Were you watching?'

'Actually, no. I was working in my shop at that time. But I was coming back next evening when my friend told me that Frenchman was again to be playing. This time *very* fine local chess player is coming. Some more Indians now coming to watch, and once again this Frenchman is wreaking havoc with our man!'

I couldn't help chuckling. Indians, perhaps with good reason considering that they grow up in such a hugely populated society, seemed possessed of a stronger competitive streak than most.

'So what about this man's chances?' I asked. 'He seems to know what he's doing.'

'*Great* champion,' said Amir. 'Captain of Varanasi District Chess Association. Best player for long distance in actual fact. Brain is tip-top.'

Another man, keen to join in the conversation, sidled up to Amir. '*Bahut samay se dekhā nahīṁ*,' he said. 'Long time no see.'

'My friend Rajesh,' introduced Amir. 'You should visit him. He is making excellent horoscopes.'

'Handy,' I said. 'An astrologer. Can you make a prediction about this match?'

Rajesh grinned, exposing gleaming teeth. 'No need for *Jyotisha* in this instance. India has already lost too many wickets.'

This was certainly true. The Frenchman, in a display of skill which appeared almost insulting, had plunged his queen into a nest of the Indian's pawns, then proceeded to make a kind of systematic culling. Each further conquest prompted yet more riffling of the chess book, and the occasional whimper of frustration from the beleaguered Indian. Opposite him, almost luxuriantly, the Frenchman lit his cigarette.

Very soon it was over. The competitors shook hands, pats on the back were awarded to both men from the admiring throng, and the defeated Indian was animatedly praising the Frenchman's technique. 'Not for many years have I been beaten like that,' I heard him say. 'He knew *every* strategy I employed. Every one! An encyclopaedic knowledge, I tell you.'

After that a few days went past and I forgot about the match. But as I sat in the rooftop café of my guesthouse one evening, who should walk in but the chess player. He looked even more sickly than I recalled and sank feebly into his chair.

'You're the chess player?' I said. 'I saw you play a match on Monday. On the ghats.'

His bleary eyes lifted. 'You saw that. It was fun, no?'

'Not for your opponent. How did you get so good?'

He shrugged and flicked a Gold Flake cigarette from its packet. His nails were filthy. 'I am not so good, actually.

I was better once. But here the standard here is . . . well, quite amateur, actually.' As he lifted the cigarette to his lips I noticed his hands were shaking. 'I am not boasting,' he added. 'But I could have given that guy half my pieces and still won. It was child's play for me. He knew the great games by rote but not . . .' he exhaled, 'but not the meaning of them. You take my point?'

He was called Honoré, it turned out, after Balzac, who had also been a chess player. He supported himself by teaching chess strategy in Paris. He had once played for the French national team, but even then another mistress was drawing his attention.

'I am a junkie,' he admitted almost at once. The confession seemed to make him feel better; he could look me in the eyes. 'Heroin. I have been in rehab twice. My father came with these two big guys to the squat where I was living, and they carried me to a car and took me there. I fought them the whole way, but then after several months I came out clean.' He rotated the cigarette between thumb and fore-finger, squinting his eyes at the blue smoke. 'Then I fell back into it. Down the rabbit hole, yes. More re'ab. But since then . . . three years, I 'ave this habit still. I cannot shake it. Perhaps I don't want to . . .' He gave an involuntary shiver.

'Why the hell not?'

'I like it too much. I mean, perhaps it's stating the obvious, no, but when you've felt that good, one wants to again. Nothing else in this . . . world can really compare.'

We talked on. Between cigarettes he rolled himself hefty joints and smoked them down to the nub. He was the kind of character a writer dreams of: charismatic, highly eloquent, possibly doomed. His inner life flowed out in jump cuts and memories. He spoke of chess players as if they were movie stars: Bobby Fischer, Mikhail Tal. He knew their legends and their quirks. Not being much of a chess player, I struggled to follow as he replayed the games which had inspired him, relating the winning moves Kx5 as if mere mortals could hope to share the genius he so clearly saw in them.

'Fischer always said that chess is war. You're trying to *crush* the opponent's mind. I think at one stage I felt invincible. My mind was so strong no one could touch me. But the heroin has taken the edge away. As much as it delivers me to a plane that not even chess can touch, it lessens my ability to think in that super space – that magical space, you know – where the most serious chess happens. If I 'ave a regret, it's that.'

'Magical space,' I said. 'Yes, I understand that. But you'll kill yourself if you carry on, won't you? Do you *want* to kill yourself?'

Honoré pushed a lock of oily black hair off his brow. He had a craggy butcher's face, but with a pair of eyes that radiated intelligence. 'No, I don't want to die,' he said frankly, 'but I don't want to live enough to stop doing it. *Comprenez?* Chess was always a path for me, a way of getting somewhere that life could not take me. Heroin takes me *so* high. One floats above all of it.'

I saw him again the next morning as I walked down to the Burning Ghat. He was wearing the same clothes as the day before, but he seemed upbeat, more lucid.

'Come, we walk together,' he said. 'I am going to see Baba Sananda, who is a *sadhu* I know. He is *Niranji Akhara* . . . quite senior. He has a great energy about him. Maybe good for your research, no?'

We lowered our voices as we crossed the funeral ground, then started up again on the far side. 'How do you know him?' I asked.

'We met here,' he said. 'Eight years ago. I come here every

year, so I see him. He is always in the same place. He makes me laugh.'

And why India? I asked Honoré. What was it about this place that drew him?

The answer was partly an obvious one, partly intriguing. Drugs were cheap here, he said. He could live the whole winter on what he earned in France. Heroin came overland from Pakistan and Afghanistan. And India itself was the world's largest legitimate producer of opium poppies for medical uses. Part of that got illegally siphoned off for refinement into brown and white, and it was just getting cheaper.

'Economy 'ere is exploding,' he said. 'So the syndicates began to realise that instead of smuggling through India, from the Golden Crescent, there was an 'uge potential market on their doorstep. I think there are more than fifty million addicts already, and growing very fast. My God! I've been to dealers where you've got kids – maybe six years old – chasing the dragon in the corner.'

'Why is it growing so fast?'

'Oof!' He gave that most quintessential French exclamation, a kind of overstated sigh that seems to suggest that what follows is the most obvious thing in the world. 'Opium has always been an Indian drug. You British once had them growing it in 'uge amounts to export to China. And it's important in many religious ceremonies. But that India is gone now. India wants to be America. It wants to run *fast*. Opium is an old-world drug, something to drift away the afternoons on. Heroin is full power.' He scuffed the stone with his dirty boot; we were heading west along Kedar Ghat.

'It's not just cheap drugs, is it?' I pressed. 'There's something about India which draws you. It's in your blood.'

60

Time passed before he answered the question. His stubbled cheeks, sunken under the weight of his addiction, seem to bunch up with disquiet. With the gesture, the years sloughed off him and a frightened child seemed to shimmer, like an old photograph, beneath the skin of this unwashed fugitive. 'It is true,' he muttered, 'that I find a lot to admire in the Indians. They are *so* kind, no – even to someone like myself. But more than that, they see God so clearly, don't you think? More than any other country in which I've travelled. They see Him. One can be walking through the poorest slum and this woman will step out, so *beautiful*, and light incense before a statue, and then she is set, you know, knowing that all is OK.' He sighed, and his hands, reflectively, began to pat his jeans' pockets for cigarettes: props to ward away the present. 'They know something, I think,' he chuckled, lapsing back into badinage. 'But it's out of reach for someone like me.'

We came to a small encampment of tents beside the river where Baba Sananda was to be found. We had reached Niranjani Ghat, and Honoré explained that locals did not bathe here out of respect for the *sadhu*'s ashram. I watched Honoré greeting his old friend with genuine delight. He admired the old *sadhu*, that much was clear. For a moment I wondered if, even in the depths of addiction, Honoré came to India because it offered him a view of the only transcendent thing that might rival the drug which had him in its grip. Perhaps he wanted what the *sadhu* had . . . a different kind of freedom?

Baba Sananda turned out to be a venerable *sadhu* of about fifty, with good English, seemingly radiant health and one of the heartiest belly laughs I've ever encountered. Within minutes, we were sitting on cushions while Baba Sananda stoked up the fire for tea.

'My young friend is interested in *siddhis*,' said Honoré,

accepting a chillum from one of the younger *sadhus*. 'What can you tell him about your *sadhu* magic?'

Baba Sananda added powdered sugar to the boiling water, then green cardamom, pungent cinnamon bark, a handful of cloves. He seemed to move very thoughtfully. 'Some can do,' he said, his ash-smeared face turning towards us. 'But these days, many are boasting capaciously, and actually doing nothing.' He added some peppercorns. 'Why is this being your interest?'

'Long story,' I began. 'In Western life, there's not much magic left. Perhaps I wish there was?'

He blinked. His eyes were a duck-egg blue. 'Many foreigners wanting this, actually. Always asking *jadoo*, asking miracles. But I tell you *none* of this is possible without *Him*. He is the true miracle!' He held a finger vertically upwards. His fingernails, I noticed, were painted crimson.

I smiled and tried to look placated. He was right in many senses – how tiring it must be for the *sadhus* to be continually confronted by these spiritually bereft Westerners, asking them to demonstrate the one thing which, according to the tenets of their religion, was a pitfall, and indeed mere tomfoolery beside the larger achievements of the path! And yet, how to explain that, for us, coming from a culture overtaken by 'scientism', those paltry miracles were the raft we castaways hoped for.

He stirred the pan, tucked a glowing log more tightly into the fire and asked one of the other *sadhus* for the metal cups. We were sitting in a low canvas tent, strung up in a haphazard manner, and decorated with devotional flowers, icons of Shiva and a wooden statue of Hanuman, the monkey god, sitting in a meditative posture. It was a temporary structure, not dissimilar to the tents I'd seen at the Mela ground, and yet it exuded a homeliness: a place of order and retreat.

'I understand Hanuman performed many miracles,' I said, pointing to the statue. 'He could assume any form. His strength was superhuman.'

Baba Sananda nodded. '*Acha*. That is so. You have been reading our 'Gita. He was master of *siddhis*. Also there is one temple in Ahmadabad where Hanuman statue is granting anyone who asks visas for America.'

I couldn't help smiling.

'This is absolutely correct,' said Baba Sananda without a trace of irony. 'Even after all applications are being refused, merely one visit to Hanuman-ji in Ahmadabad is resolving all difficulties.'

'Will you go to America then?' I asked. 'Nearly everyone else in the new India seems to want to.'

'I love my India,' said Baba Sananda. 'Besides, in this *Kali Yug*, America will be very bad place. India is best.'

He was referring, of course, to the Hindu view of time, according to which we are now in the last of the four great epochs: a tempestuous age, showing a deterioration of moral values, corruption, natural disaster and darkness. In recent years the phrase *Kali Yug* (literally, 'Age of Kali', 'Age of Vice') has almost become a leitmotif in circles far outside Hinduism, because of its seeming aptness for describing current events. I've heard it used at dinner parties, as explanation for almost all the ills of the modern world ('It's just *Kali Yug*, isn't it!').

'Why will it be so bad?'

'Scripture tells us that in *Kali Yug*, men will imagine that they know everything,' said Baba Sananda didactically, 'even though they know nothing. They will also forget how to worship Him. They will have no humility. They will be arrogant. Are you getting my point?'

I said that I was. For a wizened religious mendicant he seemed to have his finger on the pulse.

He served the tea with a kind of ceremonial dignity and as I sipped the scalding liquid – slightly dazed, perhaps from passive *charras* smoking – I felt very contented with life. Through the tent entrance, all the colour of the ghats went past; we could hear the far-off calls of the *mallahs* (boatmen) ferrying pilgrims across the water. Around me, the living embodiment of Indian spiritual life: this convivial bunch of *sadhus*, sharing their chai with allcomers, and spending a good deal of their time in laughter.

'There is actually one *sadhvi*,' said Baba Sananda at last, 'in our Benares who is having some powers. Very *peculiar* lady, she is. Sometimes having a very bad temper! Shouting at peoples for no reason like a crazy person. But you can find her up there some evenings.' He pointed out of the tent, downriver a little. 'One old fort is there, abandoned by Maharajah. Now it is a place only for birds and *sadhus*.' He chuckled. 'We are enjoying view from there some days, and practising yoga *asana* in early mornings.'

'Who is this woman?' I asked. 'Will she talk to me?'

He shrugged. 'For some people she is telling future for money,' he said. 'She is not in any *akhara* either. She may talk. Or she may not. You will see.'

I thanked him.

'But remember what I said,' he cautioned. 'Only Him!' The bony finger, once again, extended to the heavens. The smile was limitless.

Some of the younger *sadhus* showed me their fort a few days later. By climbing over a stone wall and through a window frame, one could gain access to a palace inhabited only by crows. It was guarded by a hoary custodian: single-toothed, armed only with a frayed besom. He allowed the *sadhus* free access, they assured me, but should I see him I must pay the appropriate respect and perhaps a few rupees.

How had such a place, along the busiest stretch of one of India's busiest pilgrimage sites, been left untended? That it was a former palace, bathed in both sunlight and soft breezes, only heightened the appeal. Feeling the momentary guilt of the trespasser, I climbed through the window frame into an echoing chamber of winds. Grasses protruded from the gaps in its brittle stonework, between colossal stone bricks. Climbing fig trees swayed like verdant banners from the bastions. There were enormous columns with scalloped arches, small balconies under miniature domes, and below ground a bathing pool – empty now – fed by the Ganges itself during the monsoon. The *sadhus* showed me their playground with delight.

'We own nothing,' tittered one of them, a man named Dishama whose coal-black beard reached almost to his waist. 'Yet we sit each evening in this private palace!'

'Here,' said one of them, miming the playing of a flute, 'is where the royal musicians entertained their master.'

'This place,' whispered Misri surreptitiously, pointing out the remains of a central dais, 'was for beautiful Nautch girls.'

'It is said,' added Ananda, pointing to the open parapet that provided us this extraordinary view of the Ganges, 'that once the Maharaja of Varanasi was facing attack. He took his horse and jumped straight off this into the holy Mother. She carried him to safety on the other side.'

I went to peer over the parapet, far below which the shimmering surface of the water carried boatmen, merchants and the occasional corpse along the stream. Below us, I could see buffaloes at the water's edge, and hear the far-off tinkling of bells. They were hundreds of feet below: tiny pieces on a gaming board.

'When does the *sadhvi* come?' I asked.

'*Sometimes* she is coming, sometimes not,' said Dishama nonchalantly. 'She is not following any routine.'

After that I came every night, partly for the view, partly hoping to catch a glimpse of this mysterious female *sadhu*. Now and then the holy men were there and we would sit together, practising each other's language, and probing ways of life which, on both sides, seemed to exert a fascination. Other times I sat alone, reading in the fading light, or watching the riverfront from this privileged eyrie, an arena of devotion, colour and dignified death.

In the end it took several weeks; I was beginning to give up hope. But at last I saw her. She appeared one evening without a sound, shuffling across the worn flagstones on her leathered feet. Paying me no heed, she sat down, cross-legged, on the edge of the parapet. Around her neck, she wore a *mala* necklace of bone skulls – a sure sign that she was a tantric practitioner of some kind. She had a long dreaded braid of hair which fell to beyond her waist, and very pale skin.

I watched her furtively, my heart suddenly racing. Was she an enlightened one in the guise of a crone? Or just another wandering charlatan of the kind that Prabir Ghosh spent his days debunking? The *sadhus* said she told the future for money, but was she wilfully deceiving people? Did she believe she had such an ability but actually did not? The third possibility – one that made me inwardly flinch even as it occurred to me – was that she had actually gained super-natural abilities.

This last idea seemed to stir up all the conflicting ideas that, to this point, I'd been struggling to keep apart. Though I was intent on understanding the varied mystical paths of India, I remained deeply sceptical – a product of scientific empiricism, a cynic. Buddha, with his non-dogmatic, ostensibly rational mysticism, seemed entirely credible. But these Hindu saints, who flew through the air, passed years without eating, claimed the ability to give and take life upon a whim – were simply stretching my beliefs too far. And yet if I was entirely sure then why was I here, sitting in this abandoned fort as the dusk fell . . .

That evening we made no acknowledgement of each other. Neither did we on the next, when she appeared at about the same time, walking in like some ethereal Miss Haversham, trinkets swinging from her neck. On the third evening, however, feeling that the time had come to see if she would talk to me, I approached her.

'I am *not* a Westerner,' she said, as I came close.

'I didn't say you were.'

I was surprised that she had spoken at all.

'People *think* I am,' she said, in a voice that seemed ill-accustomed to conversation. 'I was born in Kashmir, before Partition. There we have white skins, a relic of the Aryan invasion. Mine is even whiter than most.'

'You speak good English.'

'I was a scholar once. My father educated me in the finest schools. English once came very easily to me.' She was looking ahead. Was she talking to me, or merely to herself?

I sat down beside her tentatively, as one might approach a wild animal. Up close she seemed feral, her breath as rotten as that of an old wolverine. She had the glassy, milk-blue eyes of an effigy.

'Can I talk to you?'

'Are we not talking already?' she said. 'Do you want something more?'

'Just to talk.'

She tilted her head. 'Have the people told you I'm a witch, then? A *daayan*?'

'No. *Are* you a witch?'

She shook her head. Perhaps there was even a smile. 'Some

of the locals are thinking so. They avoid me most of the time. But then when they're having troubles, they come to me. Is human nature not strange?'

'Do you tell them the future?'

'Future is not possible,' she hissed. 'But patterns are there. Patterns can be discerned. Likely outcomes. Not always correct.'

'Would you look for me?'

'Why?' she snapped. 'Have you lost your way?'

'Who wouldn't be interested in the future?'

'The wise,' she said. 'The wise are not interested. The foolish look forward.'

'Perhaps I'm a little lost,' I confessed. 'I'm looking for something. I'll keep looking until I find it.'

This seemed to animate her. For the first time, she really met my eyes. It was a palpable effort for her to rouse herself from the dreamlike state she'd been in.

'I had that feeling once,' she said. 'My father cried out behind me as I left home. But I didn't look back. I was still a child.'

'Do you mind me asking why not?'

'Because he was dealing with his own attachment. Nothing I could do would change that. But I *could* see it — could see that the only thing worthy of my attention was absolute liberation. And so I left him, and I had no regrets, not even a desire to turn round and wave my hand. To do so would have been to draw him deeper into the fire.'

I peered from the parapet to the surface of the Ganges, turning brown now as the sun descended. On the other side of the river, a flat plain stretched out until it disappeared into mist. I could see several cows walking across it, seemingly unaccompanied.

'Why are you always alone?' I asked.

'How do you know I am?'

I felt embarrassed. 'The *sadhus* told me. I asked them who you were.'

'My path has always been one of solitude,' she said gently. 'I've never needed people, neither a family nor an *akhara*. With those things come rules and regulations. Expectations. Constrictions. My life has been about discarding those things. I do not consider myself a *sadhu*.'

I thought for a while about what she was saying. Despite the slowness of her speech, she was highly eloquent. I could believe that she'd been a scholar once. And then she turned her back on it all, in search of the numinous. Perhaps that was what I was trying to do, although I lacked the will to cut myself off entirely from the past.

She raised herself to her feet with the help of a bamboo staff. 'I will see you again,' she said.

I returned the following night, immensely curious to find out more but unsure whether she'd return at all. If the truth be told, I wasn't sure if she was entirely sane. Something of her manner, her rags and rank smell, made me think she was barely hanging on to the world.

And yet there *was* something which fascinated me. The other *sadhus* who'd shown me the abandoned palace, despite their kindness, showed few outward signs of being more spiritually evolved than anyone else. They were cheerful, fond of badinage; they seemed to lack any special gravitas. This old woman, however, filled the room with her presence. Her eyes, when they settled upon me, seemed to burn with an unwavering flame. Amongst the spiritual crowd, the word 'enlightenment' seemed to hang upon everyone's lips and yet both the true nature of the state, and the means of recognising an enlightened person, remained mysterious to me. 'How does one rooted in wisdom speak, sit, walk?' asks Arjuna, protagonist of the Bhagavad-Gita.

The answer, like much in the Hindu scriptures, reads cryptically. 'When a man completely casts off, O Arjuna, all the desires of the mind and is satisfied in the Self by the Self, then is he said to be one of steady wisdom!'

Sure enough, she appeared as the sun was setting. I was reading in my usual spot, and watching a boatman's son fly a kite far out on the surface of the Ganges. He was shrieking with glee as he cut his opponent's kite from the sky, and his father was hastily rowing over so that they could collect their prize before it tumbled into the water.

Just then a scuffling sound turned my attention back to the empty palace. The old women shuffled into view, looking neither to left nor right, wholly absorbed in her own orbit. I raised my hand to wave and she came over, wordlessly, and sat beside me. If anything she seemed even more dishevelled than before, her long braid almost brushing the ground as she crossed her legs beneath her. She wore red robes, a fur hat despite the warmth of the evening and, on a dirty finger, a white skull ring made of bone.

'What does the skull mean?' I asked.

Silence. Then, 'The *kapala* reminds us we are impermanent,' she said faintly. 'It is made of human bone.'

'Are you a Hindu?' I asked. 'Or a tantric of some kind?'

She smiled at me. 'You like books. You're hungry to learn. I can't tell you much. I'm just a poor old woman.'

'Why are you speaking to me?' I asked. 'The *sadhus* said you didn't speak to anyone.'

'I felt like speaking English,' she said. 'I haven't spoken this tongue for a long time.'

She was quiet again; she had sounded unwell. There was a stain on her robe. She was old, I thought. She should be surrounded by grandchildren, warming her feet before the fire.

'Do you live here in Varanasi?'

She shook her head. 'We can have no home once we begin,' she said. 'The scriptures say we should be girdled by wind, eat only air. All activities should be aimed at purification of the self. That is the path to enlightenment.'

'When did you know you could read the future?'

She scowled a little. 'Such things are child's play,' she said. 'In the great silence, many things are revealed. Sometimes I use stones: the ways in which they land can be understood. The Chinamen use I Ching – do you know of this method?'

'I've seen it once.'

'And did this convince you?'

'It seemed compelling,' I admitted.

'Exactly! Not miraculous but scientific. The falling tells a story. To a mind that is clear, this story can be spoken. That is all.'

Almost roughly, she grasped my hand. She pulled me nearer so that my upturned palm was resting on her robe, so close that her rotten breath blew against my face. I struggled to compose myself.

Her palms were coarse. I could feel her sharp black nails probing various parts of my hands on both sides. Perhaps two minutes went by in this fashion. I watched her eyes as they scanned the whorls and patterns of my hand. Her hand felt scarcely human – an animal's hand – impassive and tough. But there was a hurriedness to it all; she seemed anxious to get it over.

'*Acha*. You are highly sensitive,' she said finally. 'Health is good except for a slight imbalance of the humours. You think and live independently from your family. You do something creative, is that so?'

I nodded.

'*Acha*. But you are determined. A little stubborn. If you

meet a woman she will have to live with your work. You will not give that up for anyone. But better if she has a skill of some kind – a weaver, a potter.'

Another pause.

'You are a sensualist, in that you like food and drink. You would rather see velvet than burlap.' She paused reflectively. 'There's nothing wrong with that, as long as there is no attachment. You can enjoy food but try to distance yourself from the pleasure of it. That is important. In attachment begins all the problems of the human mind. And yes,' her eyes flicked momentarily up to mine, 'you are not as peaceful as you would like.'

All this was true, I thought. Not miraculous but a little disturbing in its accuracy . . .

'You are drawn to emptiness,' she continued. 'You're looking for it, *burning* for it a little. But you should know that there are no immutable truths, no enlightenment which is graspable. That you will have to let go very quickly if you are to evolve.' She laid down my hand. 'That's all I can tell you.'

I was disappointed. She hadn't said much.

'One more thing,' she added. 'You are frightened. You're very aware of mortality. At one point in your life your spirit felt the great emptiness itself –' she tilted her head. 'Part of you wants to return to that emptiness. But you have to find the courage to live in this world.'

I froze upon hearing this, astounded and a little afraid. I had a scar on my face which might be telling, but what she said smacked of a deeper knowledge than this. Beneath the outward chaos of the hit and run I'd been involved in, I'd felt a peace that was limitless. But how could she have known this?

That was it. She would say no more, no matter how much I pressed her. Neither did she ask for money, as I cynically imagined she might. Rather, she turned her attention to the river, which was now filling with oil lamps set adrift on the evening current. Every evening, people set their prayers upon the water, commending them to that which, it is believed, once filled Brahma's sacred vessel. After a while her eyes seemed to film over, as they had been when I first saw her, and when I stood to leave she seemed not to notice. To the sound of roosting crows I climbed from the palace courtyard and made my way back through the narrow streets to my guesthouse.

That night I couldn't sleep. Monkeys clattered around on the corrugated roof outside my window, and the moon shone so brightly over the river it was like sunlight sheering off glass. At last, utterly awake, I pulled my blanket around my shoulders, opened the window and sat upon the ledge watching the dormant city. The air was chill, tinged, even now, with wood smoke from the funeral pyres at the Manikarnika Ghat.

Perhaps there will never be certainty, I said to myself. Perhaps every encounter in this strange journey will be like my meeting with the *sadhvi*; simultaneously profound and unsatisfactory. Even after many months in India, nothing seemed to stay in clear focus. This country, these myriad paths and traditions, were like the river itself, each wave made up of infinite drops, each one of them breaking apart to form a million others. Everything was in constant flux.

And yet despite the ambiguity of India, or perhaps merely its complexity for someone like myself, it was by far the most absorbing place I had ever been. Religion, as I had learned it in childhood, seemed to divide the world into two halves: one sacred, one profane. In India that division was gone. Here everything was sacred, everything was set apart for the worship or service of God. People saw Him everywhere – in elephants, in river stones, in the whorls upon a human hand. Were they ridiculous? Should we be against religion because, as Richard Dawkins suggests, 'it teaches us to be satisfied with not understanding the world'?

Or was it that we were searching for a new understanding of the world to combat our chronic levels of depression, disease and disconnection? Was it we who were so cut off from the idea of the earth as 'sacred' that we were close to destroying it altogether? Was it we who were so bound up in epistemology that we were confining ourselves, before the journey had even begun, to languishing in unsatisfactory scepticism?

In all likelihood, I would never know if the female *sadhu* had really mastered the *siddhas*. But this experience, far more than in some limited quest for proof, had brought me in contact with a person who had spent fifty years in the most rigorous search for transcendence. For the first time I had met someone who, it seemed clear, had earned a knowledge of the spaces which lay beyond the veil. Whatever the outcome of this strange pilgrimage I seemed to be on, I was glad of the journey that had led me to that.

In what I sought next, this experience might also serve me well. An ecologist friend of mine had remembered something highly intriguing from his time spent in Ladakh. While working near Zanskar, he'd come to know the village 'oracle': a trance healer who had some local renown as a healer and diviner. When not in trance she was a normal member of the community, a wife and mother, he told me. But once a week she donned the ceremonial robes of a *lhama* and left her body completely. When she was in such a state, the villagers would come to her with their problems, both physical and psychological, and, for the most part, she treated them with complete success.

'There aren't many oracles left now,' he said. 'It was ten years ago when I saw this. But if you're interested in spirit worlds I strongly suggest you go up there. I only saw her in trance once, but it was the most extraordinary experience of my life.'

Oracles in the Land of the Snows

In north-west India, bordering the vale of Kashmir and the trans-Kunlun territory of East Turkistan and Tibet, lies Ladakh, Land of the High Passes, one of the most isolated cultures on earth. More even than Nepal and Tibet, both of which are now easily accessible, Ladakh retains the allure of a forgotten kingdom, a place of vast mountainscapes, amongst which Buddhist monks meditate towards enlightenment in their ancient monasteries.

Beyond the chance to see oracles, there were other reasons to reach Ladakh. It would be a chance to explore a unique desert eco-system. Cut off from the monsoon, Ladakh usually receives less than fifty millimetres of rain per year. Its vistas are a combination of weather-beaten cliffs and alpine desert, blown into uncanny shapes by the dust-laden wind, and immense open plateaux upon which little grows. In this surreal setting, a distinctive culture of some 150,000 people survives. The town of Dras in Kargil district has the dubious distinction of being the second coldest inhabited town in the world.

Given the immensity and loneliness of the Ladakhi landscapes, it seems little wonder that Buddhism, reaching Leh via Kashmir in the second century AD, should have found such fertile soil here. Most of the Buddha's teachings stem from his insights concerning *sunyata* or the essential emptiness of all phenomena. For the Buddha, the world, as human beings imagine it to exist, is an illusion. Nothing exists in isolation or possesses a separate 'self'. Instead, he taught his disciples to view the material world as a complex web of interdependence and connectivity. Things – a flower, or an individual human self – only exist in relation to each other.

For the Ladakhis, eking out a difficult existence amidst the vagaries of a harsh natural world, this teaching of connectivity must have been profoundly life-affirming. Before that time, most of Ladakh practised a pantheistic animism in which aspects of their environment were worshipped as the abode of cosmic deities. This natural world was seen as a fearful place, full of spirits, demons and 'hungry ghosts'. With the coming of Buddhism, a systematic philosophical system linked the Ladakhis to the world around them. It also espoused inner silence as the ground upon which to plant the seeds of nirvana. Silence, as any visitor to Ladakh can attest, is something Ladakhis know well.

As is often the case in the transmigration of beliefs, it didn't take long before the Buddhist teachings began to merge with what had been there before. Elements of Hinduism, sympathetic magic and shamanism blended with the incoming Buddhism, resulting in a form of practice which is some distance from what the Buddha taught. This Vajrayana school (common to most of the Himalayan regions) is a highly esoteric religion, often involving great secrecy. It also contains a great number of magical formulas, the exorcism and destruction of demons, divination, auguries, and – if I could still find them – oracles.

Prior to my experiences in Ladakh, I knew next to nothing of oracles. The classical world, I remembered from school, had believed in oracles, most famously in Delphi. The priestess of the oracle at Delphi was known as the 'Pythia' and it was said that Apollo spoke through her. Generally an older woman of blameless life chosen from among the peasants of the area, the oracle sat on a tripod seat over an opening in the earth. Some theories suggest that the fissure over which she sat may have released a type of natural gas with the power to induce trances. Under the influence, the oracle spoke in riddles which were then interpreted by the priests of the temple. Seekers from all over the classical world came to see the oracle, and she was consulted before all major political undertakings.

From Delhi my plane flew north-west towards the Zoji La Pass. Before the coming of air travel, this was the lowest western land approach to Ladakh, at 14,000 feet. Even by plane, the experience is astounding. For some time one creeps above serrated peaks, peering into deserted snow bowls, before suddenly dropping into the Leh valley. Kushok Bakula Rimpoche airport, the highest commercial landing strip in the world, turns out to be a kind of military encampment, ringed by barbed wire and hills of brown shale. Officially part of the Indian sector of divided Kashmir, Ladakh retains one of the strongest military presences in India and, from the first, this is powerfully evident. Tourists, in fact, have only been allowed into Ladakh since 1974.

Stepping out in the piercing clarity of Leh, one is struck immediately by the air, so thin and pure, one's lungs marvel first at the sheer sweetness of this nectar, and only then begin to feel its scarcity. At 3,050 metres, visitors to Leh invariably feel some symptoms of altitude sickness, and especially those who arrive by air. By early evening I was wishing I'd made a more conservative approach, as a throbbing headache set up shop for the night.

Nevertheless, Leh in summer is an enchanting sight. Soon

after leaving the somewhat forbidding environs of the airport, one arrives in the town itself, a jumble of traditional mud buildings, ringed by apricot and apple trees, rich vegetable patches, willow and poplars. More even than the natural environment, fed by trickling glacier-melt for the short summer months, it's the Ladakhi people who enliven their surroundings. Weather-worn like almost no other people on earth, they bear the distinctive pink complexion of high altitude dwellers, as well as the most evocative smiles I've ever encountered.

For the first few days I lay low, reading in the garden of my guesthouse, while the elderly patriarch of the family hoed onions in the clear light. Initially I had trouble sleeping, and the slightest exertion left me panting. But soon – thanks to a diet rich in blood-thinning garlic and litres of water – my body began to acclimatise and I was able to begin my explorations of Leh. Another guest in the Oriental Guesthouse fared less well. Beset by fever, vomiting and diarrhoea, she showed all the signs of chronic altitude sickness. The local doctor came to visit, recommending her glucose and apricots, which, due to their high iron content, help the body to produce red blood cells more easily. The patriarch, a spry seventy-eight but with the mischievous grin of a teenager, seemed unfazed by the American girl's travails. 'All will pass,' he whispered to me, as the American sucked on her oxygen tank. 'According to Lord Buddha everything passes . . . although perhaps more slowly for Americans.'

From the guesthouse, a rutted track led down towards the town. I walked slowly, my senses alive to the Himalayan light, the chattering of finches, the wild flowers lit up on the verge. Behind a low stone wall, a newly born *dozo* calf, the hardy half-cow, half-yak breed which serves the Ladakhis as farm animals, lay soaking up the sunlight. Still wet with afterbirth, it struggled to its feet, then slipped, then struggled up again. Steam rose from its back.

I stopped for a minute, overwhelmed by the wonder of it all, the smells of wood smoke and newly turned earth. Not even a murmur of wind served to break this endless silence. That old, obscure longing felt in cities seemed entirely absent here. There was nowhere I was trying to get to, nowhere I needed to be. My heart was overflowing with the simple delight of the moment.

Towards the town, however, all was less serene. A small hump-backed bridge had collapsed due to the storm-fed river, and a group of military engineers were erecting a temporary replacement. It was dangerous work, with the icy cold water bolting over the rocks below, gurgling and sucking down-stream. One intrepid Sikh, tied on with ropes, was lowering himself an inch above the white water to hammer in some bolts. He stopped from time to time to realign his turban.

'Big problem is there,' shouted a young soldier to me above the noise of the rapids. He beamed as if this were all a huge adventure. 'Too much rain is coming. Bridge has been smashed to pieces!'

As I would learn over the weeks to come, this was just one incident in a worsening series. In recent years, global warming has changed the weather patterns considerably here, to the point that rainfall had exceeded the total yearly average merely in the two weeks prior to my arrival. For a self-reliant culture, whose entire social structure has carefully evolved around agricultural practices designed to make the most of an exceptionally short growing season, such changes are poten-tially catastrophic. Their crops – barley, millet, apricots – do not fare well in too much rain. Nor do their houses, made of mud and brick. Or their animals, their roads, even the clothes they wear. Ladakhi culture is a marvel of invention and evolution – but how can a culture attuned to its landscape over millennia be expected to adapt within a few short seasons?

'We're very frightened about the future,' one dusty farmer later told me in a small workers' café. 'This year we have seen a month of rain! Never, even in the memory of my grandfather, has this happened. People in the Markha valley have lost everything.'

The town itself – aside from the occasional rumbling truck, and the ubiquitous backpackers' cafés – has changed scarcely, perhaps, for millennia. It was once a major trading post, and merchants from Persia moved through the Karakoram mountains to the great Silk Road at Yarkand here, carrying their precious cargoes of gold, silk and opium.

Along the thoroughfare, sun-beaten Ladakhi women sat before their piles of produce – luminous green beans, rosy-cheeked apricots, stunted carrots – with which they eke out a meagre wage to buy the goods they cannot grow themselves. Some of them had travelled many miles to bring their wares to market. With them were donkeys hopping with fleas, a lumbering yak, monks en route for their monasteries in the deep interior. Noticing one of them, a contemplative young boy of no more than ten or eleven, I wondered whether this bustle was exciting for him, a welcome respite from his duties, or if – to the contrary – he longed for the silence of the inner passes.

Finding a small café with tables shielded from the sun, I ordered some rolls with thick apricot jam, and ate my breakfast. They even had coffee – a fortunate by-product of tourism in these parts – and I sipped it contentedly, noting Kashmiri merchants en route for the mosque, an old woman spreading apricots out to dry on the flat of her roof, two backpackers arriving on heavily laden Enfield motorcycles.

An Indian man approached me: 'You want meditation classes?' he asked. 'I teach yoga system of Patanjali, Tibetan yoga, Astanga yoga, kundalini yoga and bhakti yoga. All types are possible, depending on budget.'

'That's very comprehensive,' I said. 'Why so many types?'

He leaned closer. 'Honestly, sir, foreign people are liking *too* many choices. It is how they are. But actually, all systems the same!' He roared with delight. 'Our little secret, yes.'

Over the next week I begin to frequent the library of the Ladakhi Ecological Development Group, set up in the 1970s by veteran activist Helena Norberg Hodge. Here, as well as coordinating various efforts to preserve Ladakh from the marauding shock of the new, a well-stocked library houses books in many languages and dialects. None of the librarians knew much of a continuing oracle tradition, however, despite their keen interest in my project. 'I have heard that this is a practice of the villages closer to Tibet,' one of them told me. 'But we do not have such things here – not for a long time. I would not know where to begin. If you had been here fifty years ago, perhaps . . .'

Rather despondently – since this answer was becoming somewhat familiar – I contented myself with reading about the oracles in such dusty tomes as *Oracles and Demons of Tibet* by one René de Nebesky-Wojkowitz. This Austrian ethnologist, who died in 1959 at the age of only thirty-six, spent many years in the Himalayan region, prior to and during the Chinese invasion of Lhasa. According to Wojkowitz, Tibetan Buddhists believe in the existence of a special group of deities called *chos skyong*, believed to protect them against adversaries. These wrathful and generally ferocious beings, who can be enlisted for good or sometimes evil purposes, are ritually called upon by the use of skull drums, thigh bone trumpets, or sometimes a libation of blood or bile. Many of those deities, Wojkowitz goes on, take possession of certain men and women who act as their mouthpieces: these are the oracles – who generally enter their first trance around the time of puberty.

Time passed. After several weeks without success, during which I'd seemingly visited every scholar in the district, I decided to temporarily abandon my quest and spend some days exploring. Real life was passing me by while I sat in libraries and offices, talking to people who, invariably, seemed to shake their heads dolefully and tell me I was wasting my time. Outside it was high summer and all about me trekkers were coming and going en route for Zanskar and Lamayru, places I'd long dreamed of visiting. If life had taught me anything thus far, it was that I should take the opportunity of seeing these things now, for who knew if I would come this way again.

So I turned my attention instead to the monasteries of the interior. Few dwellings on earth feel so remote or suggestive of spiritual aspiration as these tiny *gompas*, set amidst jagged peaks and hills of steep scree, cut off for months of the year by the weather. In winter, everything turns white and the ground sets like iron. The days fall dark early, and the wind, coming down from Siberia, can be one of the coldest on earth.

In summer, however, this lonely stillness vanishes before an equally formidable adversary: the armies of camera-wielding tourists. Rarely have I felt so ashamed as when I walked into ancient Hemis monastery one Monday morning, to see an Italian woman ordering one of the monks to break from his conversation and move so that she could take a photograph. When the monk looked up at her in amused bewilderment, she began to gesticulate wildly, shouting aggressively at him that he was spoiling the shot. The scene was inexcusable and yet hardly surprising. It is little wonder that modern tourists, transplanted from their own culture with a speed and ease resembling magic, fail to exhibit the sensitivity that former generations, moving on foot or by public transport, may have learned by observation. Perhaps, too, a cultural arrogance remains as we move from the developed to the developing world. Do we think that by dint of our wealth and technological superiority, it is we who are civilised and others who are 'primitive'? In this – as perhaps with our rationalism – we may have thrown the baby out with the bathwater.

Later that day, as I was sitting on the parapet of Hemis monastery, I spotted the American girl who had been so ill in my guesthouse. She looked healthier now, with some colour in her cheeks, and was inspecting a copper-gilt statue of Lord Buddha. We soon got talking and discovered a common interest in the mystical. Zoe was a yoga teacher from Ohio, and had come to India, somewhat like myself, on a spiritual pilgrimage. She was travelling alone, visiting only places of spiritual interest.

'I just felt a bit ridiculous, you know, teaching these kids yoga when I hadn't been to India,' she said. 'I didn't want to be one of those Westerners who think they're like gurus or something just because they can do a back bend.'

Zoe seemed to frown continually as she spoke. She was a young woman, barely twenty-five, with an angular, earnest face and blonde, shoulder-length hair. 'My Mom thinks I'm nuts: going to India on my own, practising Hinduism, which, to her, is like this foreign cult or something. She's a Baptist and takes Jesus kinda seriously.'

We went for lunch together in the small teahouse at the entrance to the monastery, ordering *thukpa* (Tibetan noodle broth) in dented aluminium bowls. It was the kind of café that did a brisk business because of its location, thereby absolving its proprietors from even the most cursory effort. Two chickens confronted each other on the concrete floor. Tables glistened with congealed food. We sipped the soup warily.

Zoe was a New Ager, in the best sense of the phrase: her spirituality was a personalised miscellany of Native American, Wicca and Hinduism. She'd read F. Max Müller's translation of the Upanishads, had spent time in South America studying shamanism. Like me, she felt there must be something at the end of a journey like this: if nothing else, the fact of having shattered habitual ways of seeing. But more than that, she confessed, she really was searching for transcendence. Many travellers I met professed an interest in the Eastern religions, but she was the first to openly profess the desire for enlightenment. 'Once you begin to recognise how the structure of the ego manipulates our every interaction,' she said gently, 'I don't see how you have any choice but to try and get to grips with it. It's become the central purpose of my life.'

'And how does one do that?' I asked. 'That's the crux of it. So many methods. Easy to go wrong.'

'I guess I'm figuring that out as I go. But all these traditions, I think, offer methods that work. If we practise hard enough, there's a way through all the difficulties of the human condition. If we conquer the ego, we can become free.'

I would think upon these words a lot over the months to come.

After lunch Zoe and I followed an old monk into the interior of the monastery. Clutching a medieval fob of keys, he unlocked a six-inch door, then led us into murk and smells of yak butter and incense, the former faintly rancid, the latter pleasantly astringent. Inside the prayer hall, our eyes drew focus on an almost unbelievable array of *thangkas* – the exquisite geometric scroll paintings of Tibetan Buddhism. From every wall, a cosmology of Buddhas and demons stared down at us, laid out on a systematic grid of angles and intersecting lines. Up close, the detail seemed too precise for any human hand. Despite the gloom, the colours – made from pounded minerals and rocks – seemed to glow with a phosphorescence, giving the scenes a supernatural radiance. The Buddhas were impassive or smiling faintly. And the angry demons were hellish forms that even Dante might have baulked at.

Hemis, the monk told us, owns the world's largest *thangka*. At sixty-two feet in length, it is unveiled only once every twelve years, at the monastery's summer festival. Elsewhere in the *gompa*, he added in hushed tones, the hands of the monk who painted it are preserved as a sacred relic.

'Aside from *thangka*, summer festival is very important,' added the lama, his grey-green eyes twinkling under tufted eyebrows. 'It is written in the *Padma Kathang*, the prophecy of Guru Padmasambhava, that on this day the most faithful and sincere devotees are blessed by a vision of Guru Padmasambhava himself.'

Zoe asked who Padmasambhava had been.

'Guru Rinpoche,' explained the monk, 'was a very great Buddha. Sometimes called "Second Buddha". He brought Vajrayana Buddhism to Tibet, and destroyed many demons there. A powerful *siddha* yogi.'

'And have *you* seen him,' I enquired, 'at this summer festival?'

The monk smiled, so that his whole wrinkled face lit up with delight, jangled his keys musically and strode away. Like many encounters in Ladakh, a smile seemed the only answer I could hope for.

★　　★　　★

86

It was the following morning when the breakthrough came. On my way to the German bakery in Leh, I took a short cut down a narrow street. And it was here – through good fortune, sheer coincidence or a glimmer of magic – that I noticed a small handwritten sign propped up outside a particularly shabby-looking travel agent's. 'We take visits to oracle,' it said.

In this dusty back street of Leh, before an open sewer, a new direction had finally opened up. I almost glanced up at the heavens in gratitude.

Inside, a young man of about thirty sat wreathed in blue cigarette smoke, reading the morning newspaper. This was Norbu, dressed in North Face and Patagonia, but with the high Mongolian cheekbones of the Ladakhi people. His eyebrows arched in thick parentheses. The radio was playing Bryan Adams, with whom Norbu was humming softly under his breath.

Over sweet tea, we sat in the dim light and talked of oracles. Norbu seemed little surprised at my questions; I may as well have been asking him to lead me trekking. It was his sister who was the local oracle, he explained. He took people to see her not for money – he made no charge – but because he was proud of this Ladakhi tradition, and felt that it had potential to help people when Western medicine had failed.

'I do not take "tourists",' he began. 'I take people who are really interested, and who are respectful of our traditions. No cameras allowed. First rule.'

'When did you know your sister was an oracle?' I asked him.

He thought for a moment. 'My sister little older than usual when she got the spirit inside her. She was something like twenty-five. Most girls more like sixteen.'

I asked him how they recognised her symptoms when they first appeared.

'When spirit is inside her she has no fears, no shame; she is acting like a mad person, actually. Completely crazy if you have never seen it before. In Ladakh we know the symptoms so we took her to the monastery and spoke to Stakma Rinpoche in Shishod. He is what we call a *lapok* – one who is able to train the oracles. He said she was becoming an oracle and therefore needed some training.'

'It must be very frightening for a young girl,' I said. 'To have these visions, and be hearing voices. How did she know she wasn't going mad? If this happened in the West we'd probably lock that person away for the rest of their lives.'

'Here it is not frightening,' said Norbu. 'Oracles have no memory of the spirits once they have gone – you will see. Spirit comes – maybe one hour, two hours, and all kinds of crazy things are happening, and afterwards she is normal again. But training is *definitely* necessary to control the spirits. *Rinpoche* told us that when the spirit comes first both good and bad spirits are there. Training is necessary to separate them. If not, person can go mad permanently. So my sister went to Sabu Lamu for guidance, and she stayed with her for some time. When she came back she was fully trained oracle, and recently she has become the main oracle for the town of Leh. This is a great honour for our family.'

'Why has it been so difficult for me to find an oracle?' I asked Norbu. 'So many people who must have known about them professed a total ignorance. I must have asked thirty people.'

Norbu looked embarrassed. 'These traditions can be secret,' he said, 'and some people not liking foreigners coming to ask questions. Some people have asked me to take down my sign. But I have no problem with people seeing things, and nor does my sister, as long as they are interested people, or people with real trouble who need help. No problem for us. Sometimes Western medicine is not working, and oracle helps.'

'So she won't mind if I talk to her?

'Why would she?' said Norbu lightly. 'Come tomorrow, eleven o'clock, you can see. One German fellow is also coming – he has some problems.'

I got up to go, but first I had one more question.

'You seem quite Westernised,' I pointed out. 'Your clothes, your music, your brand of cigarettes. What do you think about the oracle? Do you really *believe* she is speaking with gods?'

He raised his eyebrows. 'Of *course* I believe. Many times I've been sick and my sister has cured me. We do not believe "blindly"; we believe because our experience tells us it works. Once I saw my sister treating a cow. They had taken it to the vet and he could not find out what was wrong with it. They had given it antibiotics and still it was getting thin – you could see the ribs through the skin. And my sister pushed her hand into the cow's side and took out a big nail which the cow had eaten.'

'She cut the cow open?'

'No, there was no cut. Hand went inside, and then nail was out. Afterwards cow was better.' Norbu grinned. 'When we ask the gods for help, they listen.'

Next morning I was up early, in time to gather my thoughts at a chai stall in Leh before departure. Around me, the ancient market place hummed with life. There were khaki trucks carrying troops to repair the roads and bridges; a muleteer, wearing traditional Ladakhi clothes, goading his unruly beasts onwards with a willow stick; several diminutive boot-blacks, carrying boxes of polish and brushes, tapping the Western tourists on the shoulder to tout for business. Many of them were from Bihar, one of the poorest states in India, and came up here during the summer to earn some money. Who knew where they slept, who took care of them? Some of them seemed scarcely ten years old, like characters from Dickens.

After an unusual juice made from sea buckthorn and a few momos, I paid my bill and walked to Norbu's travel agency. He was waiting outside, smoking as usual, and talking with a lanky German man of about forty. The man looked gaunt and his skin was stretched tight over his cheekbones. He had red hair, shaved almost to the scalp, and a depleted smile.

'Stefan,' he said, proffering his hand. 'You are coming to see this oracle too?'

I said that I was.

'You too have some problems?'

'Just interested.'

'I have rheumatoid arthritis,' he said. 'My body is failing me. Doctors tell me I have the limbs of a seventy-year-old man already. So, everywhere I go, I visit healers. In India, I did a *pancha karma* – a three-month Ayurvedic cleanse. *Scheibe*, the things they made me eat! This has actually helped a good deal. But the problem is still bad.'

'I'm sorry.'

He shrugged. 'Nevertheless, this journey has changed my life. Even healed, I could never get back to the work I was doing. Not after this!'

I asked him what he did back at home.

'I was doing a PhD in robotics. And I worked for a small artificial intelligence company, doing research.' He looked awkward. 'I am kind of a nerd, actually. Good with numbers. Or at least, I was. It seems numbers have failed me.'

I asked him how he'd found out about Norbu.

'Two years ago, Norbu took my sister trekking. She met the oracle with him too. She is quite a cynical person also, but was quite convinced. She suggested I come here and see whether it could help.'

'I'm surprised *you're* not more sceptical. You're a scientist after all.'

'I do not know if this will work, my friend,' said Stefan, massaging his swollen knuckles. 'But I am quite desperate now, and when that is the case you will try anything, *ya*. Soon, I am worried that I will have to walk with sticks or be in a wheelchair. My movement is increasingly restricted. Arthritis, you may know, is an auto-immune disorder, which means that the body is falsely sending an immune response where none is needed. In my case, that may end up killing me. So what have I got to lose?'

Crammed together in Norbu's weather-beaten hatchback, we left Leh. Quickly, the patina of development that has changed Ladakh so quickly petered out. Asphalt returned to dust, concrete to mud, and the twenty-first century, despite a few subtle flourishes, retreated to a time in which Ladakh had neither reason nor desire to seek self-definition from America or Europe. It felt stirring and somehow appropriate to this adventure to be leaving the modern world behind us.

Outside Leh, the looming mountainscape appeared through the morning light. At a military checkpost, primary-coloured Tibetan prayer flags trembled in the breeze. 'This is a desperately hard landscape; without solace,' I wrote in my notebook. 'The rocks seem remaindered from some primordial conflict, the fauna reclusive.' Norbu, displaying some of the human warmth which seems to bloom so brightly here, leaned back with one hand on the steering wheel and offered us some bitter apricot seeds, said to be a cure for all ills. In the spring, he said, the hills of the Leh valley explode with white blossom. 'There are more than forty different varieties of apricots here,' he says. 'After the snow – no colour anywhere! – it is so beautiful.'

We came at last to a small hamlet. Perhaps fifty people lived here, along with the usual pye-dogs, *dozos* (half cow, half yak), sinewy chickens: those animals which can survive up here, providing sustenance or protection. Tibetan Buddhism, unlike other schools, does not interpret the Buddha's statements on non-violence to mean vegetarianism. In any case, it would be impossible at this altitude, with the Ladakhi diet already restricted to largely *tsampa* (roasted barley meal), wheat noodles and dried vegetables. Religion – like much else in this world – adapts to the geography of place.

Stepping out, we saw that ours was the only car in evidence. Wisps of yellow roof straw drifted from the new thatching; cow pats were drying in the sun for winter fuel. Outside the ramshackle building, there were three local women all in black, their necks covered with scarves. One of them held a young girl in her arms who was sobbing. There was not a bird in the sky.

Following Norbu, we ascended some uneven wooden steps, pausing to add our shoes to the mound of sandals and cheap trainers already there. It was dim inside, and thick with juniper smoke. I felt my breath quickening a little. Here I was at last!

Perhaps thirty people were seated before a somewhat rotund Ladakhi woman, wearing an ornate crown and a flowing black robe, and beside her a younger girl, similarly attired but without the crown. They were chanting softly. The room was small, with a low ceiling of twigs and a concrete floor. The light from a single dirty window was muted.

'My sister,' whispered Norbu. 'Come, we will sit at the back and watch. I will translate.'

As we shuffled to the back, several of the villagers looked round, including a young man, lean and dark from the fields, and an old woman, yellow-eyed; both projecting that interested but non-judgemental stare that I've found all over India. I sat down cross-legged against the wall, trying to keep as low a profile as possible. Already, a current of energy was filling the room. Although I couldn't put my finger on it exactly, it was enough to send prickles of unease down my spine.

When the chanting stopped, the oracle moved slowly to her altar and knelt down before it. There were several brass pots containing offerings of barley grains, oil, yak butter, incense sticks. Beside those, there was a pot of juniper. She picked it up and waved it around so that the room filled with the intoxicating smoke.

I could see little of her behind the crown, just the raven-black hair, the small mouth above a round chin. She began chanting again, *sotto voce*, her pudgy hands clasped together before a picture of the Buddha and an image of the Panchen Lama – the young *tulku* (an enlightened Tibetan Buddhist lama) kidnapped by the Chinese. Her voice was strange, growing higher and more other-worldly by the minute. She turned round to the young girl and gave her a hand bell.

'That is a new oracle,' whispered Norbu, close to my ear. 'My sister is training her. Her parents have brought her here to help bring out the bad spirit from her.'

With her eyes half closed, the young girl took the ritual hand bell (known as *dril bu* in Tibetan), and began to shake it rhythmically, so that its sound cut out harshly into the cramped room. Now the oracle, already swaying in time, picked up a drum and joined the beat. The hollow drum rumbled behind the high monotony of the bell to create an eerie harmony. Together, they moved in time, the oracle's heavy frame jerking sharply, involuntarily.

'She is going into trance,' murmured Norbu. 'Oracle is coming!'

Now, the oracle picked up the smoking vessel again, so that one hand continued to beat the drum, the other to wave the smoke. Along with the drumbeats, the ringing of the bell, the swirling smoke, both heads were shaking, both women chanting louder, unintelligible words, but which Norbu later told me are of no language anyone but they can understand. It is a language which comes upon them when the spirit does, he explained: a god-given language, beyond human speech or comprehension. I could make out repeated phrases, however, each one sending them deeper into the trance.

What happened next was bizarre, even terrifying. Abruptly, as if the spirit had suddenly gained entrance to her consciousness, the oracle stiffened and her eyes seemed to blaze with energy. There was little I could relate it to, save for horror movies involving spirit possession. Norbu's sister, to all intents and purposes, had vanished, and in her place was a far more powerful energy: a wild, unruly madness that subsumed the personality beneath it. With her eyes flashing, the oracle began to speak in tongues again, shaking her head so that the enormously heavy gilt crown swayed violently this way and that.

With my heart pounding, I leaned as far back against the wall as I could manage. Whatever was going on, there was palpable force coming out of this woman now. Whether it was a state of self-induced psychosis or a genuine case of spirit possession as the Tibetans believed, this village woman seemed no longer on our plane of consciousness. Can this be real, I thought to myself?

When the oracle spoke at last her voice was booming. Startlingly deeper, more forceful, it sent a jolt of fear running through me. Throughout the room, no one moved a muscle.

The villagers looked on gravely, both dread and reverence on their faces. One small girl began to whimper quietly. Suddenly, the drum ceased and all fell silent.

'Now it begins,' said Norbu gravely.

A mother began to speak. Perhaps thirty, she breastfed a baby within a muslin sling. Beside her was another child – pink-cheeked, with fearful, angry eyes.

'My seven-year-old is constantly angry,' she told the oracle. 'He won't go to school. He's always making trouble with the other children. He won't help in the fields.'

Hearing this, the oracle tensed, invisible currents moving through her body. She held out her hand and the young mother urged her son to the front. Terrified myself, I felt for the poor child as he nervously shuffled forward, his cheeks taut with apprehension.

What happened next was almost too much to take in. Getting to her knees, the oracle lifted up the child's shirt and began to probe his stomach with her hands. Her hands were small and thick-fingered, the hands of a woman who works the fields. Finally, she located the spot she was looking for and bent her head. At first I assumed she was examining the spot closer, but before I knew what was occurring, she put her lips forward and sucked, much in the manner of a man drawing out the poison from a snake bite.

'Aaaaaaaaaaaaaaaaaaaaaaaaaaagh,' she roared. Then, leaning forward, she spat a quite stupendous amount of liquid into a bucket.

It was hard to stop myself from recoiling. She put her lips to the spot again, and repeated the process. The child's eyes began to well. Again, what seemed like half a litre of dirty water spilled into the bucket! The third time, the liquid flowed almost black, and I turned to the side, fearful that I was going to vomit. Never had I seen anything so revolting!

'She is taking out the bad,' whispers Norbu. 'Boy has some evil spirit inside him.'

Finishing her healing, the oracle wiped her mouth with the back of her hand and began to speak.

'This boy must wear some protection from a *rinpoche*,' she advised. 'Take an amulet, or a slip of paper upon which the prayers of a trusted *rinpoche* are written, and give them to the boy to wear around his neck. He will be protected.'

Before I'd even recovered, the next healing began. An old lady had stomach troubles – one of the most common complaints, according to Norbu, because of the extremely high consumption of grain amongst Ladakhis. The matriarch had a burnished copper, deeply lined face and the tight traditional braids of Ladakhi women. With little compunction she pulled her robe aside to show her rounded stomach, lined with age, while the oracle leaned forward and puckered her lips to suck out the poison.

In this case the oracle herself flinched, as if encountering some particularly bitter liquid, before spitting heavily into the bucket. More of the liquid sloshed from her lips – faintly yellow this time. Where the *hell* is it coming from, I wondered. If this was a hoax, as I imagined most scientists would postulate, it must be coming from the oracle's own stomach . . . regurgitated in some manner? With this thought in mind, I scrutinised her throat as she sucked from the old woman's belly, searching for the telltale constrictions of the oesophagus which might signify such trickery. I could find nothing. The throat appeared still.

Over the next hour, the healings continued. All of it was shocking, vaguely repulsive, but also astounding, continually prompting me to consider how extraordinary this was, how fortunate I was to be seeing this before it vanishes for good. Later, in an attempt to understand what I had seen, I read numerous scientific papers: psychotherapic interpretations of spirit possession, anthropological treatises on 'emotive healing'. One theory suggested that becoming an oracle was a pre-industrial method of dealing with schizophrenia, allowing the individual to reconcile twin personalities; another that it was caused by epilepsy. The Indian psychologist Sudhir Kakar concludes that trance healing provides 'a cultural container for a psychic state that threatened to become chaotic'.

But while all of these theories were, in their way, plausible, none of them really explained the subtlety or the sheer power of what I was seeing. Clearly, on a purely psychosomatic level, there was a level of reassurance to be gained from visiting a trusted healer. But that alone didn't account for what was happening here. I wasn't sure if this *was* just 'transcultural psychiatry', to use Emile Kraepelin's term. Nor was I satisfied, as Emile Durkheim suggested at the beginning of the twentieth century, with the notion that the source of ecstatic religious experience was society itself, a group coming together in 'collective effervescence'. To stand in front of an oracle in trance is to feel an other-worldly force that seems far beyond the human realm. Later, I would hear that the Tibetan state oracle has been known to bend an iron sword in half as if it were paper. Where does it come from, this supernatural strength? Do higher levels of consciousness bring the power of healing?

As the last of the villagers finished their treatment, the German, Stefan, was called to speak. Norbu shuffled forward to translate for him, and a long conversation ensued in Ladakhi, so that the oracle could understand the nature of the disease. Stefan spoke calmly and clearly to the oracle, and I felt a sudden wave of admiration for this sickly-looking German fellow whose quest had brought him here, so far from home, and so far from conventional Western attitudes.

At last the oracle seemed to nod her head, and a flurry of high-pitched babble broke out. When the speaking hushed, the oracle moved forward to a wooden box and withdrew a long copper tube. I noticed Stefan's eyes flickering nervously but, to his credit, he merely assented while she rolled up his trouser legs. Finally, using the same sucking technique but through the tube, she placed the copper against his withered knee joint and pursed her lips. Now, in a release of water so monumental that the room let out a collective sigh of wonder, she spat what might have been half a litre of clear, thin liquid into the bucket. Once again my stomach churned.

Moving from joint to joint, the elbows, knees, ankles and wrists, the oracle continued her bizarre therapy. Within ten minutes, the five-litre bucket she'd brought in for the ceremony was almost full, and another was produced. At the back I'd been surreptitiously making notes but now, I simply laid down my pen. This was the strangest thing I'd seen yet, and I was too incredulous to think.

When Stefan, at length, came to sit back down, he kept his eyes dead ahead and seemed to betray nothing of what he thought or had experienced. With everyone treated, I now expected the ceremony to be over, and for everyone to file out, but there was one further surprise. The oracle spoke again, and to my right, Norbu responded. Suddenly, he leaned forward to whisper in my ear.

'Oracle wants to see you.'

My blood ran cold. 'What do you mean, she wants to see me? I've got nothing to say.'

'She is calling you,' he said excitedly. 'Go forward. I will come too. You cannot refuse her!'

With my heart racing, I stepped forward. Certainly the oracle was looking at me, and there was something acutely unnerving about this strange being, deep in trance, fixing her eyes on me. Up close, she was crackling with energy, and I knelt down in genuine panic before her.

Again came the wild-sounding speech, accompanied by flailing arms. Norbu bent down to whisper.

'I know why you are here,' she says. 'You have come on business.'

I was shocked. How could she know this? Norbu must have told her . . .

'This is acceptable to me. But you must not misuse this knowledge, or it will be bad karma – for you, not me.'

I nodded weakly.

'There is something more. Your brain is full of too much pressure,' she continued, 'like a machine that breaks with overuse. You must become calm, quiet, you must let it go and live quietly.'

Again, I bowed my head. All my rationality suddenly ceased to matter.

'For your well-being you should be helping others,' the oracle continued. 'Give happiness and it will gain you more. And religion – Buddhism, Christianity, Hinduism – they do not matter, as long as you follow the right precepts, only the truth, avoid bad things, clean your mind, no bad thoughts.'

All of this seemed good enough advice. But far less specific than what she'd first said. And then, she made her final remark. It seemed to speak more powerfully to me than any voice yet on my journey, to a place deep within myself. I felt struck by wonder.

'You are afraid,' she says, 'and it is this fear which needs to be released. You must do two things. First, take some prayer flags and write your birth date on them. Then take them to a mountain. Tie them up, somewhere where the great wind can touch them, and then with each breath of wind, your fear will find release.'

She fell silent for a second; one could hear a dust mote falling in the room.

'The second thing,' she said at last, 'is that you must buy an animal. You must find an animal which is going to be eaten. Go to a butcher and buy a pig, or a lamb, or a chicken, or a pigeon, and let it go.'

'In the street?' I asked.

'No. Because then someone will find it and eat it. You must find someone to take care of it. Someone who will keep it, let it live, allow it to survive. In this manner, your fear will be freed and you will become peaceful.'

And with that it was over. Turning away, the oracle gave a sign that, for the day, she would make no more pronouncements. One minute I'd been kneeling before her, the next I was making my way, amongst Ladakhi villagers, children eager for the sunlight and the quiet, shuffling Stefan, for the doorway. Outside we stood in silence by Norbu's car. Beyond the village, a dust plain, bathed in waxen summer light, stretched out until it rose up into steep cliffs. There was not an animal to be seen and only a few stunted trees.

Feeling the need for a moment by myself, I walked to the edge of the hamlet and stared out. I felt the press of light against my face and saw sharp blue sky without clouds. What I had just experienced was beyond my ken, mysterious in a way that rendered rational analysis unimportant. Being out here, far from everything that was familiar to me, was to dispel some of the blind spots that come to all of us, comforted by home and family and the mundane. Do we shy from exploring the magical realities accepted by indigenous cultures everywhere because we believe our understanding of the world surpasses all others? Or is it that we fear uncertainty because we don't want to question the structures and ideologies that keep us safe?

Behind me, the villagers returned to their fields, or to a long tramping journey home across this desert landscape. None of them, I felt sure, was questioning the validity of what they had seen, probing its edges for clues, or trying to *understand*. Rather, they were reassured, confident that a higher power than themselves had been called upon for advice and diagnosis. In my case, that higher power, whatever it was, had given me my own set of instructions. And so that, for better or worse, was exactly what I would do.

The following day I spent some time in the dusty markets of Leh searching for a prayer flag, or 'wind horse' as the Tibetans call it, to enact the first stage of the oracle's advice. After finding one I liked, I wrote my birthday upon it, October 25th, and tucked it in my pack for the long walk up to the Shanti *stupa*, a peace pagoda set upon the highest hillside in Leh. After the first hundred steps I thought my lungs would burst but a glance behind me, at the Leh valley ringed by mountains, reassured me that it would be worth it. Several hundred more and I arrived, drenched in sweat, before a gleaming statue of the Buddha. Below me, the town was like a child's model.

Aside from a few workmen who were repairing the temple wall, I was the only person about. To one side of the hillside, across a precipitous slope, some prayer flags already fluttered and I stepped out warily, bracing myself against the wind, and tied the first string to a metal rod someone had hammered into the rock. Ten feet away across an even more vertiginous drop, I tied the other end, then edged back to safety.

Below me, the brightly coloured flags caught like sails in the wind, and the mantras written upon them became a blur, spun out across the rim of the world.

In the Footsteps of Paul Brunton:
the Cave of Sri Ramana Maharshi

Returning to Delhi one morning, I disembarked my overnight train from the Himalayas. Dawn was breaking; it seemed that the most restless nation on earth had at last found a moment of repose. Around me the city slumbered. Even the cigarette sellers and coolies lay dozing amongst their blankets.

Outside the station, I found a chai seller making his first brew of the day. He was a fat man, clad in a sooty white vest and *lungi*. His moustache would have looked grandiose on a general wearing full regalia: it suggested an outrageous self-belief. The accoutrements of his trade were simple: a gas burner, a pan, a sieve, one calcified spoon and a dozen cracked glasses. With this he offered a service and made enough to survive, perhaps support an entire family. He brewed, I suppose, many hundreds of cups per day, and yet to each one he gave his full attention.

Beside the chai stand was a single rickety bench, on which the customers could sit for the minute or two it took to drain their glasses, and take respite from the city. Hefting my dusty pack to the ground, I sat down on this beside another customer, an elderly gentleman perusing *The Times of India*. Above me, the distinctive red-bricked arches of Old Delhi station were changing colour in the weak sunrise. Beyond them, kites screeched in the mist.

Groggy from the journey, I wanted to sit for a while and reacclimatise to the capital. Before me lay exhausting bargaining with rickshaw wallahs, the fending-off of hawkers, the shooing of urchins, a hectic drive across Delhi to my guesthouse. Before then, a moment of silence: a quiet emergence into the metropolis.

I accepted my tea, which was pungent with *adrak* (ginger) and black cardamom, and felt a great sense of well-being as the sweetness entered my system. As I began on my second cup, I took out my book. It was Somerset Maugham's *The Razor's Edge*, which I had found languishing on the bookshelf of a backpackers' lodge in Manali, between a Clive Cussler and a copy of the Torah. I opened it and began to read.

'Very fine,' said a voice to my left. 'Very fine to see the works of William Somerset Maugham are still appreciated.'

It was the *Times of India* reader, a gentleman of at least seventy, I now noted, whose small, benign face was contained by a shock of ash-white hair.

'Yes, I'm halfway through,' I replied. 'It's a real discovery.'

The old man looked at me quizzically and laid down his newspaper. 'Isn't it?' he said. 'That title is a quote from the Upanishads, you know, one of our holy books.' He thought for a moment: ' "The sharp edge of a razor is . . . difficult to pass over; thus the wise say the path to Salvation is hard." '

'That must refer to Larry Darrell,' I said.

The old man laughed shrilly, his eyes gleaming. 'Of course! I had forgotten the name. Larry Darrell. A young man who ventures East in search of esoteric knowledge and returns utterly changed. Isn't that why all you foreigners are here? Searching for some . . . guru who will make your life better.' He cackled at his own joke.

'I'm not entirely innocent of that charge,' I said. 'But I've got my eyes open.'

The old man pursed his lips. 'That is prudent, young man. Our India is more full of tricksters than saints.'

'You've read much Somerset Maugham?'

He nodded. 'He spent time in India, of course. Just before the Second World War.'

'I didn't know.'

The old man blew steam noisily from the top of his chai. 'Sir, did you know that Larry Darrell existed?'

I shook my head.

'Yes, yes. One theory suggests that Somerset Maugham based his character on a man named Paul Brunton. Have you heard that name?'

I shook my head.

'Then you may consider this meeting very fortuitous,' he said. 'Because I can safely say that for anyone interested in the mystical traditions of India, the writings of Mr Paul Brunton might be considered essential.'

At this moment the chai seller cut in, holding his weather-beaten kettle above our empty glasses. 'Allow me,' said the old man at once, fishing in his pockets for change. 'Amit Rajkowa, at your service.'

I introduced myself and we shook hands formally. Folding his newspaper delicately along its seam, Mr Rajkowa shuffled closer to me along the bench.

'Too many travellers have come to our shores with some-what fanciful ideas,' he said animatedly. 'But Mr Brunton travelled here with a *genuine* fascination for Indian spirituality. *The Razor's Edge* is a good yarn, but whimsical, and without any real depth. Brunton's book, however, was the product of real insight. I tell you this as a man who has studied our philosophies for many years.'

I said that I would buy a copy.

The old man nodded and his rich brown eyes narrowed for a moment. 'If only my granddaughter would buy a copy. Always she is reading these . . . fashion magazines! *Cosmopolitan* and such things. Nothing of our Indian spirituality interests her. You know, I have much affection for her but I think she will never wake up in this lifetime. The West is a hypnotic jewel for the young Indians: they will strive for it their whole lives, but it is not till they have it in their hands that they see it is a lump of clay.'

'So you don't mind that there are so many Westerners here, looking for . . . gurus? You don't think we're somehow ridiculous?'

'Quite the contrary. Because the thing is, my young friend, India is a land filled with a great river of spiritual wisdom. But many Indians have largely forgotten how to drink. So when we see you foreign people, so *thirsty*, it reminds us that we should also be.'

We sipped our tea quietly for a time, both of us provoked into introspection. Mr Rajkowa, I noticed, had almost completed the daily crossword. Finally, the old man spoke again. 'Brunton met a great sage in India, perhaps one of the greatest we have ever produced. You will read of this in the book, but it occurs to me that – time permitting – you should visit the place where they met, a small hill town in South India. That is one unique place.'

I said that I would certainly try to.

'Each year,' he continued, 'there is a pilgrimage to this town. From all across our India, people travel in their thousands to walk round a holy mountain, Arunachala. I will tell you sincerely, that if you want to understand something of what makes India tick, you should see this. On the final night, a great beacon of fire burns out so brightly it can be seen for many miles.'

'When is this festival?' I said.

Mr Rajkowa's eyes twinkled once more. 'It is beginning in two weeks,' he said. 'And although I am not knowing your commitments, I am heartily suggesting that you cancel them.'

A week later, I was on the train heading south. Plans had been rearranged, meetings postponed, tickets transferred via innumerable sheets of waxy blue triplicate. Although I've never been much of a person for signs and portents, I couldn't help but feel that what had happened was fate. A chance meeting had spun my compass through ninety degrees, and placed in my hands the account of a journey which seemed, with every passing page, to mirror my own.

On the top bunk of my berth, by torchlight, I marvelled at the book. Brunton, a journalist who had served in the First World War, was a curious man by all accounts, intensely private, and claiming certain occult abilities since his youth. He went East, like so many before him, in search of mystical knowledge. What set him apart from most Englishmen of his era was his attitude towards both the Indians and their religious traditions. There are two types of traveller to India, he wrote: 'The white tourist who "does" the chief cities and historical sites and then steams away with disgust at the backward civilisation of India . . .' Or alternatively, a 'wiser kind of tourist . . . who will seek out, not the crumbling ruins of useless temples, nor the marbled palaces of dissipated kings long dead, but the living sages who can reveal a wisdom untaught by our universities.'

Brunton himself fell very convincingly into the second category. During his travels around India he found yogis who could stop the beating of their own hearts, who claimed the powers of telepathy, who could drink the most deadly poisons without suffering the effects. A natural sceptic, he remained unaffected by almost everything that he saw, until one day he arrived at the small hill town in South India called Tiruvanammalai. It was here that he would meet Ramana Maharshi, one of the most revered Indian saints of the twentieth century, who would change Brunton's life for ever. Brunton's writings, in turn, would inspire thousands of Westerners to make their way East, and his account of his meeting with the sage remains a classic account of spiritual revelation:

There is something in this man which holds my attention as steel filings are held by a magnet. I cannot turn my gaze away from him . . . But it is not until the second hour of the uncommon scene that I become aware of a silent, resistless change taking place within my mind. One by one, the questions which I have prepared with such meticulous accuracy on the train drop away. For it does not now seem to matter whether they hitherto troubled me. I only know that a steady river of quietness seems to be flowing near me, that a great peace is penetrating the inner reaches of my being, and that my thought-tortured brain is beginning to arrive at some rest.

The expression 'thought-tortured' seemed to me to be especially significant. As a symptom of Western life – addled by data smog, overstressed and anxious – it seemed one of the most likely causes for our modern turn East. Certainly, on my unhappiest days I felt that my brain was a machine with overloaded circuit boards, and that if only I could hush it I might find peace.

This 'inner silence', then, was part of what I was here to find. To practise meditation is to begin to still the endless chatter that most of us live with in our heads. It's to come fully into the present, to achieve what the Zen Buddhists call a 'one-pointed' mind. For Hindus this silence is even a divine state, a state of *samadhi*, and it is said — as Brunton discovered — that certain realised masters have the capacity to allow those who sit with them to share in it, a state of complete absorption in the present moment. Those moments of my life when I'd felt most struck by the numinous had also, I realised, occurred when 'thought' was entirely absent.

'One more thing before you go,' Mr Rajkowa had added to me, as we bade farewell at Delhi railway station. 'If you make it to Arunachala, please visit the cave on the hillside there. Although Sri Ramana Maharshi is no longer in his body, the cave has a stillness that is very rare in this world. I sat there myself in early 1984, by chance at the very period Indira Gandhi was shot. And though I feared greatly for what might happen to India, I emerged from that cave in a state of unique tranquillity. Perhaps I have never achieved it since?'

A week later, I found myself outside Ramana Maharshi's ashram. It was late November, and the sun was a glowing halo in the sky. Unsteady on my feet after three days of dysentery, I walked gingerly along the road, barely able to focus on the men and women who passed me. Along the lane I saw a vendor of tender coconuts and stopped to buy one. The vendor, a minuscule woman of about sixty, pushed herself to her feet and picked up her machete. She had the most deeply calloused hands I've ever seen: a lattice of brown ridges across each palm. Laying the coconut down on an old stump, she swung the machete with a practised air and sent a disc of green spinning into the ditch. Three more chops, then she used the knife's tip to prise open the milky crown. Inside, the precious liquid seemed startlingly clear and pure amongst all the filth, and as I drank it down the first inklings of strength flooded back into my body. Nonetheless it was curious to be back on my feet, and a wave of dizziness passed through me. She noticed and offered me her own stool.

'Problem?' she enquired, pointing to my stomach.

'Yes. Big problem.'

'*Acha.*' She tilted her head and held her palms up acquiescently. 'One day, two days only,' she added brightly. 'Only cleansing!'

I smiled at her. In a few sentences, the entire Indian world-view was evident, and I found it intensely heart-warming. For the price of seven rupees (ten pence), she had given a stranger her chair and a maternal kindliness. It was what made me love the country from the first.

I wandered further along the road, taking in the sights of the town. Decrepit structures roofed with corrugated tin. Sellers of snack foods: crispy *dosas* and soft white *idlis* topped with filigrees of coriander leaf. Buffaloes, their horns painted sky blue. Bamboo lean-to's, concrete painted in garish hues, an internet café boasting one primeval machine.

As I walked on, the nature of the town as a pilgrimage site was instantly apparent. Rickety stalls offered garlands of flowers, fruits and sweets. *Naivedya*, an important element of *puja* rituals, are gifts given to deities or saints, and one of five required daily offerings amongst orthodox Hindus. Different vendors – an old crone, a portly man swathed in a billowing orange shirt – entreated the passers-by not to forget their spiritual dues. Between all this, buses painted with deities roared past honking their horns, dust devils cavorting in their wake.

Presently, already sweating from the heat, I came to the archway that signalled the entrance to the ashram. At least five beggars were in position outside, vying for alms.

Scarecrow figures, emaciated from a life in the open, they held out their bowls, offering toothless grins. It was hard to look at them unmoved. Behind the ashram, the mysterious cone of Arunachala, a wild uncultivated hill, rose up under the flaming sun.

Inside the ashram gates, I passed quickly through the streams of devotees, and followed the signs for the path towards the summit. Behind the meditation hall, and past the placid buffaloes which provide fresh milk and ghee for the ashram kitchen, a narrow trail led up towards Arunachala. Even before Ramana Maharshi made his way to the hill a century before, there were tales of saints secluded in the caves there, and I was anxious to see for myself just what about this hill was so remarkable. Added to this, my landlady in Tiruvanammalai, Mrs Vasikari, had told me that there was, even now, a great sage who dwelled upon the summit.

For the worshippers of Shiva, perhaps nowhere in India is so revered as Arunachala hill. That, in fact, was why so many pilgrims were at this very moment swarming into the town in their thousands, camping out under makeshift tent structures, snoozing in doorways and on dusty verges. As one version of the legend tells it, the hill was formed after a dispute arose between Brahma, the Creator, and Vishnu, the Preserver. While both of them argued over who was superior, Shiva manifested himself as a vast column of light, thus asserting his dominance. When the people prayed to Shiva to reveal himself in a more comprehensible form, he revealed himself as Arunachala hill. The yearly Karthigai Deepam festival is thus a recreation of this event, and the giant fire lit on the hill's summit is supposed to represent Shiva's divine pillar of light.

But for now, the bustle of the town was behind me. It was still barely eight a.m. and the tapered path heading upwards through dense scrub appeared empty. I walked briskly, breathing the clean air, taking in the broad plain encircled by groups of hills about me. Above me was Arunachala, the highest hill for miles around. It is said that years ago this whole area was studded with great trees, but the growing demand of the nearby townspeople for firewood has wreaked havoc. Now there was largely a stony soil, interspersed with scrub, lemongrass and the occasional basking lizard.

Off in the distance, I heard the shrieking of wild monkeys and the trilling of a peacock. Then silence. Only the crunch of my feet on the stones, and the sound of my breath coming faster now that the path grew steeper. It was pleasant to be alone in nature, a surprisingly difficult feat in much of India. In the brush I noticed wild neem growing, often used by Indians as a medicine. Vast boulders, which looked as if they had been tossed here by a giant, appeared at random on either side of the path, and I felt a surge of great happiness to be walking in this sacred place.

Round the next corner, I stopped suddenly. An old man was sitting cross-legged on a boulder. He was dressed in pure white, his hair shorn to the scalp, and there was a broad smear of ash across his forehead. I raised my hands in *namaste* and drew closer.

'Do you speak English?' I asked.

There was a pause. Then the old man gestured to the flat boulder beside him. He may as well have been waiting for me. 'Please be seated,' he said, in well-articulated English.

I did as he suggested and we observed each other for a time. He was quite elderly, with fair skin for an Indian and an impressively hooked nose. His eyebrows, as well as the faint tufts which protruded from his nostrils, were chalk-white. His robes were immaculate; by his side was a faded brown bag of the type doctors carry in old black-and-white films.

'You are a pilgrim?' he asked.

'I suppose I am.'

'And you are going to Bhagwan's cave?'

I nodded.

'Then you are blessed. That is one very special place. Many auspicious births will have been necessary to bring you here.'

'May I ask who you are?'

He paused for some time. No feature of his face moved. 'They call me the Wandering Swami,' he said at last. 'And that is a name I do not dislike.'

'Are you the swami from the top of the hill?' I asked. 'I think I've heard of you.'

'No, no. That is a different man. He was there a long time. Had you come here even *one* day ago you would have found him at the summit. But yesterday, I myself witnessed him being carried down and taken to hospital. Stomach problems, I believe.'

'I heard he hadn't eaten for fifteen years,' I said, trying not to sound too facetious. 'I suspect he might have major stomach problems.'

The swami smiled faintly. 'Cup of milk he was taking every morning. That is all. Some yogis, it is true, need not take any food at all. Air is enough. But that man, he had one cup of buffalo milk in the morning.'

'And he *never* spoke?'

'Correct.'

'I had hoped to see him,' I confessed. 'I heard he had a great spiritual presence.'

The swami nodded reflectively, smoothing his cheeks with one of his hands. 'Energy was there, yes. But for the one who is attuned, Bhagwan's cave may also show the way. Whole hill, in actual fact, has great spiritual power. And there are many other yogis here.'

'There are?'

He shook his head. 'You cannot meet them, friend. They are invisible. Perhaps if they wanted you to see them. But why should they? They are *siddhas*, tantric yogis. They are ethereal beings who have moved beyond this world.'

I looked across the hillside. 'Have you seen them?'

'No. But, over time – and I have been here for a long time – one comes to know when they are close. Human being is very special,' he added. 'And of humans, *siddhas* most of all. They have the power of *kundalini* – the divine energy of the feminine creative power. They are alchemists who have understood the way to immortality. Not even the squirrels and the birds can do this.'

'What do they do exactly?'

He tucked his knees more tightly beneath his robe. 'Only *within* can you find this answer. God is what we call the macro, and man is the micro. The goal is to merge these two into one. That is the goal and the answer also. *Siddhas* know this.'

'Do you sit here all the time?' I asked.

'When it pleases me,' he said. 'Now you must go to the cave. You are the first pilgrim this morning, so you will be alone. That is best.'

I got to my feet and thanked him. Clearly, the interview was over. He smiled again, a warm smile, and reached down into his Gladstone bag, taking out a small picture. It was of Ramana Maharshi.

'You must take this,' he said. 'For many are the saints who have stayed here on Arunachala, but none have been like Bhagwan. Do not worry that you have not found the one on the hill. Another will come. If you go on working with the light available, you will meet your Master.'

I walked on, bemused, holding the photograph. I tucked

it into my bag. The view was spectacular now, and the peace made me forget the remnants of sickness. Over the next rise I came to Skandashram, the original hermitage of Ramana Maharshi in the early days, and the site of his meditation for the first six years. A simple lime-washed building stands around the cave, with a small courtyard before it; smells of earth and devotional incense; no one about.

The path dropped down some two hundred feet as I headed towards Virupaksha cave, where it is said Ramana lived for almost two decades in retreat. It is named after a great yogi of Tiruvanammalai, who preceded Ramana Maharshi. One story recounts how, at the end of his life, Sri Virupaksha told his students that he wished to be alone for some time. After a while, the students started to wonder where their guru was, but when they entered the cave, all they found was a pile of ashes. Ramana Maharshi, during his residency, formed these same ashes into a tall pile.

I went inside. It was dim and musty, but someone had already lit oil lamps. Perhaps the Wandering Swami had already been up here? Perhaps there was a caretaker, whose sole purpose in life was to watch over this sacred place and keep it tended? I stooped down to enter the cave and found myself in a narrow, dry enclave where, I imagined, the great saint must have found respite from the elements. Not a single noise was discernible, and the air smelled of ghee and camphor. Old mats lined the ground, providing a peaceful place to sit, and as I sat down, legs crossed, I felt the world outside diminish. What brings a man to give up everything for such a life? I wondered. What lessons emerge from year upon year of pure silence, immersed in the mystic consciousness of *samadhi*?

I concentrated on my breathing, following the breath in and out as I'd been taught. The gentle noise echoed from the roof of the cave. In meditative practice this is known as *pratyahara* – withdrawal of the senses – and it involves the removal of cognition both from the external world and from the images or impressions in the mind field. With practice it comes easily.

Gradually, a silence came over me, a peace that was primal, born of the absence of mental chatter. One minute I was sitting there trying to get somewhere, the next I was merely sitting, effortlessly, without aim or thought. A great serenity filled me completely and I let myself sink into it, as if I were falling through space without any fear. My breath came smoothly, deeply, quietly.

Some time passed – perhaps an hour or more. When I came to it was as if from a dreamless sleep. My eyes opened slowly. I knew I hadn't slept. I became aware again that I was in a cave, halfway up a tall hill in south India. What was I doing here? How did I arrive? How much time had passed?

Outside, the sun seemed impossibly bright. Emerging, I felt that I'd come to the closest point yet on my journey to glimpsing what lay on the other side of the 'self'. Ramana Maharshi taught that, behind our compulsive thoughts, there is no 'I', as we commonly suppose, but something far deeper. And yet how difficult, for us egocentric Westerners, to give up the self and all its quixotic pieces. If we give it up, we suppose then we are nothing. The great paradox of Eastern thought, however, is that the very opposite is true: we are everything.

As dusk fell – shades of umber and sienna behind the cone of Arunachala – I arrived wearily back at my guesthouse. My landlady, Mrs Vasikari, had moved her plastic chair out and was surveying her neighbourhood with a proprietorial air, oblivious to the mosquitoes. She was a pensive, angular woman, with something of the look of Indira Gandhi about her. Perhaps it was the clearly defined stripe of white across her tightly drawn black crown, or the fine boned stoical features. But every time she spoke to me, I felt myself scrutinised, as if before the steely gaze of India's former prime minister.

'You have been to Sri Ramanashram today?' she enquired.

I said that I had been to the cave.

'And how did you feel in His presence?'

I thought for a time. Perhaps I couldn't answer that question for myself at this point. 'It's a peaceful place, Mrs Vasikari. I'm not exactly sure if I felt his presence. But something happened . . .'

She tittered. 'Questions are there, yes. Too many questions you foreigners carry round with you. But wait a little time here in Tiruvanammalai. Bhagwan's grace will touch you, I can assure you of that.'

'Can you tell me about the Deepam festival?' I asked. 'Even since this morning, the town seems to be getting fuller.'

'Just wait!' she said. 'Within one week this town will look like every person in India is here. Just now there are only first few arrivals. Deepam is our oldest and most important festival. Like a South Indian *diwali*. On that day, every person is cleaning their house. Not half cleaning but *full* cleaning is done on that day, so that everything is sparkling. Then, when darkness comes, we are putting *too* many oil lamps outside our house. Whole town is shining! Finally, at stroke of midnight, *sadhus* are lighting huge fire on top of Arunachala. Fire is so hot it can be seen for miles in every direction. Fireworks are being lit. Explosions are occurring.' She sighed. 'This was my husband's most favourite day of the year.'

'I'm sorry,' I said. 'I didn't know your husband had passed away.'

She shook her head. 'Husband is not dead. He has taken *sannyas* since four years.'

I had heard of this. In Hinduism, after the three main stages of life are fulfilled (student/householder/retirement) a fourth may be adopted – that of *sannyasin* or renunciate. While most men defer this final stage to a future life, the most ardent bid farewell to their families and possessions and set out, during their final years, to find detachment from all worldly pleasures and thus draw closer to *moksha*, enlightenment or liberation from the wheel of rebirth. As a cultural institution, it is perhaps the greatest signifier of just how much orthodox Hinduism venerates the spiritual quest.

'Did you always know your husband would become a *sannyasin*?' I asked.

Mrs Vasikari nodded. I looked at her, expecting to see sadness there, or regret, but there was none. Instead, her face was shining, even proud. 'My husband was always very devout man,' she said fondly. 'Every day he was doing *puja*, going to temple. But also he was very good family man. We have three children: two daughters and one son. Husband worked at post office for forty years. And although he never talked of *sannyas* during that time, I said to myself, he is a good Hindu, it is his duty.'

'Will you see him again?'

She shook her head. 'No, no. He is dead to this world now. Perhaps I will see him in the next?' She waved suddenly to a young girl passing in the street, a regal wave. 'Tell me, Mr Piers, do you take *sannyas* in your culture?'

'We don't,' I said. 'For us retirement is the final stage. Many people, you know, do not believe in God in my country.'

'God is everything,' she said simply. 'And after God, duty is most important. Many people are forgetting that these days. I will tell you one story my husband would often discuss. There was a holy man rescuing a scorpion who had fallen into a pond. Scorpion was stinging but holy man would not stop until he had saved it. One student asked holy man why he was prepared even to be stung so he could save tiny scorpion. And the holy man laughed and said: "Duty of scorpion is to sting. Duty of *sadhu* is to save other beings from suffering. Since scorpion does not give up his duty, why should *sadhu*?" '

'What does this mean?' I asked.

'It means we must do our duty,' she said, rising to her feet and picking up the plastic chair. 'Even if sting is there.'

In the evenings I took to eating in Manna, a small café frequented by travellers, not too far from Mrs Vasikari's guesthouse. Amongst the coterie of Westerners who wind up in Tiruvanammalai, a larger proportion than usual seemed to me to be genuine spiritual seekers. The usual tie-dyed crowd was there, the hedonists, ageing flower children, trustafarians playing at spirituality, but there was also a noticeable crowd of serious, usually older, devotees of Ramana Maharshi. Several of them had made Tamil Nadu their home for many years and seemed to live serious, contemplative lives, drawing little attention to themselves. Others amongst them, such as Dave, the owner of the Manna Café, seemed to enjoy a different role.

'I used to smuggle acid into Goa back in the day,' was his opening line to me, as I chewed my banana cake in the corner. 'We used to bring in sheets of LSD blotters and just walk down Anjuna beach lighting people up. Man, that was the day. Five hundred, a thousand people tripping. We did it for free sometimes! That was a special time, you know. We thought we were changing the world, one consciousness at a time.'

I asked how he'd come to Tiruvanammalai.

'Well, you can't play the party game for ever, mate,' he said, a trace of his East London accent coming back. 'And the acid turned us on to God – it gave us a glimpse – but we couldn't sustain it. So I started on the ashram circuit. Wanted to find that high permanently. I ended up here. Fell in love with a girl. Had a kid. Bought this place. Stayed twenty years!' He held up his palms and gave me a wide-boy's grin.

'That's what happened to Ram Dass, wasn't it?'

I was referring to the well-known Californian teacher, formerly known as Richard Alpert, who'd been one of the pioneers of LSD use in the 1960s, lost his professorship at Harvard as a result, and then journeyed to India. He'd had a profound experience with an Indian master and changed his name to Ram Dass: servant of God. Over the last thirty years, perhaps no one has so eloquently translated the central ideas of Indian philosophy to a Western audience.

'Fucking *Richard*,' said Dave. 'We used to see that guy around all the time. I knew him in Rishikesh way back in the beginning, when he was living with Neem Karoli Baba. Guy was refusing to wear shoes. Wore all these beads and dressed like a *sadhu*. Even then, he was intense, though. He had this Jewish intellectual vibe going on. I mean he *really* wanted to get enlightened, you know!'

'And what about you?' I asked. 'Did you find what you were looking for?'

Dave looked disconsolate, then clapped his hands loudly. A young Indian girl came in, and he ordered her to fetch his whisky. 'Well, you know my priorities changed,' he continued, some of the bluster leaving his voice. 'I opened this place, had to start raising my daughter. Perhaps some of the fervour went out of me? Perhaps I just accepted that I'd gone far enough this time around.'

The girl returned with his plastic bottle of cheap whisky and a tumbler. I finished my banana cake while he poured himself two fingers, sipped it gingerly, and ran his tongue across his lips.

'Fuck it, I don't know,' he muttered, talking more to himself now than to me. 'The thing is once you've been out here long enough, you *can't* go back. I know that much. Here I have this place, a quality of life. Back home I've got nothing. I'd be in a council flat, government pension, dying in some shit-hole run by the state. No fucking way. I'd curl up and die. That wasn't the freedom I set out to find.'

'Inner freedom?' I suggested gently. He was drinking the whisky in short, angry draughts now. 'Wasn't it inner freedom the hippies wanted?'

'Sure, mate,' he said, refilling his glass. 'Thing was, it was easy to pop a pill and feel *that*. But to get there without chemicals . . . Jesus.' He swatted his hand at some imaginary fly. 'It takes a lifetime. Many lifetimes, if you believe the Indian system of things. And you have to give up *everything*! You can't have family, can't have commitments. When you're ready to walk out of your own front door naked and never look back . . . then you're ready to begin.' He lit a Gold Flake, blew a plume of smoke. 'I guess I wasn't. So in this case, I'm talking about external freedom. The freedom to work less, live more. That counts for something in my book.'

After Dave had left, I took out my notepad and began to catch up on my notes. Manna was filling up now with the evening crowd, some of whom I recognised from the night before. The room we were in was floored with cow dung, in the traditional Indian fashion, on top of which lay mauve and lime silk cushions, squat wooden stools and two low tables glimmering under candlelight. People sipped clay cups of chai, fruit juice and lemon and ginger tea spicy enough to placate even the hardiest chillum-smoker's sore throat. It was in stark contrast with the poverty outside and represented both the privilege and predicament of being a traveller moving on the strength of a foreign currency. People ordered green salads, couscous and real coffee, highly sought-after commodities for travellers keen for a taste of home.

To my right an English guy named Mike was continuing where Dave had left off, only this time, rather than boasting about his drug smuggling, the theme was a more common one for this particular locale, that of spiritual prowess. In Australia, I recalled, backpackers boasted about the biggest wave surfed, or the highest bridge dived off with a bungee rope. In India, predictably, such bragging is delivered in deadly solemn tones, and relates to how long one has meditated, or how outlandish a yoga posture one can sustain.

Around the table was Chris, an earnest young Californian from San Diego, Sue-Ellen from Vermont, Mike from Birmingham and an older couple, Ron and Lily from Switzerland. All of them, to varying degrees, were dressed in the accoutrements of New Age spirituality: kaftans, sacred crystals, amulets. Ron, a seventy-year-old Swiss chemist, wore Tibetan beads made of yak bone, which he claimed had belonged to an important lama. Together we seemed to represent a bizarre cross-section of Western life, but all of us were united by the feeling that there was something here, some truth or lesson to be found in India that would enrich our lives. Only Mike seemed intent on establishing himself as further down the path than anyone else, and I found my hackles rising at once.

'I was lost before I met Papa-ji,' Mike announced, referring to one of Ramana Maharshi's most well-known disciples, who had died, apparently enlightened, in 1997. 'Before then I'd travelled around most of India. Stayed in scores of ashrams. I met Ramesh Balsekar, Guru-mai, Shree-maa. But while I recognised their holiness, they weren't the guru for me.'

'But why do we even need a guru?' said Lily, who had a soft, musical voice. 'Can't we get there by ourselves?'

'I don't think so,' said Chris, the Californian. 'Most of the Eastern religions stress the need for a teacher. You wouldn't try and hike through the mountains without a guide, would you? And the mind is a far more dangerous place . . .'

'If you'd met Papa-ji, you would *know* why,' said Mike. 'I mean *one* minute in his presence took me further than ten years in India. "Wake up, you are already free!" he said to me. For a moment or two after he said that, I *was* free. I was pure consciousness. No ego!'

'And then it came back?' I said, without intentional irony.

He glared at me. 'Sure. The ego came back, of course. But now, at least, I know what I'm searching for. I've tasted it . . .'

'What about you?' I asked Sue-Ellen, who was a middle-aged schoolteacher at a Vermont high school much of the time, but a keen traveller for the rest. She had brown ringlets and a soft, melancholic face. All this time she'd hardly said anything.

'I'm not such an expert in all this stuff, Piers,' she said quietly. 'I mean I was forty before I even began on the path. But I just felt, you know, like there was something *missing* in my life. Everything was fine – I mean I wasn't . . . real miserable, but I just felt . . . you know "is this *IT*?" It wasn't enough. And then I went to a Buddhist retreat one day, on the instigation of a friend, and I just saw a whole new level of existence. It was like my brain had only been tuned on to this one radio station for all these years and suddenly I saw that there were all these other ones . . . more subtle, harder to hear, but so much more beautiful. So then I came to India in my vacation – that was five years ago – and I've been meditating ever since. My friends think I've joined a cult or something. I started throwing a lot of my stuff away, just trying to be more aware of what I really need. And they look at me like I've become a Hare Krishna.' She laughed. 'But that's OK.'

'And why here? It's not exactly on the backpacker trail.'

'It was the funniest thing,' she said. 'I was in this bookshop in Montpelier, Vermont and I found a book about Ramana Maharshi. So I sat down and started reading it and, well, I just knew, then and there, that I had to come here. You've seen his face . . . Well, one look at it was all it took to make me want to come here.'

I patted my pocket, remembering the picture which the Wandering Swami had given me. I took it out, and Sue-Ellen and I gazed at the benevolent face for a time, smiling out at us from the past.

'You know, when Sri Ramana died, Henri Cartier-Bresson happened to be staying at the ashram,' she said, reaching for her journal. 'He saw something quite incredible.'

She leafed through the pages thoughtfully, scanning her own girlish handwriting. Finally, she found the passage she was looking for:

It was a most astonishing experience,' wrote Cartier-Bresson.

I was in the open space in front of my house, when my friends drew my attention to the sky, where I saw a vividly luminous shooting star with a luminous tail, unlike any shooting star I had before seen, coming from the South, moving slowly across the sky and, reaching the top of Arunachala, disappeared behind it. Because of its singularity we all guessed its import and immediately looked at our watches – it was 8.47 – and then raced to the Ashram only to find that our premonition had been only too sadly true: the Master had passed into mahanirvana at that very minute.

The Deepam Festival

The morning of the Deepam dawned fine and clear, with the South Indian sun rapidly searing off the haze. I'd been up since dawn, watching the light change on Mrs Vasikari's porch. At sunrise, the grey sky purpled, then turned blood-orange, while a gathering of common babblers clustered at my feet to feed off crumbs of chapatti. Through binoculars I saw a white-breasted kingfisher come to rest on a nearby telephone wire, with the torso of what looked to be a cricket disappearing into its beak. Its plumage was the most iridescent shade of turquoise, and its musical call, *chake-ake-ake-ake-ake*, was the only sound I could hear. A tranquil start on what I knew might be anything but a tranquil day.

Soon after sunrise, Mrs Vasikari appeared, pink dressing-gowned and yawning, just in time to greet the boy who brought the buffalo milk in a small metal can. It was rich with cream and sloshed against the lid. I felt like a member of the family as she patted me gently on the shoulder. 'I will make tea,' she said. 'Today, you will be needing much energy for the walk.'

What she referred to was the principal activity of the Deepam for the several hundred thousand-strong group of devotees who had now arrived: that of a fourteen-kilometre perambulation around Arunachala hill. During the walk, we would pass some 360 holy tanks, *mandapas* (pillared outdoor halls or pavilions for public rituals) and ashrams, as well as eight important Shiva *lingams* (squat, phallic shapes resembling worn river stones). More enticingly, as far as I was concerned, legend suggests that the walk burns off the karma of 10,000 births.

'No, no. You should not be wearing those,' said Mrs Vasikari, pointing to my boots in horror. 'It is *much* more auspicious to be walking barefoot.'

'Barefoot!'

'I have done it too many times,' she said with a casual wave of her hand. 'When one has Bhagwan in one's heart, blisters are impossible.'

As I considered the walk ahead of me, I realised that practices such as this – a form of pilgrimage – were far more common aspects of Hindu spiritual life than some of the more esoteric things I had seen. While Hinduism has numerous weird and wonderful subgroups, it's largely a devotional religion in which everyone finds their own form of the divine and pours all their human energies into its worship. Most Hindus will perform a pilgrimage at one stage of their lives, following a journey to a supremely sacred place, or if following the advice of the Mahabharata (one of the two major Sanskrit epics of ancient India), visiting a number of them. Hindus call this *tirthyatra* – *yatra* embodying the notion of travel, *tirtha*, as I had discovered in Varanasi, that of a meeting place between the human and non-human worlds.

As with Arunachala, many of these sites are linked to the landscape of India itself: rivers, caves, sacred groves. There are seven particularly holy rivers in India, seven holy cities, four *dhamas*, or dwelling places, of the gods. For those who make these sometimes arduous journeys, pilgrimage allows a temporary moving outside of family responsibilities and attachments, a useful social function. It may also be done with the ashes of a family member in tow, so that special merit may be gained for the departed soul.

Finally, there is something about making the journey with *others* that is important. With the expansion of public transport in the twentieth century, pilgrimage has even become one of the most popular forms of tourism in India, something to be done with family, both a temporal and a spiritual adventure in one. My part in today's events would be to share in this, and to feel – perhaps for the first time – part of a multitude who were trying to unite with something larger than themselves. It seemed to me that this experience, which wasn't esoteric at all, was a primal aspect of my journey.

After a quick breakfast of curds and honey, and reluctantly leaving my shoes behind, I strolled along the main causeway, quickly joining the enormous crowds that had already amassed. Although the pace was slow, the ground was pebbled with cow pats and sharp stones, and I quickly cursed my decision to go barefoot. Bhagwan or not, there were going to be blisters by the end of the day.

Nonetheless, the atmosphere was jubilant. As with many Indian religious festivals, the sacred element of the occasion was happily married with an air of fiesta. Everywhere, men, women and children walked side by side, laughing merrily with each other, catching up with old friends and stopping to buy snacks from the never-ending array of vendors who lined the sides of the road. (Food, as ever in Indian life, remains paramount in religious festivals.) Hindu chants blared from loudspeakers, while at certain way stations bullocks and goats were traded for fistfuls of rupees.

Mixed in with this inordinate mass, Saivite *sadhus* from all over India had come to join the throng. This was, in effect, an important work day for them, with Shiva himself in attendance. Many of them wore their hair long and flowing, in imitation of their deity, while others puffed small fragrant pipes. One terrifying individual wore sharp hooks through his flesh weighted with dried lemons, and I walked behind him for a time, transfixed by his slow, methodical steps and the empty stare of his eyes.

After several hours, I fell into discussion with a girl walking along side me. Neela, although Indian in appearance, wasn't a national at all but a doctor from Los Angeles, completing her residency in Tamil Nadu. She'd been to India many times, visiting her grandparents in Bangalore, but somehow she'd never been out of the cities. 'I'm actually kind of glad I ran into you,' she confided, 'because the locals have been looking at me like I'm some kind of freak-show. I should have dressed a bit more appropriately for the occasion.'

Wearing a fairly skimpy lycra tank top and designer jeans, she would have fitted in perfectly in a Mumbai nightclub, but was a fish out of water here. Although she spoke Kannada (one of the fourteen official languages of India), her knowledge of India was confined to an affluent corner of Bangalore, around which she was usually driven by her grandparents' chauffeur. In Tiruvanammalai, a traditional South Indian pilgrimage town, modernity might have arrived in the form of satellite dishes and mobile phones – and even in the form of ragged-looking foreigners like myself – but to see an Indian woman dressed and speaking like an American was a shock too far. The young men stared at her with both astonishment and abject lust.

When I told her why I was here, it was her turn to look at me with surprise. 'I've never been to a yoga class in my life,' she told me. 'We're Hindus of course but only in the sense that most of my American friends are Christians – it's a cultural thing. We celebrate *diwali* but that's about it. To be honest, my parents are of that generation that were so proud to make it to the States that they've spent most of their lives trying to be American.'

'But you're here,' I said. 'What made you come to the Deepam on your own?'

'I was curious,' she said. 'Actually it was my grandmother who told me I must promise to come to the Karthigai Deepam just once in my life. This year, I've been working in a clinic in Bangalore, so I figured now was as good a time as ever. I have to admit, though, this is a different world for me – I'm not sure where I fit in.'

We chatted for the next few hours as we walked. She seemed, I reflected, both the promise and the drawback of the new India. With her modern clothes and an Ipod in her pocket, she represented the dream of so many young graduates, most of whom, prompted by television, still believe America to be the promised land. She was almost a fully qualified doctor at twenty-five, a keen advocate of women's rights, and had probably never known a moment's hardship in her life. And equally, the garish gods and goddesses of the Hindu pantheon were for her little more than backdrops to a series of rituals that had little importance in her life. She'd spent far more time than I in India and yet, until now, she'd somehow never seen or interacted with the countryside, nor felt the power of the great spiritual current which keeps India's heart beating.

'It's so funny,' she said, 'how many of my friends do meditation and all this stuff. And they think just because I'm Indian I must know all about it. But I haven't a clue. Why should I?'

'It's a stereotype, isn't it?'

She leaned forward to whisper. 'For the same reason, every guy I meet brings up the *Karma Sutra* – thinks I'm going to be some kind of expert. I mean, *Jesus!*'

We strolled on. I had never seen so many people. Everyone was moving at their own pace; some trundled in ancient wheelchairs, the small ones carried aloft on the shoulders of parents. One *sadhu*, whose retinue carefully swept the path in front of him free of sharp objects, rolled along like a barrel, his face locked in a mask of self-absorbed devotion. To our right side, the hill loomed, its top obscured now by a wreath of clouds. Do the Saivites believe that the hill is actually animate or is it a metaphor for God's presence on earth?

Rabindranath Tagore, I would later read, had his own theory about why so many Hindu sacred sites correspond with the landscape itself. 'India chose her places of pilgrimages on the top of hills and mountains, by the side of the holy rivers, in the heart of forests and by the shores of the ocean,' he wrote, 'which along with the sky, is our nearest visible symbol of the vast, the boundless, the I.'

But what was this boundless I? Increasingly now, I thought about it, peering beyond the signs and metaphors of Hinduism for the essence that lay beneath. It was the ineffable mystery itself – what the Tibetans call *Tong-pa-nnid*. Many other cultures hinted at it too: the ancient Scandinavians used the word *Ginnungagap*, meaning 'yawning or uncircumscribed void'; the Chinese called it *tsi-tsai*: the self-existent. All of these words pointed at something limitless, the womb of all cosmic existence.

Neela and I fell silent for a while. It was sweltering now, the air pregnant with moisture; added to this, the fug of incense, chatter and the singing of *bhajans*, devotional songs expressing love for the divine. There was indeed something stirring about processing within the flow of a vast crowd, if only for a sense of uniformity, of being part of a larger entity than oneself. I imagined staring down at the hill through the window of a small plane and seeing the immense crocodile of devotees, perhaps half a million strong, weaving their way clockwise around this hill. A majestic sight.

In Sanskrit, the circumambulation of Arunachala is known as *Giri Pradakshina*. *Pradakshina* – walking in a circle – is a common practice in both Hinduism and Buddhism, as any morning visitor to a temple will have noticed. Hindu devotees walk clockwise around the innermost chamber of the shrine housing the temple deity, often chanting to keep their minds clear. Indian marriage ceremonies also involve a sacred circle, as the wedded couple walk around the fire seven times to seal their vows. There are many theories about why the circle is important, the most obvious being that circular movement mimics the spinning of the earth upon its axis. Other explanations involve the representation of cosmic unity and the infinite, perhaps the reason that both Hindu temples and Buddhist *stupas* have based their architecture on the circle.

At lunchtime we stopped for a rest at a *dosa* stall, where there were lines of makeshift tables and benches, beside which sizzling pans fried the fermented rice-batter pancakes, with their distinctive sour taste, which are such a feature of the South Indian meal. In all my worldwide travels I have never known such good value. For just five rupees (three pence), it was possible to eat as much as one wanted. No sooner had one *dosa* been devoured than a boy would come past with a stack of fresh pancakes, rolled up like papyrus scrolls, or a great vat of piquant coconut chutney, to replenish the plate.

It was a good opportunity, too, to rest my feet. Neela had sensibly opted to keep her trainers on, while my unseasoned soles were smarting with a thousand tiny scrapes and bruises. ('Very pious,' she said with a grin, 'but I prefer my Nike airs.') A few metres away, the great retinue continued onwards, like some vast migration. We watched them pensively, and had no sooner finished our plates than it began to rain. Grape-sized balls rattled the corrugated shelters, and a thousand concealed umbrellas bloomed in an instant.

A little tiredly, we rejoined the throng. The ground underfoot was already slick from the multitudes. The coconut fronds were jerking in the rain. Ahead of us, buffalo were moving across the highway to a different pasture. We navigated through them, their chocolate-grey muzzles puffing steam, their eyes enviably still. They walked with their heads down, their mouths chomping in small concentric circles. The smell of them, bestial, elemental, seemed as timeless as India itself.

Soaked to the skin, we walked on. Children splashed in the puddles, while those who'd forgotten their umbrellas tore banana leaves from the wayside and held them over their heads. Neela and I quickly embraced the soaking, joining a group who were splashing about jubilantly in a newly formed stream. The sheer intensity of this sudden rainfall was magical: it had the capacity to wash away everything. We held up our faces to the onslaught, children ourselves again, shrieking with laughter. And when the rain stopped, the jungle to either side of us rang with that peculiar silence that succeeds a storm: a sense of the world slowly emerging again, flower buds creaking open to the nascent sun.

Several hours passed. Conversations began and finished. Neela and I soon felt like old friends. She told me of the clinic she'd been working at in Bangalore, a refuge for those without the necessary funds for Western medicine. Her stories disproved my theory that she knew nothing of India's under-belly: she'd seen children dying from cholera, and dysentery and typhoid fever. What had most shocked her, she confided, was the plight of the women – who could they turn to if abused? Some of them looked to her, she said, because she was independent and, as a foreigner, seemingly empowered. She felt helpless. Five thousand years were against her.

Along the road, we stopped at the site of each sacred *lingam*, placed at a different compass point around the hill. The *lingams* were surrounded by devotees, for whom they were resonant with power: women with pleated marigolds in their oiled hair, men chanting with their hands in prayer. Before each *lingam*, a fire was burning in an ornate brazier, and devotees would come and throw balls of camphor on the fire, sending the flames roaring. One man knelt in the dust beside his small daughter, a girl of about five dressed in marshmallow pink. To see him showing her how to pray, how to pass her hands through the flame, was extraordinary.

By the evening, with aching limbs and glowing cheeks, we neared the town of Tiruvanammalai. With dusk falling, the whole town was lighting their *agal vilakkus* – tiny earthen ghee lamps that give off a warm yellow light. In every door, window and balcony, and in some cases arranged along the eaves, scores of these tiny lamps were being lit. The effect was magical, each lamp representing a small human connection with the divine. To blur one's eyes was to see a kaleidoscope of flame.

An old man, hearing me speaking English, addressed me. 'Lamps are warding off evil forces,' he said. 'And they are also small version of *Tejolingam*.'

'What is *Tejolingam*?' asked Neela.

'Great fire on Arunachala.' He grinned, exposing ruined teeth. 'When fire is lit, light of Shiva will be there. Mind and intellect will be illuminated. Ultimately, heart will be illuminated!'

We walked on towards the temple, pushed back and forth by the enormous crowds. A few young men were jostling each other excitably and I sensed that, before too long, this crowd would become a writhing mass, like a hundred football matches in one. Those that lived along the roadside were standing on their balconies, dressed in their finest clothes, while still more candles were appearing, so that the whole town seemed to shimmer with light, with spirals of smoke rising over the streets.

As darkness fell, the atmosphere grew more and more frenetic. Approaching the Arunachaleswarar temple, Neela stayed close to me as pilgrims began to let off firecrackers, fiery red *petard* lit from a small fuse. Unlike the tiny bangs I remembered from childhood, these were like primitive bombs and it was necessary to keep a vigilant eye out to avoid being caught in the blast. Bonfires were also being lit in the streets, fed with ghee, camphor and anything else which happened to be lying around: a broken chair, the stump of a palm, armfuls of leaves that caught like moths' wings. To stand too close to one of these was to risk a serious burning, as at any minute a pilgrim might throw on a handful of some accelerant, sending the flames leaping.

More than anything, the atmosphere itself seemed to be approaching boiling point. The crowd was filled with a mounting excitement that was beyond that of, say, watching a sporting event. One might call it religious fervour, save for all the distasteful associations that such a term brings with it. Rather, it was as if they were simply letting go of all their conditioning and their routine, to fall into step with something larger themselves, a belief in the total harmony and structure of the universe. It was fire worship – that most primeval of human beliefs – and to see the people dancing and holding up their hands to the flames was to be suddenly cast back to a time older than civilisation itself, when the first Indo-Aryan peoples began to forge together their beliefs, when fire protected them from the dark.

Just as the noise began to reach thunderous proportions

and the explosions to be so excessive that I feared for our very safety, a profound hush descended over the crowd. It was as if a switch had been flicked. Instantly, I felt a chill run down my spine – it was impossible to remain dispassionate as, up through the gloom, glimmering on the distant peak of Arunachala hill, something began to shine. No one made so much as a whisper – not even a child cooed. All of us, in harmony, strained our necks to see upwards to where the great pyre was being sparked.

Suddenly, prompting the loudest roar I have ever heard a crowd muster, the hilltop flame caught and surged up. At first a tiny glow through the smoke, then growing in size and ferocity, eventually it was a giant luminous tear of fire, many metres high. Instantly, all about the town, around all fourteen miles of Arunachala hill, the people bent their knees and began to chant *Om*, the one sound, the ineffable sound of the universe. *Om, Om, Om*, the people chanted, and the noise of it was so loud I thought my heart would break.

Om, they chanted, every man, woman and child bending their knees and touching their foreheads to the ground. *Om*, came the prayers, until I too found myself turning and bowing to the mountain, that vast conical godhead, which represented if not exactly Shiva in my own mind, then the goal of human existence – an ultimate truth, a unity, which was perhaps what Shiva represented anyway.

Om, they chanted, again and again in great rumbling waves, and at the same moment, all the thousands of *sadhus* and the most ardent of the devotees – clutching their vats of ghee – began to run towards the hill. On the summit – several hours' climb away – they would add their own fuel to the fire, so that the flame itself, burning throughout the night, would come to reflect their own ardour. Never, as long as people live in India, will that ardour die out.

For a second, I was apart from the crowd again – a mere witness – and I felt something of my old loneliness course through me. I couldn't yet believe, with *all* of myself, that we were doing anything but going through the motions here – putting our faith in a structure that, when investigated, might prove an empty shell. But then the wonder and immediacy of the moment washed my fears away and I was a participant again, just happy to be there, alive, to be looking for something that seemed – even if I had yet to find it – the most important thing there is.

Mata-ji: the Divine Mother

After the Deepam I returned to Varanasi. I loved the ancient city, with its ever present worship and decay, its crumbling architecture, its plethora of tricksters and saints. Installed in my old room, I felt a sense of homecoming, even the welcome of the hotel staff offering comfort after so many months on the road. Honoré, the chess-playing junkie, was gone now – to Thailand, said Bhapuji, the manager. 'He is bearing a great burden,' he added mournfully. 'What a difficult incarnation.'

Certain things were becoming clearer to me, too. If I had set out uncertain of the differences between mysticism and magic, and indeed resolute that it was not religion itself that I was searching for, I was beginning to narrow my focus. Central to both the mysticism of the *sadhus* and Ladakhi oracles, as well as the more prosaic gathering of the fire ceremony, had been a marked shift in consciousness. For the *sadhus*, marijuana brought them into contact with Shiva; for the oracles it was drumming that gave them access to the pantheon of Tibetan deities. Although the exact nature of these trance states remained unclear, I felt that I, too, had experienced a foretaste of them, both at the climax of the fire festival and during other peak experiences of my life. That sense of the numinous had been a portal, of sorts, into mystic consciousness.

Now that it was becoming comprehensible, I joined some other dots. Could it be that beyond all religions lay the same primal state of consciousness, accessed through an infinite number of methods and substances, but allowing for the same awareness of an ultimate reality? Since magicians were playing both with the texture of perception and with our human notions of the supernatural, the parallels between the magician and the mystic seemed also far clearer than I'd previously supposed.

From here on, these states of consciousness would become the focal point of my search. William James, the pioneering American psychologist and philosopher, explored the same questions back in 1886 when, after availing himself of some ammonium nitrate, he experienced his own higher state of consciousness. James was fascinated by the untapped potential of life: that 'compared with what we ought to be, we are only half awake'. In an attempt to uncover this hidden strata of existence, James dosed himself with laughing gas, a drug which was having revolutionary consequences for the medical profession at that time. The effects of that experiment would remain with him for his entire life and his writings on it would inspire seekers and mystic wannabees throughout the twentieth century, who shared James' assertion that consciousness remained the last hidden frontier. James wrote: 'Our normal waking consciousness, rational consciousness, as we call it, is but one especial type of consciousness, whilst all about it, parted from it by the filmiest of screens, there lie potential forms of consciousness entirely different.'

But what exactly *were* those 'potential' states of consciousness? And what would reaching them mean? Even as these thoughts occurred to me, I felt a trace of my former scepticism rearing its head. From the perspective of science, this seemed the greyest of areas. But then a second feeling arrived, one which prioritised the feelings I'd experienced at first hand. In those moments I'd come to call 'numinous', I felt more alive than at any other time in my life. On the basis of that alone, this was a worthy avenue of enquiry.

With pleasure, I returned to my old routines: roving the constricted streets with my notebook; striking conversations at tiny chai stalls; hearing sitar recitals at the numerous music ashrams of the city. India's musical traditions stretch back to Vedic times, and they are notable for their religious neutrality, despite strong devotional aspects. Muslims and Hindus often play together, with Muslims singing Hindu *bhajans*, and Hindus singing Sufi compositions, everyone accepting the music's ability to lead one to the ineffable, without feeling the need to quibble too much about what exactly that means.

It was on such a night, cramped amongst a diverse audience of Indians, backpackers, musicians from East and West, that a new strand of my journey opened up. Sitting on rickety chairs, sipping spicy *ayurvedic* tea, we listened to a female vocalist, her sweet, endlessly lilting voice soaring above the other instruments. Above us, the building rose up three tiers, each with viewing galleries, to an open roof. Glancing up as her voice reached its zenith, I saw a bleached moon, full and trembling in the sky, surrounded by endless silver pinpricks of stars.

When the concert was over, I fell into conversation with a man sitting to my left, with a plump, kindly face, who seemed to know a great deal about the Hindustani music of north India. He was a tour guide by profession, he explained, but when time allowed he came here. The greatest regret of his life, he said, was he had never learned an instrument himself.

'For myself, music is a means to feel the presence of God,' Niraj confided, with a matter of factness about the meta-physical that one gets used to in India. 'And for the musicians, too, it is clearly a form of worship. One story tells of the day when the sitar player Ustad Imdad Khan's daughter died. He was practising when someone came to discuss the funeral arrangements with him. "Please wait for a time," he asked them. "I am not yet through with my prayers."'

I told him a little of my own journey, of some of the things I had seen and hoped still to see.

Niraj listened politely but I could see he thought my journey mad. 'That sounds like a very important journey you are on,' he offered. 'But a very *Western* one, if you don't mind my saying.' He adjusted his wire-rimmed glasses on his pleasantly crooked nose. 'You are bringing an exhaustive Western mindset, with all its tests and analyses, to what is a very simple question. Stop looking and simply accept God. His forms are many.'

If only it were so easy, I thought.

'You must come and see Mata-ji,' said Niraj. 'In a village not far from here is a great saint. Whenever anyone in my family has a problem we go to see her. She is a fully realised being, an incarnation of Kali. Great power is there.'

I leaped at the chance. 'Will she talk to a foreigner?'

Niraj considered. 'I will go to see her this Sunday and ask her permission. Assuming she consents, then we will return the following week.'

I thanked him. But what did it mean, I asked, to be an incarnation of Kali?

He thought for a second. Niraj was articulate and confident, and yet this, perhaps, made him hesitate in answering my question.

'Mata-ji is a human form of the divine mother,' he began.

'She is also Durga, Bhagvati, Lalita – there are many forms. Are you following me?'

I nodded, only half sure if I actually was. About us, attendants were beginning to pack away the chairs, while the musicians were eating their evening dal and rice at one edge of the stage.

'She's an avatar? A goddess in human form?'

'Mata-ji is a normal village lady, of course. But when she wishes, the spirit of Kali enters into her. At that moment we believe we are not talking with Mata-ji but with the *force* behind her. Kali is *actually* there. Her energy is manifest.' He searched my face. 'Such things do not happen in London, I am sure. But here they are relatively common. Many villages have such people. But Mata-ji is the most powerful I have known.'

A week later, perched on the back of Niraj's Enfield Bullet, we left from the main bazaar. Mata-ji, apparently, had found no problem with a foreign visitor. After twenty sluggish minutes of weaving through shoppers on their way to market, the traffic thinned and we leaped forward, past bony cows, flamboyantly decorated Ambassador taxis, white-buttoned traffic controllers. Soon, we headed north along the crescent-shaped bank of the Ganges, past Indian Railways' bustling diesel locomotive factory, and finally into the green and rich brown countryside of rural India. To be riding a motorbike, the sun just tinged with winter, felt enormously pleasant.

We rode for a few hours, stopping only for tea and to buy marigolds for Mata-ji. Beneath us, the conditions of the road seemed to speak volumes about the direction in which we were heading. Smooth asphalt gave way to potholes, then dust, then finally little more than a rutted track. The concrete buildings returned to an organic mud and brick, and the people lost their Western clothes, their sunglasses and their ever-present mobile phones, to be replaced by hand-loomed saris, pitchforks and buffaloes straining at the end of worn hemp ropes.

For the last half mile, the motorbike could not be driven. We left it basking in the sun, and walked along the narrow path, open fields stretching out in every direction. Three quarters of the working population of Uttar Pradesh, India's most populous state, work in agriculture. Here that was evident in the corn, millet and lentils which studded the red earth. In the distance, I could see cotton tufts blowing in the breeze, and I felt a great well-being flood through me.

Niraj, on the other hand, seemed nervous, so I asked what was bothering him.

'I have been leading quite a bad life recently. Smoking and drinking profusely, and neglecting my religious duties. I am worried Mata-ji is going to give me a talking to.'

I suppressed a smile. 'You're certain she'll know?'

He nodded. 'Oh yes! She knows. Last time she was so angry I did *puja* for a month! She is quite frightening, actually.'

'But she doesn't mind a Westerner coming here?'

'No, no. But make sure to give her some rupees. When she tends to people, it is taking her away from her main work, which is farming. So she needs the money to buy food. She is not profiteering, you understand.'

At the end of the track we saw a cricket match in full swing. Outside the small hamlet, an open field had been planted with cricket stumps, and a wicket drawn out in chalk. Most of the adolescent male population of the village were involved, with those too young to join in seated cross-legged at the boundaries, or in several cases perched in the lower branches of banyan trees, punching tiny fists in the air when the shots made it past the boundary. Seeing the arrival of a *gora* – a white man – many came over to say hello, and Niraj was soon involved in lively explanations about just what I was doing here, in a village where a foreigner had rarely – if ever – appeared. I stared into their faces, which were full of friendly curiosity.

The village itself was small, scarcely more than five or six buildings, and populated with the usual goats and chickens. A tiny girl was rolling a wheel through the dust with a stick. To one side was a rammed earth platform, a temple of sorts, pillared with concrete and crowned with a tiny red pennant. I could see a large crowd and, over the bobbing heads, I could make out who I assumed to be Mata-ji sitting cross-legged: seemingly a regular village woman, surrounded by some fifty people.

Closer, I saw that she was tough-looking, with the thick arms and muscular neck of a rural peasant, a face older than her years and the slightly thinning hair of the Indian matriarch. In her parting she wore the traditional vermilion powder, and amidst her dark complexion there was a pair of unusually deep-set eyes. She was muttering quietly beneath her breath. A fly had landed on her cheek but she seemed not to notice.

That Niraj had said she was an incarnation of Kali told me something. This put Mata-ji in the school known as 'Shaktism' – a system outside the Brahminical tradition in which a local priestess becomes a channel for the person-ality of a goddess. In some villages, particularly in the largely communist state of Bengal, these figures have been driven out, much like the European witches of the Middle Ages. Elsewhere they remain, albeit on increasingly shaky ground as Mr Ghosh's forces of rationalism sweep through India, labelling trance healers and tantrics fraudulent. Certainly, they are unusual figures, professing knowledge of ancestors and ghosts and often the ability to avert natural disasters and infertility, or to exert control over an unpredictable world. As with the trance healers of Ladakh, it's a gift that often appears in adolescence, the medium falling into trances for no reason, speaking with beings that cannot be seen.

Viewed as a positive force, these women are healers of a sort, versed in herbal medicine and the power of mantras, and with the ability to make amulets to counteract evil influences. Their prayers involve a spectrum of major and minor goddesses from the Hindu pantheon, and they provide primary counsel for men and women often cut off from conventional medical and psychological advice.

They are also interesting for being the last vestiges of a goddess tradition that reaches back long before the arrival of Hinduism as we know it. According to these beliefs, divine energy is a feminine rather than a masculine principle. Called *shakti*, this primordial force is responsible for creation and destruction, for curing diseases and punishing wrongdoers. The goddess is called upon to help with agriculture and birth, to bring marital happiness and sexual enjoyment; in some forms she is Mother Earth herself.

Slightly apprehensively, I sat down beside Niraj on the edge of the temple. Aside from a few cursory glances, no one paid me too much attention. Some of these people, he told me, had travelled a hundred miles to see Mata-ji – they were here for any number of ailments: professional, mental, physical – and thus were more concerned that this living incarnation of Kali should help them than by the presence of a foreigner.

For the first hour, I watched and listened. Mata-ji wore a brown tunic, beneath a turquoise sari. She smoked enormous *bidi* cigarettes – made from hand-rolled tobacco leaves and ground cloves – almost constantly, dragon-like plumes of smoke pouring out of her large, somewhat masculine mouth.

Several blue bangles jangled on her left wrist, pink on her right. She listened intently, giving each *bidi* merely a few hefty puffs before tossing it away in a shower of sparks. She laughed often, and it was that, more than anything, which suggested some kind of altered state. It was one of the most raucous, booming laughs I've ever heard on a woman, and it seemed to heave up from her chest without restraint. In her eyes was a daunting strength: there was nothing it couldn't subdue.

'That fellow has money problems,' explained Niraj, as a shattered-looking man with a hennaed beard pleaded his case. After touching Mata-ji's feet reverently, he knelt before her, unburdening himself with an occasional wringing of the hands. 'His hardware shop was always successful, but recently something has happened. Customers are not coming. Within a few months, he will lose his business if something doesn't change.'

Mata-ji listened sagely, her eyes flashing through a fringe of sweaty grey hair. She held out her hand and the man passed her a package wrapped in newspaper.

'He has brought earth from the floor of his house,' explained Niraj. 'She needs it to understand the situation, and to see if any curses are there. Earth is best, although rice is also acceptable if the house is modern.'

Mata-ji unwrapped the twist of newspaper and poured the earth into her hands. There was barely a teaspoonful of dust; she stirred it gingerly with her forefinger, then brought it up to her nose to smell. I felt there was something immensely logical about all this: that soil and rice, two objects at the very heart of rural Indian life, should be the telling substances.

Niraj translated as she asked her questions:

'Has anyone in the house had dreams of an old woman or a small child?' she asked. 'If they do, you must pray for those people – they are spirits seeking peace.'

The man said that no one, to his knowledge, had dreamed of such things.

Mata-ji nodded, tossed away another *bidi* like a missile, and then held up her hands.

'Now she will begin,' whispered Niraj. 'She will speak with the Deities.'

What followed was garbled at best, much of it verging on pure stream of consciousness. But some of it was translatable, and Niraj did his best to keep up. Had I not seen the oracle in Ladakh I might have been more bewildered. As it was, it felt not too dissimilar, and I watched with interest as her eyes lost their focus, and her voice turned thin; the woman she'd been vanishing somehow.

'Oh Durga, Brahma, Kali,' she cried. 'Why are you meddling in human affairs? We, who give you *pujas* and offering, who worship you in form and beyond, are humans trying to lead peaceful lives. What have we done to offend you? What must we do to avoid your anger? Why won't you leave us alone?'

Five minutes of this was followed with wailing, gnashing of her yellow molars and a final surge of anger.

'Now she is *cursing* the gods,' whispered Niraj. 'She is threatening them. Oh dear, this is too much.'

I nodded without comment, but inwardly impressed at the astonishing confidence it must take to openly curse the gods in such a pious society. And truly she was herself a wrathful presence, both formidable and commanding, and with a gruff, crashing voice that suggested a weird and powerful state. For these few minutes, at least, my inadequacies of language were rendered unimportant: I could understand swearing when I heard it!

When her speech tapered out, she spoke again to the nervous shopkeeper.

'Has anyone given you anything to bury in your house?' Mata-ji asked.

The shopkeeper paled very suddenly. He was so startled he almost fell backwards off the temple dais and he put out a frail hand to steady himself. Several of the spectators began to tut beneath their breath.

'Yes,' he confessed. 'Oh God! An old friend has given me something to bury. Three months past. He told me it was valuable and I was to keep it for him until he asked for it back.'

'Give it back at once!' said Mata-ji, flatly. 'That package is *cursed* and is bringing harm upon your household. Take it from your house this very night and return it. Then you must bring a Brahmin to your house and have it cleaned. *Puja* must be given to Kali. Incense must be burned. Several offerings will be required to bring peace.'

With his eyes fixed on Mata-ji the entire time, the man knelt before her, stammering his thanks.

She patted him on the head affectionately. 'Don't worry, my son, Kali has helped. Soon, business will be profitable again.'

After he had left, the next person explained his case. He had urinated beneath a tree, apparently, which had allowed a bad spirit to gain power over him. For a time, though, I was too stunned to pay attention. How on *earth* had Mata-ji known the other man had something buried in his house? More than anything I'd yet encountered on my quest, that truly seemed to speak of the supernatural. Sitting here, in this unlikely spot, I found myself blinking in amazement, and yet no one else around the temple seemed in the least perplexed. I resolved to carry on listening, to see if her other pronouncements showed such acuity.

The next woman, it transpired, had back problems. She

could no longer stand up properly. Had someone cursed her? There was a woman in her village known for her ability with the evil eye – was it her? To my astonishment Mata-ji was shaking her head before the woman had even finished speaking.

'This is a medical problem,' she said. 'You must visit your doctor. I cannot help you.'

After her came another patient, an attractive woman of about twenty-five with a gold stud through her nostril. She had metal hoops through her ear lobes and an agitated mouse-like face. When she began to speak her voice came in stutters, the words spilling over themselves. All of this reminded me that this wasn't, in these people's minds, merely a village elder giving advice. Mata-ji was an incarnation of divine power, a goddess in human form. Could anyone look upon the face of God without quailing?

'I'm from Varanasi,' she began.

'*Acha*, I remember you,' said Mata-ji. 'You came before, two months past. Did you bring the rice I asked for?'

From beneath her white pashmina, the woman produced a package of cooked rice skilfully tied up in muslin. As with the earth, Mata-ji examined it for a time before beginning her dialogue with the gods.

'That girl is wanting a child,' explained Niraj. 'Her husband's family are becoming angry with her because she cannot conceive. See, behind her is the husband. He thinks it's her fault.'

I made out a young, bullish man behind her, mobile phone protruding from his shirt pocket. He stood sullenly, crossing then uncrossing his arms, unable to look Mata-ji in the eyes.

Mata-ji put down the rice and began berating the gods once more. It went on longer this time, and her bony finger jabbed the sky insistently. Finally she bade the couple stand before her. She joined their hands together, then began to examine the palms of each, using the tip of a kitchen knife to trace the lines.

'Brahma has written the story of our lives on the hand,' she said to the husband. 'Her hand is clean. But on your hand there are seven bad signs. Is this your second wife?'

The man's eyes widened, and he nodded fearfully. All of a sudden the sullen confidence vanished to reveal a frightened boy.

Mata-ji tilted her head. 'Other wife is deceased, is she not?'

Another nod. His lower lip fell open.

Mata-ji smiled. It was hard to tell, of course, but it seemed a knowing smile, seeing the bigger picture. 'Take these flowers,' she said, reaching to one side and picking up a garland of orange marigolds that someone had brought her. 'Tread them on the crossing before your house, one by one, and I won't need to see you here again.'

Clutching the flowers in a plastic bag, I watched the young couple walking away across the village. Again, Mata-ji seemed to have displayed an almost preternatural knowledge of their lives. How could she have known he had been married before? Nevertheless, no matter if her prescription worked or not, I admired her for what she'd done. Now at least, the young girl would not face pressure for failing to conceive: Mata-ji had laid the responsibility firmly at the husband's door, straight from the gods themselves. It was almost poetic.

The morning stretched on. In every case, Mata-ji listened, enacted her strange dialogue with the Deities, and then offered her help. Perhaps the most serious case of the morning came when an old woman appeared, skeletal and slick with fever. Mata-ji summoned an attendant to bring a chicken from the farmyard, then nicked its crown so that a tiny fleck of blood dripped on to the blade. Although I was interested in the healing, I couldn't help but feel for the chicken. It was released squawking back into the farmyard, and the other chickens began to peck at it savagely, aroused by the sight of blood. The poor bird ran this way and that, pursued by a rampaging mob. Finally, in a last desperate attempt to find safety, it leaped back on to the temple dais, then ran up to me and tucked its fluffy head beneath my leg. It lay there motionless, trembling faintly, and finally fell asleep.

As the last of the villagers thanked Mata-ji and went on their way, Niraj and I went forward. She greeted him warmly and accepted the money he offered without looking at it. Then she turned and looked at me properly for the first time. I felt a great kindness emanating from her. She gave one of her booming laughs.

'What does this white man want?' she asked Niraj. 'Does he wish to ask the goddess something?'

'Can I ask her how she got this power?' I said.

She acquiesced. 'I can tell him,' she said. 'I was twenty-two when I had a dream that I could heal people with problems. Kali came to me. The next day it so happened that someone came to ask me for help. Even as they stood there, I heard voices telling me how I could solve their problems.' She shrugged, as if it were the most natural thing in the world. 'Since then I try to do the best I can. Sometimes people go to priests for help, but the solutions they offer are only temporary ones. Problems can return. But when I get rid of something, it is gone for good. Kali works through me.'

'My problems aren't acute,' I said. 'At times I've suffered from depression and inertia. I'm seeking something beyond all that – but I can't seem to reach it.'

Mata-ji smiled and beckoned me over. I sat cross-legged before her, looking respectfully down and waiting for her to begin. Before I knew what was happening, I felt her hands on my head, two rough hands, but full of maternal kindness. They were warm and they kneaded my scalp vigorously, then my shoulders, then came to rest.

'Too much tension,' she said, chuckling. 'Mustard oil is good for the muscles. You should be doing this daily!'

I looked up aghast, wondering if I, too, was to receive practical rather than mystical assistance. But she was looking to the heavens now, and her eyes were glazed over.

'Oh Durga, Brahma, Kali,' she wailed. 'You who remove all obstacles, please help this man. Help him find quietness. Help him find peace. Mahadev, please drive out the spirits from him.'

Suddenly, I felt the hands release, and I opened my eyes again. Mata–ji was smiling at me, and the interview was over.

That evening, back in the quiet of my room above Manikarnika Ghat, I reflected on the day. If Mata–ji was a goddess, then she was certainly one of the most down to earth, practical incarnations one could hope for. Her advice seemed largely sensible, and from what I'd seen there was nothing of her work which either took advantage of people or offered the potential for serious harm.

To decipher, in practical terms, what exactly she was doing was difficult, perhaps impossible. What was important was to understand the world-view she represented, and the seamless unity of her vision. For Mata–ji, life's panorama extended far further than my own. Included in her gaze were innumerable gods, goddesses, protective spirits, demons and ghosts, all of which she had learned to control or placate. It was a holistic world-view, with nothing left unexplained.

Whether these gods and goddesses were 'real' might have been, at the start of my quest, far more important for me. But the more I saw of these things, the more it appeared that 'reality', as it seems to our rational consciousness, might be a concept far less relevant to one in trance. In such a profound state of attunement, who *knew* what Mata-ji was seeing and experiencing? Just because we couldn't see something or prove it, did that make it less real? Could it not also be, that in the case of an entire culture fed by the same myths, that the same beings might appear again and again: the expression of profound human archetypes that push aside the conscious mind to come forth and express themselves?

Mata-ji, it seemed to me, was fully at home in the world she lived in, and had a world-view that functioned far more accurately and successfully than any alternative. Equally, I refused to believe that she would be in such demand, and others like her in villages across India, if she failed to help people – if, in short, her magic didn't *work*. Something then *was* happening: a strange, imprecise power that smoothed away the boundaries and resistances of everyday life. Recalling the way she'd held my head that morning, I felt a nostalgia for a way of life I had never known. For who, in Western life, can we go to when things become too much, outside doctor, therapist, or friend? Mata-ji was that distant figure, authoritative but kind, who could advise on problems of any kind, ask the very gods themselves for help, and leave one heading home with a lighter heart.

At midnight, still restless, I wrapped a blanket round me and went down the cow-pat-strewn lane towards the Burning Ghat. As ever in Varanasi, the process of death and rebirth continued and even now a corpse was being lowered on to the pyre, the flames sending faint reflections of themselves across the Ganges, shadows of one life passing. I sat on the cold steps, wrapped in darkness, and watched the primal scene unfold, and heard faint sounds of chanting at the water's edge.

For scientists, I reflected, even these sacred rituals of death would be considered somehow 'false' or fabricated. And yet might it not be, rather, that those feelings which occur in the human psyche seek natural expression in the world of form? Are not every culture's religions and bodies of myth merely the manifestations of human awareness, vessels to make the transcendent comprehensible?

If this was true, then Mata-ji was indeed fighting off spirits with the ability to make trouble in the human world. To believe in them was to give them power. In the week to come this notion would come to haunt me. For I was about to see the dark heart of a magical world-view: a ceremony intended not to heal, but to kill.

Black Magic

'I was telling my friend about our visit to Mata-ji,' began Niraj, enjoying a fizzy green Limca on the rooftop of my guesthouse. 'And that you were interested in the traditions of Benares. He asked me if you would be interested in meeting some Mantriks.'

'Mantriks?'

Niraj paled. 'Very unpleasant men, actually. Also worshipping Kali, although when they invoke her name it is not for purposes of healing or assistance. It is for death. They have the power to kill people through curses and charms.'

I froze. I'd heard rumours of such people, but certainly never expected to meet them.

'Are there many such people here . . .?'

Niraj looked uneasy. 'Bad men are there in every country, I think. For myself, I do not like such people. I want nothing to do with them. But yes, there are some such fellows around. I'm assuming you don't want to meet with them.'

'I think I do,' I said, tentatively. 'What if I give them a false name and pretend to put the evil eye on someone who doesn't exist?'

'This may be possible. But you must be careful. And you will have to go alone.'

'Alone!'

'I will drive you to the village,' said Niraj. 'But after that I will go no further. I am afraid of these people.'

In the event, it took some time to organise. Niraj's friend knew of the Mantriks through his cousin, who had some recourse to seek revenge a few years back when a local crime syndicate threatened his business. They were cautious men, it seemed, who wanted money up front and certain assurances. What I did glean was that they were of the Dom caste, the untouchables who worked the cremation ghats. As untouchables they were entitled to handle corpses – a source of ritual impurity for orthodox Hindus – and it was their lot from birth to manage the rituals of death. Because of their trade, however, most Hindus were reluctant to even brush past them in the street. Their village was apart, and they were expected to marry amongst themselves.

Over the week before the ceremony, I discovered as much about the Dom as I could. They were not vegetarian, offered one pious Hindu with a shudder, but ate the bodies of animals that had died a natural death, even rats. Another person suggested that the Roma, the gypsies who first originated in India, stemmed from their caste. Doms were supposed to stand when a higher caste person walked past them; they were forbidden from wearing new clothes; their children were illiterate; their women amongst the likeliest to work in prostitution. Even at weddings they were only allowed to make four sacred rounds of the fire, as opposed to the seven traditional for Brahmins.

With all this in mind, I began to feel an increasing sympathy for those downtrodden members of society. But neither had I forgotten that these Mantriks were, in effect, paid killers. They made their living from causing harm and that, when all is said and done, is a choice.

It seemed important to meet them, however. They were evidence of the dark heart of a magical world-view. It was easy enough to blame science for our disenchantment and to lament the wonder we had lost. But the truth was more complex than that. Black magic remains a serious problem in India, with occasional horrors appearing in the press. In 2005, the state of Maharashtra introduced its Eradication of Black Magic and Evil and Aghori Practices Bill in an attempt to stem a rising tide of incidents. And one only had to glance at the classified ads of any newspaper to see astrologists and numerologists offering cures for the effects of witchcraft, proof of an endemic problem.

India is not alone, of course, in such beliefs. In many parts of the Middle East and the Mediterranean, belief in the evil eye remains prevalent, with any number of charms and talismans adopted for protection. Disks of concentric blue and white circles are held to be, as well as certain prayers, particularly powerful.

The evil eye, evidently, is merely one aspect of a belief system which stretches back to the earliest origins of man. My own culture, I reflected – in the days before I was to meet the Mantriks – had once waged its own war against such beliefs. It was Pope John XXII, in 1320, who formalised the persecution of witchcraft when he authorised the Inquisition to prosecute sorcery. Almost overnight, those people once esteemed for their ability to manipulate the supernatural were seen as being in league with the devil. The trials and discrimination that followed, culminating in the mass hysteria of the seventeenth-century witch trials, were the beginnings of our European disenchantment.

More than that, I supposed, these historical events had also helped form the type of society the West had now become. The Enlightenment marked the beginning of a new era, still with us, in which reason and science were held as the ultimate arbiters of reality. Little did the Protestants know that this process, which was intended to gain them precedence over their Roman Catholic brethren, would eventually begin to erode the commonality of Christian monotheism itself. It would leave behind a society in which natural science was held to have authority over all interpretations of life, where the numinous struggled for air, only the faintest embers still glowing.

Nevertheless, it was with some considerable trepidation that I met Niraj on the appointed day. Suddenly, the calculating light of reason seemed a life-raft as I considered the possibility that these men were genuinely in touch with malevolent forces. Pacing through the main bazaar, I resolved to keep my mind open whilst keeping my wits about me. This was going to be a strange and unnerving day.

Niraj was waiting outside the Ganesh Chai Stand, puffing a *bidi*, when I arrived. He looked edgy and drawn, and said little as we sped through Varanasi in his cousin's auto-rickshaw. Away from the ghats, the thick mist that had ushered in the morning burned away. The sky was cloudless and the ancient stonework was lit up with a flaxen light. At the traffic lights Niraj handed two folded bills to the traffic policeman, a fat bully in a sweat-stained uniform, who nodded and waved us through without a word. These bribes and pay-offs are the norm in Indian society, so that people such as Niraj, struggling to haul themselves up, are preyed upon at every level.

It was one more reminder of the challenges the poor face. The public image of India seems increasingly one of success and economic boom. But for the most part it is the middle classes who are enjoying the benefits. UN statistics show that 700 million Indians still live on less than two dollars a day and a fifth of children don't go to school. Driving through Bajardiha, the Muslim weavers' district, we saw scenes of harrowing poverty. Open sewers ran down the streets; undernourished children peered out from doorways. Here even auto-rickshaws were a rare occurrence and we caused a palpable surge of interest as we sputtered through the constricted lanes. I felt self-conscious, a voyeur, and crouched back beyond the canopy.

'Silk market is in grave decline,' said Niraj quietly. 'Some weavers are dying from starvation.'

I asked the reasons for the crisis.

'These people use traditional hand looms,' he explained. 'But now some factories are using machines, so that they can't compete. Also, too much cheap silk is coming from China.' He shrugged. 'What to do. World is changing, isn't it.'

For the last several miles, the rickshaw bumped unhappily down a dirt track. There were very few people about. At the roadside, a mound of burning plastic exuded a noxious yellow smoke; an old woman squatted beneath a peepul tree. Hairy black pigs rooted for grubs. Women pounded clothes on stone blocks, their flashing eyes acknowledging our arrival. There seemed something significant in occult traditions on the margins of society, a psychic as well as geographic hinterland. Shamans, I had read, often built their houses beyond the perimeter of villages, partly for privacy but also to subtly encourage the rumours that can only circulate in their absence.

What kind of men came here to seek out these Mantriks, I wondered. A slighted husband, a businessman wishing to edge out the competition? On some level, it was not dissimilar to hiring a gunman to achieve the same ends, and yet, perhaps because death was less certain, the weapons less tangible, it conjured a different feeling in me. Equally, could I ever really understand the primal fears and impotence that gave rise to a need for black magic? Like most visitors from the West, I travelled in the developing world supported by the full gamut of tablets and inoculations, not to mention the money to seek whatever help I needed. But what would it feel like to exist in a world where those options were not possible, where the only real source of help lay in places like these, amongst whispered spells and mantras?

We pulled to a stop. In the distance, beneath the dappled shade of a tree, we could see three men loitering.

Niraj pointed distastefully. 'Over there. You go and talk to those men. They will take you.'

'You're sure I can't persuade you to come?'

He shook his head, and touched a tiny icon of Hanuman hanging from the wing mirror. 'I'll wait here.'

I got out and trudged across the scrubland, inwardly cursing myself for too much curiosity, for not staying in the reassuring confines of the backpackers' district like the rest. It was after three o'clock and the sun seemed to sear the top of my head. Sweat was trickling down my back. Up close, I raised a hand in greeting. The men wore turbans of a distinctive pale-pink hue, and were dark-skinned and angular about the face. Two of them had impressive moustaches, the third a long, effeminate face, with smears of kohl beneath his eyes. They were waiting for me.

I walked forward tensely, standing out in my Western clothes, and shook them by the hand. From the first I was struck by their ease around me, their lack of surprise at having a white man here, seeking out their somewhat objectionable services. Their gazes disclosed little. For a time we stood beneath the tree while they finished their cigarettes and then, with a faint inclination of the head, the one who'd introduced himself as Baskar led the way. I fell in behind them, saying nothing.

We came to a small settlement, with perhaps three or four dwellings. There was dust beneath our feet, peppered with cow shit and windblown plastic. A hundred yards beyond, I made out a house built of mud bricks packed in with rammed earth, a sheet of corrugated iron serving for a roof. Outside, there were several unfinished baskets and a spool of rope. I could feel my eye twitching, as it sometimes does during moments of intense unease.

'Inside,' barked Baskar. 'Come.'

There were no windows inside the Mantriks' hut and it was surprisingly cool. Outside the sun had barely begun to dip, and heat lines still danced above the red earth. Beyond the cloth door it was silent; a single blade of light exposed dust whirls descending slowly to the floor. There was no furniture, save two coir mats, a battered wooden chest and a large bulging hessian sack. Instantly, it was as if the world outside had ceased to exist. There was only this humble room, and the belief of the men before me that they could effect real change on the world outside.

The three men sat down opposite me in the gloom, crossing their legs carefully. They seemed in no hurry to speak. I composed myself with a deep breath. Now the ritual would begin, I thought. I would have to work very hard to remain grounded.

'You would like to curse someone?' asked Baskar, who had the best command of English. 'That is why you are here.'

I nodded.

He stared at me unblinkingly. 'Do you want to kill this man?'

I thought for a time. 'Yes, I do.'

'This can be done. Death will probably not be instant – may take time. But will happen. Do you understand this?'

I said that I did.

'There are many methods, many mantras. Many ways you can bring harm on your enemy. He might fall ill, have some bad accident. In certain cases he may drop dead in the street. Even those that have protected themselves with amulets cannot withstand our mantras. They have been in our family for a long time. No one else knows them. Before us, our fathers used them. Now it is the role of the sons to continue their work.'

I nodded.

A head tilt. 'You have brought the money?'

I took out the notes – 3,000 rupees – and handed them over. According to Niraj this was the fixed rate, and they had not attempted to hike up the price once they knew I was a foreigner. They were taking great risks, to be sure, in the services they offered, but nevertheless it seemed like a lot of money to be handing over. A month's wages for a rickshaw driver, three or four for a weaver.

The man named Ajit took the notes, licked his finger, and counted them carefully. I searched his face for signs of glee, but there were none.

'*Acha*. We will start.'

Patiently, they began to remove the accoutrements of their trade from the wooden box. First, some garlands of marigolds, bright orange and unlikely amidst the dun earth tones of the hut. Then a lemon, a rusty blade with a wooden handle, some sheets of paper and finally a heavy object in a clean white cloth. I could feel my eye twitching again, faster now, as Baskar unwrapped it reverently. Inside there was a human skull.

I gave a barely concealed shudder. Years past in a science class I'd handled a human skull. But this was far from the polished, bone-white item I remembered. The occipital bone at the back was jagged and stained with blood. It looked only partially decomposed.

'From the Kali Ghat in Calcutta,' growled Baskar, as if reading my mind. 'Kali Ghat is most important place for tantric magic. This object has great power. You should not touch it.'

That was plausible, I thought. As Doms they would have free access to the cremation grounds.

Baskar laid out three strings of marigolds on the ground, then slowly lifted the skull and placed it on top.

'First mantra,' he muttered. 'We ask Kali to listen. She is the Black Goddess, source of all creation. She slays all demons. She creates and destroys worlds. If we give her worship, she can destroy for us.'

Chanting under his breath, he held his hands in the air theatrically, then in a quick motion sliced the lemon in half and squeezed out the juice on to the skull. Within seconds it began to smoke and an acrid reek permeated the hut. Some moments later, small flames appeared, engulfing the skull and the mound of orange flowers. Orange flames licked eerily from within the eye sockets.

The youngest of the three, the effeminate Ajit, looked at me expectantly, probably hoping to see my wonder at the materialisation of flames without the use of any matches. But I gave him nothing in return. The lemon juice, obviously, was the catalyst for some sort of chemical reaction. If I'd wanted to see such cheap conjuring tricks I could have gone to any street corner in the city.

As the marigolds charred and withered in the heat, Baskar began to sprinkle pinches of finely ground herbs on to the blaze, and add small shavings of wood. The flames leaped higher. Then he began to sing. His voice was low and ruined – a voice that had drunk and smoked away the harshness of life. The mantras were spoken quickly but I was able to jot down some of them.

Sat guru sat masan. Rabu chandal ban chandal – kam kamacha devig chu – Sat guru sat masan. Rabu chandal ban chandal – kam kamacha devig chu – Sat guru sat masan. Rabu chandal ban chandal – kam kamacha devig chu

When the mantra was finished he passed me a scrap of paper and a pencil.

'Write the name of your enemy on this,' he commanded. 'Spell it correctly. Then close the paper and hand it back to me.'

I wrote down the name I'd prepared. It was a name at random – a name with no possible meaning for me. And yet, even as I scrawled it, I was worried. What if someone *did* exist with this name: was the spell transferable? At the same time, why was I worrying at all? I didn't *believe* in this mumbo jumbo – it was superstition, a fascinating anthropological relic. And yet somehow it was impossible to discard entirely the possibility that some outcome would arise from what I was seeing here. That, I supposed, was the very premise upon which these men sold their services. No matter how rational we believe ourselves, these thoughts run very deep in the human psyche.

I handed Baskar the piece of paper. He took out a cigarette from his pocket and lit it, then blew smoke across the tightly folded square. He stubbed out the cigarette and put the paper in his mouth, chewing hard for several minutes. When he opened his mouth next, a dense stream of smoke, almost like dry ice, poured out, which he directed across the human skull, now resting in a circle of embers. Another conjuring trick, but the effect was impressive. The bloodstained skull, placed on glowing embers, was now veiled beneath a halo of smoke.

He began to chant once again. 'Second mantra.'

Akas bani patal bani bani dilkikai dohai nona chamain kachoo –
Akas bani patal bani bani dilkikai dohai nona chamain kachoo –
Akas bani patal bani bani dilkikai dohai nona chamain kachoo

'That is Ma Kali mantra,' he explained when he had finished. 'With this mantra your enemy will not be able to face you. He will *never* be able to come in front of you again. Even now he will be feeling some effects.'

Ma kamru kamacha devi jirya bangali non chamaiain kechyo – Parjare jarai kalki kai mai kamru kamacha kechoo adirat pichli pahar japoo karoo mai kamru kamacha devi taiaho jeeria bagale kechoo

'This third mantra is most dangerous,' he continued. 'You take the ashes of the marigold flowers, keep them in your pocket, then follow your enemy in the market place, or as he leaves his house, and throw the powder in his face. Just as flowers burn to dust, so will your enemy.'

I nodded uneasily. The repeated mantras, the claustro-phobia, the low light – all of it was filling me with a strong desire to get as far away from the place as possible. If only in the intimidation side of their business, they were good at their job. I gazed longingly at the door, willing this to be over.

Baskar stopped chanting suddenly and tapped the third man, Kanti, on the shoulder. The room was so full of smoke by now that I could hardly see them, but I saw Kanti move towards the hessian sack.

Ajit shuffled towards me with gleaming eyes. He rested a soft hand upon my shoulder. 'Kali is goddess of destruction,' he whispered. 'She has strength of *shakti* – cosmic power. Even Shiva lies beneath her feet. It is her we have to ask for assistance.'

I shifted back a little. The energy in the room seemed to be reaching a crescendo and I was beginning to shake.

'Kali, the black-skinned one, wears a necklace of *nagas* – serpents. Like Kali, snakes can bring death. But they are also creatures of great power. When we conduct a mantra with snakes, outcome is much stronger – Kali is listening.'

Snakes! I thought to myself. Please let there not be snakes. Peering through the smoke, I saw Kanti upending the hessian sack. He jiggled it slightly and, recoiling in disbelief, I made out the heavy, thick coils of a python unspooling into the hut. I felt mildly sick. It was sleepy – perhaps recently fed – but despite this I began to back up against the wall of the hut. This was madness; it was time to get the hell out of here.

'Not dangerous, my friend,' simpered Baskar. 'Not dangerous to you. Only to your enemy, anger of snake will be coming.' He laughed, a menacing chuckle, lifting the python around his head.

Composing himself, he began to chant the mantra again, a low intonation that seemed to rise up from his solar plexus and reverberate around the room. For a second I almost burst out into hysterical laughter. This was too absurd, too unlikely! I've been in some strange places in my life but truly none could outrank this for its sheer distance from the normal facets of my life. And yet even as this thought occurred to me, so too did the realisation that this was what I'd come looking for. In this room everything had significance. I should not complain now that I had found it.

If the first snake had made me uneasy, it was the second

one, however, that really pushed me towards the edge. The litheness of it, its subtle reed-green hue. The flickering tongue that spoke of rare sub-tropical toxins and which, more even than the venom it might bring, seemed to tap into the deepest levels of the human psyche, to envelop me with unease, to send my heart rate spinning upwards so that sweat began to pour from my skin.

'This snake from jungle,' whispered Ajit, his voice now the faintest murmur. He was relishing the performance, I was sure of it. Surely there was no need to petrify the customer! 'Small snake,' he continued, 'but very, very dangerous one. One bite is enough.'

In a second I got to my feet, edging towards the door, but Baskar grabbed my arm and pulled me down.

'Do not be afraid, sir,' he said, allowing himself a smile. 'Poison is not there. Poison is gone. Only for Kali do we have snakes. She is enjoying them.'

With the greatest reluctance, I lowered myself back down to ground level. After checking to make sure that they were cool, Baskar swept the ashes from the fire into a small paper bag.

'These,' he said, 'you keep. After they have touched him, within at least one month your enemy will be falling dead. Possibly he will be falling ill, or heart will be stopping. Death will be imminent.'

I nodded. The whole point of black magic, I'd thought, was to avoid such public confrontations. In a society which continues to fear the supernatural, running up to a known enemy and throwing a handful of dust in his face might be about the most obvious statement of intent one could think of. But then I considered the element of fear. For a believer in witchcraft, what could be more terrifying than to suppose oneself cursed? Even disallowing all the effects of the incantation, the weight of fear would be a powerful weapon in itself, perhaps even enough to make one ill.

With that it was over. All too quickly the snakes were coiled and replaced, the floor swept with a besom, the money recounted and I was out, sucking great gulps of air. Newly paid, the Mantriks were all smiles now, one of them fetching a sooty kettle from behind the hut and offering me chai. How quickly, I ruminated, had we gone from the business of calculated murder to social pleasantry. More than anything, this seemed evidence of just how normal they supposed their job to be. They didn't seem to have the same ideas of good and evil that I was familiar with. Nothing was intrinsically positive or negative; there were merely these two forces at play in the universe, and through skill, technique and piety they could be manipulated.

Nevertheless, I refused the chai. To their knowledge, I was about to throw magical dust in the face of my enemy in order to put him in the ground, so I supposed I could find better people to drink tea with. I shook hands with the men, thanked them for their time and made my way slowly across the village. A chicken ran across my path. Some distance behind me I heard the voices of children, which told me that in one of the other huts the Mantriks' families had been there all along, cooking, cleaning and surviving.

In the distance I could see Niraj's rickshaw and I almost ran towards it.

For several days after the black magic ceremony I slept badly. It wasn't the things I'd seen which left me uneasy, so much as feeling that I'd indulged an area of curiosity which should never have been part of this journey. If it was the macabre I was after, then there were innumerable avenues of exploration. In actual fact it was the very opposite I was seeking. Black magic, and the whole realm of superstition which fuels it, is a practice which draws upon the fears and uncertainties of human beings. Mystical knowledge, on the other hand, comes through hard-earned achievement, and springs from a mind unwavering in its search for truth.

It was almost time to leave Varanasi, but first I went to bid farewell to the elderly yoga teacher who'd been instructing me in the early mornings. He lived not far from my guest-house, at the end of a narrow alley in which I'd twice found myself drenched from an overflow pipe, and once narrowly escaped a savaging from a pye-dog. On the morning of departure, I arrived to find Yogi Raj, as he called himself, already enacting some vigorous *asanas* on the stone flagons outside his house. He was about sixty, with a round barrel chest, a shock of hennaed hair and a style of instruction which brooked no excuses. He had a habit of quoting the scriptures to me one minute, then shattering my preconceptions by telling me of his ambitions to fly an Apache helicopter, or visit Las Vegas. In short, he was very much today's Indian: steeped in the past, but by no means stuck there.

That morning we practised his inimitable style of yoga for an hour and then, as the morning sun took the chill from the courtyard at last, laid out some cushions in the light to take our tea. An arc of pigeons cut across the sky above us, as Yogi Raj's neighbour set his flock out for their morning practice.

'Ah, you are leaving our Benares,' he lamented. 'Just as we are making some progress. You a very restless young man.'

'I'm trying not to be,' I said.

'When you come back,' said Yogi Raj, 'you will study with me again, and my wife will cook you some special vegetarian delicacies. Non veg is inappropriate for the study of yoga: it excites the mind too much. Also, please avoid onions, garlic and spicy foods.'

I said that I would.

'Book writing is a worthy profession,' continued Yogi Raj, extending an advisory digit, 'but remember it will not bring the answers you seek. God does not come in the form of thoughts and ideas. He comes in the place that ideas end. For Westerners, this, what you might call, central difficulty.'

I sipped my tea thoughtfully. Yogi Raj had a habit of talking in riddles, but in this case I felt that he was speaking very sincerely. Increasingly, on this strange journey, it was becoming evident that mystical experience occurs entirely outside conceptual thought.

'Thought is necessary, yes. But let the mind be the servant! Beyond thought, you will find that there is something capable of watching thought arise!' He chuckled. 'This is the Witness, the one who sees. This Witness is eternal and without form. When this body dies,' he patted his arms and chest forcefully, 'it will continue on.'

Feeling rather like the lectured novice in some martial arts epic, I nodded once more, and the conversation soon turned to other things. But what he'd said stayed with me. At the heart of mystical experience was a state of consciousness which, though the different faiths call it by different names, was the highest goal of a human life. Albert Einstein, that most mystically inclined of modern scientists, seemed to capture it precisely in a letter he wrote to the Queen of Belgium in 1939:

'There are moments when one feels free from one's own identification with human limitations and inadequacies. At such moments one imagines that one stands on some spot of a small planet gazing in amazement at the cold yet profoundly moving beauty of the eternal, the unfathomable. Life and earth flow into one and there is neither evolution nor destiny, only being.'

From Varanasi, I took a night train to Delhi, where I intended to begin my investigations into the ways India's second largest faith approaches mystical experience. In the heart of Nizammudin, Delhi's Muslim quarter, a Sufi shrine attracts thousands of devotees daily. A photographer friend of mine who lives in Delhi, Hindu himself, had extolled its virtues as one of the most spiritually vibrant places in India. It would be one more glimpse into the magical; one more strand of a web which seemed, at its heart, to go beyond religion entirely.

Over the last months I'd had brief moments of euphoria, but more frequent moments of despair. I'd been piecing together a jigsaw puzzle of infinite complexity, scrabbling around in the dust for pieces which would break off, forming several more, before succumbing to any grand design. And yet at last I had begun to see the true object of my quest. Everything I'd done had been necessary to get this far, the mistakes as well as the successes. Every small conversation in India, every wrong turn, was pointing me, subtly, in the direction of something which lay not in the puzzle at all, but beneath the puzzle, a thing without form and yet which linked all the forms, a sub-surface unity. As the train rocked along its tracks, I turned over in my bunk and my mind, if only for a moment, fell absolutely silent.

Amongst the Sufis

If the modern world is experiencing a collective re-enchantment, then there can be few things more illustrative of that fact than the astonishing renaissance of interest in the poet Rumi. During the 1990s a number of articles proclaimed him the most popular poet in the world, and a translation of his works in America sold half a million copies: extraordinary figures for any poet, placing him second only to Shakespeare.

But who was Mawlānā Jalāl al-Dīn Muhammad Balkhī (or Rumi, because of the many years he lived in the Seljuk Sultanate of Rûm, in Asia Minor)? And why should a Muslim poet of the thirteenth century continue to speak with such intelligibility to the world seven centuries after his death? Donna Karan has used recitations of his poetry as a sound-track to her catwalk shows, while Hollywood director Oliver Stone is reputedly keen to make a biopic of the mystic's life.

All of this would be extraordinary in the best of times. But that Rumi's popularity should soar in a post-9/11 world says more still. He was born in Afghanistan, then in the eastern territories of ancient Persia, and his poems are almost exclusively focused on our human relationship with God. On the face of it this should make him almost unsellable, and yet, if anything, his poetry became more popular *after* the destruction of the Twin Towers. Something in the verses transcends all creeds, but more than that, it offers a path to understanding mystical experience, with its clear metaphors of transcendence. I loved them from the first.

My own introduction to Rumi came during my university years, when I discovered a translation by Coleman Barks in a second-hand bookshop. The poem that caught my eye flipped my expectations like a kind of judo hold. I may even have checked the back cover again, just to confirm that this was indeed an Islamic mystic writing the better part of a millennium ago. It sounded absolutely contemporary, speaking directly of my own life. Beyond the aesthetic experience, there were gleaming insights into the spiritual process: how to see things as they really *are*.

> Soul drunk, body ruined, these two
> sit helpless in a wrecked wagon.
> Neither knows how to fix it.
> And my heart, I'd say it was more
> like a donkey sunk in a mudhole,
> struggling and miring deeper.
>
> But listen to me: for one moment,
> quit being sad. Hear blessings
> dropping their blossoms
> around you. God.

I bought the book and soon learned that Rumi was a Sufi and that Sufism was the mystical branch of Islam. Again this confounded my expectations: I hadn't known that Islam, with its emphasis on the words of the Prophet, allowed for mysticism. 'Sufi', I discovered, was the word given to the early Muslim ascetics, because of the simple cloaks they wore, made of *ṣūf* or wool. Like the Hindu yogis, they felt that paradise could be experienced in the midst of life, by entering a divine state. They sought to experience *fitra* – meaning 'innate human nature' – a state of complete unity with the world around them, and therefore with Allah. It all sounded remarkably like 'Buddha nature' or *moksha*, as well as suggesting parallels to the Quaker belief in the 'inner light' of the soul.

Rumi quickly became a part of my life, and his books frequent stowaways in my backpack. His mystical journey, above all, was expressed in the form of love. Where Buddha talked of embracing emptiness, Rumi talked of 'the beloved' or 'the friend'. Whereas Buddhism can occasionally appear daunting to an outsider, Sufism is readily accessible to all. Rumi's poems often compare the relationship of the seeker to God with that of a lover, and are concerned, above all, with opening the heart.

> Inside this new love, die
> Your way begins on the other side
> Become the sky
> Take an axe to the prison wall
> Escape

En route through modern Delhi by rickshaw, I saw the signs of the new India everywhere. On the edge of Khan market, a gleaming Barista coffee shop, India's answer to Starbucks, offered frothy cappuccino to Delhi's middle classes for approximately fifteen times the price of a roadside chai. Four-hundred-year-old minarets protruded above serpentine flyovers, polished SUVs roared past men on juddering bicycles. In the papers that week had been news that Delhi was to rid itself of its traditional vendors of street food, now considered 'unhygienic': an act which was to put an estimated million people out of work. Thousands of *jhuggis* (slum houses) were being bulldozed along the Yamuna Pushta (a stretch of land along the River Yamuna that trickles through Delhi), leaving an estimated 100,000 people homeless.

With the Commonwealth Games approaching in 2010, Delhi is anxious to promote a new image of India to the world, and the papers are full of homilies by politicians on the 'world-class' city they are creating from the ashes. Few articles, however, address the human cost of this modernisation or consider the catastrophic effects of the changes on the city's poor – who number a third of the total population. One government plan proposed to jail the city's beggars for the duration of the Games, so that foreign visitors are not unduly distressed.

Entering Delhi's Old Quarter, one is – for now at least – returned to an older mode of being. Here there are no shopping malls or multiplexes, but an ancient, distinctly Eastern city, full of the sights and sounds of a bygone world. It's a frenzied mass of bazaars, open-air butchers, hand-painted Bollywood posters, sweating bodies, peripatetic farmyard animals and monkeys, as well as startling olfactory delights and disasters.

For a long time, it's been my favourite part of the city. As with much of the old world, it reveals its secrets warily. If the new world gives everything away in a glance, the former works in subtleties and shadings, demanding a little trust before opening its arms. One can wander for an hour in the shadowy back streets subsumed in grime, before glimpsing, in a beam of sunlight, a mother washing her child, a man throwing offal to a flock of vultures, or a greybeard tracing his forefinger over the elegant gilt lettering of a Koran.

On this morning I walked for some time, beginning at a

stand of gnarled trees in Nizammudin east, then proceeding through an area which appeared increasingly at odds with the city I had come from. By my guesthouse near Connaught Circus, a gated community protects its inhabitants from the encroachments, visible or psychological, of the Indian poor. Here the medieval lanes kept no one out; its children spun wooden tops under a pacific sky, and its food was butchered, cooked and, by the look of things, sometimes reared, in the streets where people lived.

Not far from the shrine, the roadside stalls began to take on more of a devotional aspect: CDs of *qawwali* (Sufi devotional music), handfuls of fragrant rose petals, technicolour icons of Saint Hazrat Nizammudin, books, video cassettes, bundles of heady incense and *chadurs* – cloths with which to cover one's head respectfully. Some stallholders offer nothing but a series of empty boxes. For a nominal fee one can leave one's shoes in safe keeping, before continuing to the shrine barefoot. I liked these: as business plans go, an empty box seems like a stroke of genius indeed.

At last, after moving through a closed bazaar, I stepped out into the courtyard of a tomb. In an instant, the visceral scenes of the Old Quarter were behind me, and I felt myself serene and in a place of great devotion. This was the *dargah* – the tomb of a Muslim saint, derived from a Persian word which can mean, among other uses, 'portal' or 'threshold'. That translation said a lot about the reasons so many people were here. They were here to seek remedy for their problems, material as well as spiritual, and they believed that beneath the flower-strewn marble there remained some spirit or essence of the great saint which would hear their prayers.

As is so often the case in Indian holy places, I was promptly approached by a devotee, eager to know why a foreigner was investigating such a holy place. Interestingly, I noted that I wasn't asked what my religion was, which is unusual in India: Nizammudin embraces all.

Wasi was perhaps about thirty, with flashing green eyes, a charcoal-grey jellaba and one of the loudest and most obnoxious ring tones I've ever heard on a telephone. As it rang for the second time, pumping the soundtrack to *Salaam Namaste*, that year's Bollywood hit, across the complex, he grinned sheepishly and silenced the machine with a fleshy finger.

'*Salaam Namaste*,' I said. 'I recognise that music.'

His face lit up in amazement. 'That film is *too* good!' he said. 'How many times have you seen it?'

I confessed, sheepishly, that I hadn't seen it at all, but that my landlord's daughter in Varanasi had played the soundtrack so recurrently I'd been forced to ask what it was.

Wasi told me a little of his life. He was the son of a local merchant and would one day inherit two successful shops. He liked nightclubs and fast motorbikes, but there was also another side to him, one which felt the inexorable pull of God.

'For me Sufism is the way,' he explained. 'Our India has too many problems with division, with fighting, with who has the right to temples and land and power. But in Sufism all are welcome. I come to this *dargah* every week at least one time. I ask the saint to hear me.'

'What do you ask for?'

'I ask for truth,' he said simply. 'And I like just being here. Here my problems seem to fly away. Sometimes there is *qawwali* music. Sometimes there are *pirs*.'

I asked him what a *pir* was.

'A Sufi master! They give teachings and healings. They teach us the *Tariqah*, the path. And they tell stories which I like very much. Shall I tell you one?'

I nodded. We were sitting down against the far wall of

the complex, and the spring light was warm and benevolent on our faces. To one side, an old man knelt with a fistful of incense and blew upon the tips until the smoke poured forth like a visible prayer. Emerging from the tomb, a generously proportioned Hindu lady in an emerald-coloured sari wiped tears from her face, then broke into a wide smile.

'Mulla Nasruddin once gathered all his friends and asked them if they wanted truth. "Yes, yes," they cried, "we would like to hear the truth." So Mulla Nasruddin held out his hands and asked that first they please give him money. "But how can you charge us for the truth?" said his friends. "Haven't you noticed," said Nasruddin, "that it is the scarcity of a thing which determines its value?"'

I spent several hours at the *dargah* that morning. Certainly, it was one of the most vivacious places I had been to in Delhi, with its graceful marble arches, white lattice-work added by the Emperor Shah Jahan and the mausoleum itself: a square chamber surrounded by verandas with arched openings. The dome, rising up from an octagonal drum, is ornamented by vertical stripes of black marble and crowned with a lotus flower. Beneath it, raised on a marble plinth and covered with a golden shawl, lies the tomb of the saint.

Later, I would read a description of Nizammudin in a book by Khushwant Singh, the irascible Sikh who has been one of India's most prolific journalists since Independence. In his homage, 'Delhi', Singh tells the tale of the saint Nizammuddin Auliya, and his trial for heresy at the court of Sultan Balban: 'Darvish, the ulema have complained that you make no distinction between Musulmans and infidels; that you pose as an intermediary between God and man . . . that your followers indulge in music and dancing in the precincts of the mosque and thus contravene the holy law of shariat . . .' Nizammuddin answered in a quintessentially Sufi manner.

For him, he explained, there *were* no differences between Hindus and Muslims: all are children of God. In a world clinging to its divisions as much as our own, it was a brave statement indeed.

Later that week, I returned to the Nizammudin district to meet Wasi. He had agreed to take me to the house of a great Muslim *pir*, whom he considered one of the holiest men living in India. Would a Sufi mystic, I wondered, have much the same countenance as a Hindu *sadhu*? Were they effectively tapping into the same state through different cultural forms? Or would he impress on me, as I have found in previous encounters, that Islam is the only acceptable path to God?

'A very aged man,' Wasi explained. 'Between ninety-five and a hundred years old. If you have problems − physical, mental, emotional − they will be disappearing in his grace.'

I had heard such boasts before.

From the *dargah* we branched out into the back streets. This was a place where few if any tourists wandered. Beneath a roiling, polluted sky we crossed cul-de-sacs, alleys and byways through what was once the ancient city of Shahjanabad. Despite my reservations about the way India is modernising, it was hard not to feel that these areas were long overdue for renovation. Walls crumbled into the street like old cheese, open sewers exuded a horrific stench that could only worsen with the arrival of summer. The ancient *havelis*, or private mansions, of this former imperial city were fighting a losing battle with the ravages of time. Outside a cast-iron grating, a dead rat stiffened upon its back.

After about twenty minutes, we arrived at a pair of imposing panelled doors, studded with iron bolts. A grimy lane stretched away towards the Thieves' Bazaar. After rapping firmly we heard the sounds of a lock being chivvied, and then the doors swung slowly open. Inside, I found myself in the courtyard of an old *haveli*, a formerly grand residence now in spectacular disrepair. An imperious rooster scuttled to one side as a young man, wearing a plain white *salwar kameez*, ushered us in. Heavily bearded, he had the pious, solemn look of a scholar. He bowed to us formally.

'Son of Hadji Abdul Shah,' whispered Wasi. 'Also in training to be a *pir*.'

In the courtyard, several old men on a bench sipped black tea from tiny glasses, while in the corner a tethered goat, with velvety brown ears, strained on the end of a coir rope. Several doorways led into the house, beyond which I could hear the subdued voices of women and the clanking of pots and pans. Behind ornamental shutters, I made out children peering out to get a look at the *feringhee* (foreigner), and soon a boy wearing a navy-blue crocheted *kufie* (prayer cap) peeked his head out and grinned, then vanished from where he had come.

'Hadji Abdul Shah is getting up,' said the son. 'Please take tea while you wait his arrival. You are welcome.'

We sat down opposite the old men. Spring was in its first flush, and this *haveli* felt immensely peaceful beside the bustle of the world outside. Tea arrived, and a selection of *mithai* or Indian sweets, piled high upon a silver platter.

'Your mother country, sir?' came a voice.

It was one of the old men, cultured and affluent by the look of things, with manicured nails, parted white hair and intent beige eyes. I told him I was from England, and that I had come to see the *pir*.

'*Acha*. Then you have come to the right place, sir!' He spoke in plummy Oxbridge tones, somewhat reminiscent of the voice of Jiddu Krishnamurti. 'I have been coming here forty years now. I don't miss a day.'

'What can you tell me of him?'

The man held his hands out frankly, then placed one

over his heart. 'Sir, I will tell you one thing. I believe that after today, when you go back to your country, you will say that you saw a great city, Delhi, and in this place you saw Nizammudin, and in Nizammudin you had the fortune to meet a true saint.'

'You're wearing a Brahmin's thread,' I said, pointing to his spindly wrist. 'Does the *pir* receive anyone, regardless of their faith?'

'Of course! His role is not to make conversions, but to make cures. Just the other week I heard a woman telling him her problems. She mentioned that she read the Bible and Hadji Abdul Shah said "Why *not* trust the Bible, for the Bible writes 'Surrender under to Him'." That said, he does encourage the reading of the Koran.'

I asked the old man what had first brought him here, all those years ago. He refilled my tea from a tin pot and insisted I take a third piece of *halwa*. Clearly, he was one of the fixtures around here.

'It was 1965, a bad time for us because of the second Indo-Pakistani conflict. Both sides wanted Kashmir, you see, and the violence was appalling. But actually I was having big problems in my personal life. I was restless, couldn't sleep. I lost all interest in my wife, my children, my work. I felt that some *demon* had taken residence in me and was tormenting me. And that there was no one I could confide in. Finally, after visiting many Hindu swamis and gurus, one man informed me of a Sufi *pir* here in Nizammudin. It was said he had the power to assuage even the most serious problems with a touch of his hand. I came at once, and my problems disappeared that very day. I went home and asked my wife for forgiveness, and swore then that I would visit this place every day for the rest of my life, so as not to forget what Hadji Abdul Shah had done for me.'

'You've not missed a single day?'

He shook his head earnestly. 'God has given him powers. And when we feel those powers, we feel God himself. If I am thirsty, why would I not go to the well?'

Just then a shuffling noise caused us to glance across the courtyard. The great *pir*, flanked on either side by each of his grandsons, was moving slowly towards us. Certainly, he was one of the most aged men I had ever seen, the skin stretched so tightly over his skull one could see every ridge and groove. He wore a blue jumper over which a striped shawl was wrapped; there were two silver rings on his right hand.

It was only when he reached us and I stood up to greet him that I realised he was blind. On either side of a hooked, fine-boned nose were two of the most startling eyes I have ever seen. They were so intense it was almost disquieting: a burning viridian blue, all the more striking for the fact that they seemed inert. He also had two of the largest ears I've ever seen: they stood out almost perpendicular to his face, making me think at once of Roald Dahl's BFG. It was impossible not to like him immediately.

'*As-salāmu alaykum*,' he muttered, reaching out both hands. He beamed with good humour.

'*Aleykum as-salaam*: and upon you be peace.' I held out my hands and hoped I'd got the traditional greeting right. He took them warmly; his hands were skeletally thin and lined with translucent veins.

One of his grandsons pulled a stool over and the *pir* sat down carefully opposite Wasi and me, seemingly looking straight at us. For some time Wasi explained my interest in Sufism to him, and what I was doing in India. Hadji Abdul Shah nodded, occasionally grinning to reveal the lurid purple teeth of the betel addict.

'*Acha*,' he said at last, his voice a husky whisper. 'You are interested in Sufism; that is good. I, too, was called to this path. I shall tell you how. But first,' he turned to his grandsons again, 'has our guest had tea, and something sweet? These things are important!'

They said that he had.

'Very well. Then we shall begin.

'I was born almost a hundred years ago. The exact dates are uncertain – no one thought to record it – but it was in the early years of the last century. For the first few decades of my life I was as normal: respectful of God, but without any sense of being called to him. But then, in 1940, I met a guru – Abdul Ahat Abagi – who picked me out as being one capable of serious instruction. He taught me meditation – *Muruqab* – and I did this for six to eight hours daily for some years. His guru in turn was Hasrat Charall; there is a lineage which goes right back. After three years, my third eye,' he touched the empty space between his two wispy eyebrows – 'opened, and I achieved union with Him.'

'Were you already blind?'

He concurred. 'I was born blind. I think this was in fact one of the reasons that my guru chose me as his student. "Most people are spiritually blind," he said. "You are physically blind but you have the capacity to see the true reality."' He thought for a moment. 'In Islam eyesight is *basar* whereas spiritual insight is *basira*. For *basira* you do not need eyes, you need to open the heart. Perhaps you have learned this already?'

'And after this union, you could heal people?'

He scratched his soft white stubble. 'Yes. At this time I felt a great energy in my body. I knew immediately that this energy could be used to heal people and I began to do so. With this energy I could sense and dispel the djinns which cause many of our human problems. Do you know about djinns?'

'Very little,' I said.

Hadji Abdul Shah held the first finger of each hand to the sky. 'Terrible creatures. A race of spirit beings that were here before man. God created mankind from the day, and angels from light. But the djinns were made of fire. They are mentioned in the Koran. For most people they are invisible. But for me they are everywhere.'

'Do you heal anyone, not just Muslims?'

'Of course! Beyond religion, there is only the human being. But religion is an important organising principle. For me, Islam is the right one, though I do not insist on it.'

'These powers you have,' I asked, edging closer to my real field of enquiry. 'Are they magic?'

He shook his head, the vast ears waggling a little. 'No. The Koran prohibits magic. Mohammed, peace be upon him, clearly says that magic is forbidden. But miracles are allowed!'

I couldn't help smiling. 'So you are a miracle worker.'

The *pir* tilted his head and, yes, there was just the faintest hint of a grin. 'God is the miracle, young man. I am the vessel. It is simple.'

We fell silent for a time, the *pir* accepting a glass of sweet black tea, which he cradled in his hands, blowing on its surface with puckered lips. When his glass was empty, he held out his hands towards me.

'You are a scholar, yes? You are interested in all religions. But there is another reason you have come to see me.'

I reached forward and put my hands in his, pulling my stool closer. This wasn't the first time on my journey that someone had shown unusual insight in ascertaining my true motivation.

'There is,' I admitted, 'another reason. I'm searching for something, even if I'm not exactly sure what that is.

Somehow I keep searching, moving from place to place. I can't seem to stop.'

The old man adjusted his shawl about him, and reached out his hands. I was transfixed by them: they seemed longer than any pianist's. '*Acha*. This is quite common, actually. God puts this current in us. He turns it up until we have no choice but to see Him.'

I closed my eyes. The old *pir* was very close to me now, and he put his hands out to touch my face. He traced his fingers across my cheekbones, my eyelids and forehead; his skin was as soft as a child's. Finally his hands came to rest on the crown of my head, where they spread out a little. I heard him take a deep breath and then sigh.

'It is good you are here,' he muttered. 'All will be well. Don't worry.'

Kneeling there, my mind tensed in expectation, I felt a sense of déjà vu. Several times now, I'd stood before some holy man or woman, waiting for some spellbinding act that would change everything. Now, for the first time, I rid myself of expectation. As Yogi Raj had told me, answers would never come in the form of rational knowledge.

In that instant a warm heat began to pulse across my crown. For a second my mind began to ripple with surprise, and then it quietened. I felt a great slackening of pressure, and a sense of a wise awareness passing through me. It was like an electric current travelling through circuits, or a warm liquid flushing out a blocked-up drain. Above me I could hear him chanting faintly, and as I glanced up I could see his withered lips moving, the betel-stained teeth, his eyes firmly closed.

This went on for some time. I felt calm and at peace. For a time there were no questions, no thought processes at all. It bore resemblance to the stillness I'd experienced in Ramana Maharshi's cave, and the euphoria of the rumbling *om*s echoing out over Arunachala hill. An amazing awareness of the old *pir*'s kindness shook me forcibly. Perhaps he really was a saint?

'There are no djinns,' he said at last, snapping me from my reverie. 'But I feel something. Tell me what you see in your dreams.'

I blinked a little, still uncertain what he had just done. Something very unusual had just happened. 'I remember them in the second after I wake up,' I said eventually. 'And then they vanish.'

'You must write them down. Dreams are messages from God.'

'If it's not a djinn, what could the problem be?'

He shrugged. 'I do not deal in specifics. I deal in cures. Blockage is there, yes. But I have cleared it. Problems will be dissipating in no time.'

Then it was over. He sat back upright, and removed his hands from my head. For a time I forgot to move. What had occurred was not visually spectacular in the way of the Ladakhi oracle, and yet I was filled with euphoria, a sense of having been touched by some kind of grace. I'd *invited* him to heal me and so there was no sense of violation, and yet I felt as if another person had accessed my innermost thoughts and perceptions.

'Now I will write you a *taweez*.'

'It's an amulet,' said Wasi, who had been observing courteously until this point. 'Hadji Abdul Shah will write some sacred symbols on a piece of paper, and then place them in an amulet.'

'I write verses from the Koran,' corrected the *pir*. 'A verse that is specific to you. We believe that the Koran itself is medicine. It leads us to the truth. It can protect us from djinns. It keeps us safe.'

One of the grandsons brought some paper and a pen to the old *pir*, who scribbled briefly before the paper was cut with a pair of tailor's scissors and folded tightly. From a battered-looking box, a dun metal amulet was taken, and the paper inserted. Then it was tied to a black leather cord and presented to me.

'Let me pay for this,' I began.

The *pir* wheezed with delight. 'We will not accept. We are glad you have come here today. But young man, there is something I must add. All around you is the water, and yet you try to analyse it without getting wet. This is a common problem these days. But you are a *particularly* bad case. Reach forward and drink! *Then* your life will be complete. That is all I have to say.'

He got up to go, his grandsons reaching forward to steady him. Unexpectedly, I found tears in my eyes.

'Don't worry,' whispered the *pir* in parting, again displaying that strange habit of staring right at me, even though his eyes remained blank. 'God is with you.'

It would be flippant of me to say that *all* was well after the meeting, and yet undeniably, something had shifted. I felt light and relaxed, and my sleep that night was as deep and restorative as any I'd known in years. And yet the next morning, as I ate my breakfast chapattis overlooking the Delhi skyline, I found my mind struggling to rationalise the experience. Perhaps it was merely the old *pir*'s gravitas which had got to me, or the sense of having received the advice of a wise elder? Perhaps it was the rituals which comforted, and not the treatment itself?

Even as this process of rationalisation unfolded, I was watching it happen. Would I ever escape this need to break *everything* down into its component parts? Wasn't it possible merely to accept the facts as I felt them in my own body:

that I felt healthier, more serene than I had done in months? (Freud himself declared that there are many ways of practising psychotherapy, and all that lead to recovery are good.)

After a convivial afternoon at the house of my photographer friend Ammar, I prepared to return to Nizammudin for that evening's *qawwali* session. Although the more commonly known practices of mystical experience include meditation and yoga, such things take years of practice and yield results only over time. Devotional practices, of which *qawwali* is one, tap into the innate power of music to transport the listener to a similar place. They require nothing more than one's full attention and a wholehearted desire to participate.

'It will be very crowded tonight,' warned Ammar, a long-time attendant at *qawwali* sessions. 'Actually, it will be mayhem. But in this chaotic state, with everyone swaying to the music, the Sufis believe that one can enter a state called *wajad* – a blissful state that purifies the devotee from sins.'

Drawing close to the shrine a few hours later, I could see that he hadn't been exaggerating. At the best of times these narrow lanes seem busy, but this evening they were distended with humanity. The vendors of rose petals were doing a roaring trade, the smoke from cooking fires was dispersing the scent of oily meat and the beggar children were darting this way and that, tugging at any empty hand for a few rupees.

'Not just Muslims,' shouted Ammar above the noise. 'Hindus, Christians, Parsis, Jains. All faiths come here on a Thursday night. Perhaps there's hope for India yet!'

As we drew close to the tomb itself, the prayers were just finishing. Every inch of the courtyard was packed with bodies, some people standing, others sitting cross-legged. Before the tomb entrance I could make out the musicians from the family of Nizami Khusro Bandhu, who have been leading the *qawwali* at Nizammudin for 750 years.

The music began at last. The plaintive voice of the senior singer, Ustad Meraj, cut the night air, soon added to by the other singers. To the reedy sound of a harmonium, accompanied by *tabla*, *dholak* (a classical Indian drum) and the innumerable hand claps of the devotees, he began a lament that, far outside the realms of language, seemed unbearably moving and profound.

> *Mein to naam japu Ali ka*
> *Ali-Ali se mera vaasta*
> *Ali-Ali mera maula . . .*

Within minutes the entire crowd of listeners was rapt, trapped upon the knife edge of the music, rising and falling with every breath of the musicians. By the third song, all sense of my own personal identity was disappearing. Clapping along with several hundred others, I was travelling along a song-line through our common humanity, at one with the musicians as their hands sliced the air. With each song lasting twenty minutes or more, each *qawwal* was like an extended prayer, with our individuality, our aspirations and our darkest fears suddenly subsumed into a greater presence.

The night passed quickly, with that sense of time stopping which comes only when the rational mind ceases to function. A casual observer might have supposed the crowd gripped by some momentary madness or distasteful fervour, but it was anything but that. Sufi music seems to confirm the importance mystics place on 'opening the heart', for in its mysterious flow a powerful and all-encompassing love sweeps one up.

Towards the end of the evening, I came to for a brief instant, as if from the eye of the storm, blinking around me. This journey was taking me to places I would never have believed possible, I thought. If someone had told me a year ago that I would be crammed into a Sufi *dargah* in the middle of Delhi, so filled with life, I would never have believed them. The world once again had spun upon its axis – who knew where it would spin next?

Within a few weeks, although I didn't know it just then, it would spin away from India altogether. Receiving the opportunity to write a travel article about Turkey, I suddenly saw the chance to continue my research into Sufism, and more specifically into the life of Jalalludin Rumi, the poet who had so gripped my imagination. To date I had seen *sadhus*, tantrics, an oracle and a Muslim *pir* during my time in India. But there was one thing I couldn't find here, a form of mystical experience that required neither sitting nor singing, but a kind of dance: a dance which was said to take one into the realms of ecstasy. Illegal since the time of Atatürk, this mystical practice is now an underground one in Turkey. But with persistence, and a little luck, I hoped I might still find dervishes spinning their way to God.

In Search of the Whirling Dervishes

LAW 677
Which prohibits and abolishes the profession of tomb-keeping,
the assigning of mystical names, and the opening of tekkes
(dervish lodges), zaviyes (central dervish lodges), and tombs.
13 December 1925 (1341 H.)
Quoted in Shems Friedlander, *Rumi and the Whirling Dervishes*

Late spring in Istanbul. Pale skies and a sharp, restless wind.
I stood, quite literally, between East and West. Divided by
the Bosporus, a waterway connecting the Black Sea and the
Sea of Marmara, Istanbul both connects and separates Europe
and Asia. It is, in fact, the only city in the world spanning
two continents.

All of which seemed fitting for my own reasons for
visiting. I was here to learn more about Sufism, and to see
what evidence of it – if any – remained in the country of
Rumi's birth. For although Turkey was the place where the
great mystic lived and died, and his image is still used in the
glossy pamphlets of the tourist board, the practice of Sufism
is illegal in Turkey, punishable by imprisonment. While the
rest of the world is experiencing an unparalleled mystical
resurgence, Turkey, it seems, harbours old grudges still.

I'd come to Turkey to find out more of the poet's story. He'd lived much of his life in Konya, in the south-central Anatolian steppe. After his death, the Ottoman Empire ruled his homeland for 600 years, sustained and inspired by the Sunni branch of Islam. And yet in 1925, army officer and statesman Mustafa Kemal Atatürk made Turkey a secular state. Atatürk believed Turkey needed to Westernise, both politically and culturally, if it was to modernise.

In practice, however, Atatürk's reforms would do far more than merely 'modernise' Turkey. Madrasas were shut down, Western clothing was enforced and the fez banned. The Latin alphabet was adopted over the arabic script of the past. For Sufis, their way of life was made illegal, their *tekkelerin* (convents) and *zâviyelerin* (lodges) shut down. The last Head of the Mevlevi Sufi order, founded by Rumi's son, fled to Syria. It was a forced disenchantment of almost unparalleled severity.

Three quarters of a century later, Istanbul appears to be just the kind of Westernised city which Atatürk would have wanted. Some young women do wear the traditional Islamic headscarves but the majority favour designer jeans and cropped T-shirts. A toothed skyline of blocks and office towers vies for position with the minarets, the former making no pretence at local flavour, but merely following the new 'international' aesthetic. Even my inflight magazine boasted of the city's modernity. 'The Sapphire will be the tallest skyscraper in the Levant,' the article informed me. Apartments with a view of the Bosporus, to be completed in 2009, will cost from $1.65 million to more than $6 million. 'A brand new life is beginning . . .'

Some old traits remained, I was pleased to note. In Sultan Ahmet, the area that has grown up around the Blue Mosque, I found a guesthouse which appeared little changed since the

1960s. Back then, when the great turn East was in full spate, crowds of hippies poured into Istanbul en route for India and Nepal. Stumbling in a ganja-scented haze from their buses, they brought a touch of free-spiritedness to a still conservative city. They brought Beatles tapes and guitars, kaftans and blotters of LSD. But mainly, they came looking for the mystic East and the East, true to form, rose to meet them.

My guesthouse resembled the kind of place where Richard Burton would have felt at home: knee-deep in Oriental rugs, with snaking hookah pipes and lascivious Orientalist art on the walls. The information desk offered 'traditional belly dancing shows', visits to the hammam and the spice bazaar. Scowling out from beneath his F1 racing cap, Salik the manager found it difficult to keep awake most of the time. He played in a rock band after hours, he confided, and had a record deal in the offing. 'What kind of music?' I asked. 'Groove metal or power groove,' he said casually. 'Pantera, White Zombie, Five Finger Death Punch.'

I spent a few days acclimatising. At first sight Istanbul seems closer to New York than New Delhi, its aspirations entirely American. Looking deeper, you see that the city presents a more honest face. Behind the global brand names, and the middle-class youth conspicuously consuming along the length of Istiklal Caddesi, lurks the older city, a sprawling maze of crumbling Ottoman architecture and urban poor. Out of a city of fifteen million, perhaps six million live in *gecekondus*: shanty houses built without permission, foundations or amenities. Largely populated by economic migrants from Anatolia, the *gecekondus*, I immediately felt, said a lot about today's Istanbul. They were incomplete, neither from East nor West, and most of them looked the same. But amongst them, in the sight of a barrow of unwaxed lemons piled high, or a traditional *tükürüklü köfte* (a dish of meatballs with herbs), smoking over hot coals, one gains a whiff of the city that came before. Its foundations are not of stone but of memory, and its blood will keep on flowing as long as the stories remain alive.

It was amongst these stories that I hoped to find a way into Sufi culture. Turkish friends assured me that Sufis still existed, and if I looked hard enough it would not be difficult to find one of their *tekke* (dervish lodges). Although the laws are still in place, the government doesn't waste too much time enforcing them.

Sufism, of course, existed in Turkey long before Rumi, or Mevlana (the Master), as he is more simply known in his homeland. But it was Rumi, according to legend, who first began the slow whirling dance that has become the most recognisable practice not merely of the Sufi movement, but of the mystical experience itself. According to legend, Rumi was reading poetry one day, and became so caught up in mystical ecstasy that he broke into a spontaneous whirling. Standing with his arms outstretched, eyes closed, and his long robe flowing in perfect circles, he continued for hours, utterly absorbed in the divine flow.

After Rumi's death, his followers began to practise and systematise the whirling method espoused by their master. And so the whirling dervishes were born and with them a whole culture of rituals, symbolic dress and music. A version of this whirling is still visible in many Turkish towns, principally as a tourist attraction, a kind of spiritual ballet. But whether these performers are real Sufis, or merely out-of-work dancers happy to spin for a few euros, is debatable.

'What about this performance at Sirkeci train station I've seen advertised?' I asked Mehmet, a local journalist, recommended to me as one of Istanbul's most knowledgeable and irascible sons. We were meeting in a *kahvehane*, a traditional

Turkish coffee shop that served a superb medium roast with cardamom. Around us, the hum of conversation was punctuated by the occasional shout, as one acquaintance after another hailed Mehmet loudly from across the room.

Mehmet's face, impressively craggy and with a lustrous moustache that drooped ponderously from his upper lip, creased unhappily. 'My God. These are not Sufis. They are not trained. This is a circus show.'

'But surely, if the government realises the value of dervish performances as a tourist draw, they would do it authentically?'

'Authentically!' he snorted. 'They do not care about anything but this.' Mehmet rubbed the finger and thumb of his right hand together. 'Turkey is about money now. Not Allah.'

'What can you tell me about Sufism as it persists now, since Atatürk?'

He sipped his coffee appreciatively, the cup comically small within his giant's hand. 'It is here. But it is not on the surface. Atatürk created something called the Ministry of Government Affairs to run the mosques – some 75,000 of them in Turkey – so he could monitor what was going on. He was afraid of the mullahs, of course. Afraid of the power of Islam. But the Sufis do not bow down to the state. Where they exist now, it is in private. Groups of like minds who see that . . .' his voice grew sober, 'the affairs of this world, as the Koran says, are but a sport and a pastime compared to the one beyond.'

'Compared to what there was, would you say there's a healthy Sufi community in Turkey?'

He shook his head. 'No, no. Things began to change in 1980, with the election of Turgut Özal to Prime Minister. He was a Naqshabandi Sufi, although politically it was difficult for him to admit it. Under him, Sufism began to re-emerge, at least in the sense that it was not overtly clamped down upon. But still, there are now a mere *handful* of *tekkes*. Before Atatürk there were probably thousands. Even *if* the practices remain, what has been lost is the Sufi culture: the architecture, calligraphy, music. These represented the highest achievements of Ottoman civilisation. Like much in this Istanbul . . .' he motioned disdainfully towards the rooftops, 'we've forgotten the things which made us. We're orphans, I think. The orphans of history.'

That afternoon I wandered around the city. In places the last magenta blooms of the Judas trees were visible, astonishing against the grey-blue waters of the Bosporus. According to legend, the flowers of the Judas tree (European redbud) were once a pure white. After Judas Iscariot hung himself from its branches, the leaves turned colour out of shame.

As with any new city, one watches at first through the veil of expectation. A thousand writers before me had conjured a city of pungent spices, *loukoum* (Turkish delight), covered bazaars and bright ceramics, the evidence of which I was looking for to confirm my psychic 'arrival'. But gradually, discovering the city on my own terms, through many hours of walking, a real destination became apparent.

From the harbour of the Bay of Bebek, I watched gargantuan oil tankers gliding into the Bosporus. At 17 miles long and just 700 yards wide at its narrowest point, this has been one of the world's most strategic waterways for millennia. It is said that Jason and his Argonauts passed through here on their search for the Golden Fleece. Today's prize, of course, is more prosaic. With vast oil reserves discovered under the nearby Caspian sea, oil is the twenty-first-century fleece, and the 50,000 commercial vessels that pass annually through the Bosporus are largely given over to its transport. Ecologists (and mere lovers of Istanbul) are united in condemning the sheer volume of this traffic (some of which stands as big as three football fields laid end to end) because of the danger of transporting such vast quantities of oil through the middle of a city. There seemed something glaringly symbolic about all this: East and West split by a waterway, through which oil moved like some relentless intravenous liquid.

As evening fell, I visited the tomb of Eyup Sultan, Mohammed's standard bearer, whose mosque is one of the holiest pilgrimage sites in the Islamic world. As with Nizammudin in Delhi, a mere visit to the tomb is believed to bring benedictions upon the faithful, not least because of a stone said to bear the footprint of the Prophet himself. Similarly, to be buried in the vicinity of the saint is auspicious, and the area now boasts one of the most exquisite cemeteries in the Islamic world. How often, I reflected, I seem to find myself in cemeteries. They're places not merely for the bereaved, but for those seeking refuge as well. Inside them are flowers, even in neighbourhoods shorn of almost all natural flora. And on the tombstones, stories of the past, mementoes of lives brief and protracted, like guidebooks for those of us who remain.

Wandering quietly amongst the lichen-clad stelae, I found a perfect place to appreciate the past. Here was pristine spring air. Smells of wet grass. To the edge of my field of vision, an old man wearing a skullcap laid saffron yellow tulips on a grave. In the distance, the sound of fog horns. Birds in flight. Nearest the mosque, the tombstones, reflecting centuries of Ottoman culture, watched the city rise and fall through a screen of cypress trees. The men's tombs were often crowned with a turban, depicting their rank and status, while the women's bloomed with intricate carved flowers. A third type denoted the resting places of Sufis. Above them, renderings of their characteristic felt hats protruded above the ancient stone, some of them carved with *gul* – rosettes depicting the specific Sufi order. Some lines of Rumi came to me, unbidden.

> I died a mineral, and became a plant.
> I died a plant and rose an animal.
> I died an animal and I was man.
> Why should I fear
> When was I less by dying.

Later that week, I visited Istanbul's Museum of Turkish and Islamic Art, housed in the former palace of the Grand Vizier Ibrahim Pasha. Here, amongst the relics of the Ottoman world, the years turned back and I walked, entranced, amongst the ceramics, textiles, jewellery and metalwork of a great civilisation. Most striking of all, however, was the calligraphy. Due to the Koranic injunction on depicting God (or his Prophet) in any form, calligraphy replaces painting and sculpture as the principal decorative form of Islamic art. For Muslims, copying the Koran is an act of piety in its own right, and the Arabic language revered as the chosen vehicle by which Allah imparted his message to Mohammed. But from within these seemingly tight strictures, incredible creativity and expressiveness emerges. Even without understanding the meaning, one is struck by the gravity and visual impact of these scripts. Certain of them exhibit something more: an idea of divinity beyond the boundaries of representative art, a transcendent grace.

Observing these masterpieces, trapped in their airless vitrines, I felt a pang of loss for a culture I had scarcely known until now. By banning the Arabic lettering, Atatürk felt that he was bringing his country into the present. (It is said the new alphabet, a modified version of Latin, was presented to him on a tablet of gold.) But the true cost of his actions was monstrous: one of the richest calligraphic traditions in human history was cast aside, and with it, the long genealogies of different calligraphers, the legends and fables and the schools where the very application of ink on paper was seen as a method of reaching God. (My own spidery handwriting, with which I'd been making notes throughout the morning, looked immeasurably superficial by comparison.)

After several hours I took the winding stairs to the second floor for my meeting with Dr Mahmud Erol Kilic, the museum's director. More than the museum's collection, I hoped that it would be he who could open a door on to the lost Sufi culture. Professor of Sufism at Istanbul University, he's also one of the world's foremost scholars on Ibn Arabi, a Sufi philosopher who espoused an idea of mystical unity not dissimilar to Rumi's own.

Dr Kilic greeted me warmly at the door and we sat down in his elegant office, overlooking the Hippodrome. Tea arrived in miniature glasses, and a silver bowl of powdered sugar. The morning light came in streamers through the windows. 'A donnish appearance,' I wrote surreptitiously in my notebook. 'Wire-rimmed glasses, an indoor pallor, but also a great sense of ease.'

'So you have come to look for Sufis,' he said, exhibiting just the traces of a smile. 'Did you find any?'

I shook my head.

'They are not whirling in the streets. No, they keep themselves quiet. That, given the times we live in, seems wise.'

While Dr Kilic poured the tea, I asked him about Atatürk: had he known what a death knell his actions would sound upon the achievements of Ottoman culture?

'Atatürk was a revolutionary,' he explained. 'And like

all revolutionaries he wanted to cut off *all* ties with tradition. On November 13th, 1925 he issued a declaration to ban the *tekkes*. He was a modernist, and he wanted change not through *cultural* revolution but by force. A revolution of the hat. A revolution of the script. His, alas, was a Maoist approach to changing culture.'

'Before Atatürk?' I asked. 'What percentage of Turks practised Sufism?'

He considered for a moment. 'At that time Istanbul had a population of about 500,000 people. For that number there were some 360 dervish lodges open. Based on what we know, approximately 90 per cent of the city's population were affiliated to a *tekke*! Those *tekkes* created sublime music, they created art. An Ottoman was a kind of chevalier, you see: virile but with a romantic heart. These days, I think you will find few cultured people here in Istanbul.'

'What about other parts of the world then? Has there been a diaspora?'

He described a wide parabola with his hand. 'Sufis have sought refuge all over the globe. Aleppo, Cyprus, Albania. After Atatürk, some Sufi masters hid themselves here, never once leaving their houses until they died. Not even accepting guests! Can you imagine such a thing? To stay inside your house for ever.'

What of the performances one saw advertised around Istanbul, I asked. Were they really cheap theatre?

He chuckled. 'This is registered as "Turkish classical folk dance". According to officials, this is not Sufism. But, although some of the performers consider this a job, others do take it seriously.' His face took on a sombre aspect. 'One must feel for them deeply. Perhaps this is a difficult scenario for a Westerner to grasp. *You* can belong to any club or religion you wish: yoga, meditation, tai-chi. Here in Turkey, we are not free to do this. There is one, however, which I consider authentic. I'll give you the details.'

'But it's the UNESCO Year of Rumi,' I pointed out. 'I mean, he's being recognised around the world as one of the most celebrated poets in human history. And his poetry is *meaningless* without considering the mystical states he's trying to convey. Why is this so threatening to the state?'

Dr Kilic shrugged. 'Old habits die hard. And there are new threats in the world, some of them from fundamentalism. No politician is going to risk his seat, in a country trying hard to be European, by trying to make life easier for Islamic mystics. It's just not going to happen.'

'Do you know any Sufi masters?' I said finally. 'They must be here still.'

He looked uncomfortable. 'This is not like India,' he said, 'where the gurus are public figures. Here, if you do find a Sufi, he may be wearing a suit and tie. And,' his eyes twinkled, 'he may not announce himself.'

'Would they really arrest someone?' I said. 'Or is it merely a threat?'

'It depends. I doubt they would arrest a man for whirling. But for *teaching* Sufism – the *practice*, not the history – certainly. Last year, a seventy-year-old Sufi master was arrested for just this. We are living, despite appearances, in a kind of Communist regime. In fact,' he laughed wearily, 'we have a kind of joke here in Turkey. We say there are two Stalinist regimes left in world, North Korea and Turkey.'

'It all seems so depressing,' I said. 'All over the world people are rediscovering mysticism. Rumi himself is selling *thousands*, if not millions, of books. And yet in his own country he remains effectively underground.'

'You are quite correct,' said Dr Kilic. 'Rumi, our greatest poet, our Shakespeare, is not even taught in high school in Turkey. It's a disgrace, a calamity really. But this is the new Turkey. A place where the Sufi culture no longer exerts its positive influence on our young people. Because of this, murder is on the rise, smuggling, rape – all those criminal things are going on. They have no religion now . . . except football, perhaps. Or rock music. I mean, have you seen the way young people *worship* footballers and musicians? One must see the parallels! It's beyond sport or music now, they spiritually annihilate themselves . . .'

'And then there are the fundamentalists,' I pointed out. 'Because those hungry for spiritual things are easy prey for the radicals.'

'Yes.' Dr Kilic slapped his hands together passionately. 'Paradoxically, they complain of the radicalisation of Islam, but the *only* solution for this is Sufism! When they ban Sufism they are *opening* the gates for radicalism. Sometimes I feel the sword of Damocles hanging over us.'

After my meeting with Dr Kilic, I took myself to a café on Divanyolu Street to reflect on what I had learned. The infamous Pudding Shop remains one of the best-known travellers, haunts in Istanbul, despite seemingly not having changed a bit since its golden days. It was here that the steady stream of travellers East would stop for espresso and gossip, and to check the cork notice board for errant friends and free rides to Goa. Here, too, Billy Hayes, whose autobiography *Midnight Express* was later made into an Oscar-winning film, bought the hashish he intended to smuggle out of the country. The scenes of his many years' incarceration in Sağmalcilar prison remain the strongest deterrence imaginable for would-be smugglers, even thirty years after the film's release.

The Turks, however, considered the film an abomination, deeply resenting its harsh portrayal of their culture. Sitting in the musty confines of the Pudding Shop, writing my notes,

I mused upon this, as well as the equally clichéd alternative offered by my guesthouse in Sultan Ahmet. Were all cultures so beleaguered by stereotypes? Where *was* the real Turkey, beyond the harems and the hammam, beyond the formulaic depictions of *Midnight Express*, but equally not entirely expressed by the business people, clutching their mobile phones and laptops like the aspirational class the world over?

Slicing my cake, I decided that clearly the real Turkey was to be found somewhere between all these things, and perhaps Dr Kilic was right in suggesting that Sufis offered a good example. Aside from the flowering of high culture which the *tekkes* had fostered, Sufism, in itself, represents a notably liberal and pluralistic interpretation of Islamic doctrine, much needed in a post-9/11 world. In recent years, even Turkey's staunch founding principles of secular government have come under attack from fundamentalists, who urge a return to Islamic law. Even during the past week in Istanbul, thousands were taking to the streets to protest against the possible election of a hard-line Muslim government.

Once again my thoughts returned to Rumi. 'Love's creed is separate from all religions,' he wrote. 'The creed and denomination of lovers is God.' Certainly, Rumi's own path to the divine was Islamic, and yet he excluded no one on a different route. This, after all, was why I had come on this journey in the first place: to investigate the different mystical paths that reconnect us with the Absolute. And yet nowhere to date had seemed so fraught with contradictions, nor any path so feared by the state.

Leaving the café, I strolled back through Sultan Ahmet. It was early evening and a muezzin was making the call to prayer. Thin strips of sunlight brushed the dome of the Blue Mosque, taunting the rainclouds which, even now, gathered overhead. An old man holding a tray of cigarettes, sun-bleached postcards and miniature Turkish flags in cellophane, approached me; I waved him away. On the corner, a shop sold crimson fez: cheap renderings of the felt caps which were once worn by almost all Ottoman men, favoured for their ability to allow their wearer to touch his crown towards Mecca.

I felt suddenly very low, caught, somehow, in the very place I try to avoid above all others: a tourist trap, a place where commerce has become the overt method for understanding. If I went home with a fez would I comprehend Turkey? If I bought one of the kitsch renderings of a whirling dervish one saw glinting in improbable technicolour through the windows of all these shops?

It was time to get out of Istanbul and to head towards the heartlands of central Anatolia. There, I imagined, the contradictions would be fewer, the tourist trade negligible. It was in Konya, on the central Anatolian Plateau, that Rumi had spent his life. For the pro-European, Western-facing Turks, Anatolia is often described as 'backward' these days. I imagined a patriarchal, Islamic-centred place, deeply rooted in the rhythms of village life. From where I was standing that didn't sound too bad . . .

Back at my guesthouse, Salik looked morose when I told him of my departure. 'But next week the band is playing,' he said, sadly. 'You could have seen me destroying my guitar at the end of the show.'

Regrettably, I told him, that pleasure would have to wait until my return.

But before I left, there was one more thing to do. Dr Kilic had spoken of a particular performance of dervishes which he felt to be authentic. And there was no way I could leave without seeing, in some form or another, the slow whirling dance of the Sufis. On a downcast Saturday afternoon I walked to the Galata Mevlevihanesi, a former *tekke* now a museum, at the southern end of Istiklal Caddesi. It lies on a street full of music shops, and I stopped for a while to gaze through the windows at rows of Stratocasters, gleaming cymbals, many tiered keyboards. Inside one, a novice was thrashing out a guitar riff which would have made Salik proud.

Further down the street, a stone archway marked the discreet entrance to the Dervish lodge. Unless you knew what you were looking for, you might pass it unawares. It seems designed to avoid attention behind its tall Ottoman stone wall. But inside, I felt myself immediately in a sanctuary. The courtyard was filled with cypresses, roses, a fig tree, a fountain no longer offering water. For a moment I imagined it as it had once been: a place where man could aspire towards something more than himself. Calligraphers, musicians, poets and astronomers would all have paced these flagstones.

I stopped to talk to one of the attendants who was showing people inside for the performance, a fat man, with darkly hooded eyes.

'It says this Galata Mevlevihanesi is now the Museum of Court Literature? But it was a *tekke*, yes? Is it still a *tekke*?'

The attendant gave me an amused smile. 'This is now a museum. But it was originally constructed as a *tekke* in the fifteenth century. Then it burned down in a fire in 1766 and was rebuilt.'

Was he being evasive? 'But are they *performers*, or Sufis?'

His face betrayed nothing. 'Performance, my friend, is something one does to entertain others. *Sema* is something one does to become one with God. It is not for me to decide which you will see today.'

I moved inside. A large octagonal hall spread out before me, dimly lit and filled with a crowd of about fifty people.

On the first floor, ornate balconies overlooked the central 'whirling' area – an empty space of varnished boards. Despite the fact that most people here were tourists, the atmosphere was sober, expectant. Certainly, this felt like a church or temple, the soft light pouring through the glass. In here we were far from Istanbul; it was difficult to imagine the commerce and the struggle taking place out there.

Some minutes later, even the faint chatter fell away and, from a side door, the dervishes began to file out. They wore jet-black cloaks over their distinctive white robes, and on their heads tall camel-coloured fez, supposed to resemble tombstones. I wondered what their professions were – executive? cobbler? optometrist? – and how they reconciled the world outside with what they did here.

Standing before the *semazenbashi* (master), the dervishes lined up. Above us, musicians, similarly dressed, filed forward on to the balcony, and, in low, rich voices, the sound of chanting commenced: a prayer to Mevlana (Rumi), followed by a *sura*, or chapter, from the Koran. Then the first haunting note cut through the silence, the sound of a *ney*, a reed flute, which was Rumi's favourite instrument, and an often used metaphor in his poems. For Rumi, the reed cut from its river bed was a symbol of the human condition, and the plaintive sound of it like a human voice, crying for return.

'Listen to how the reed complains,' he wrote. 'It is telling a tale of separation.'

Slowly, the dervishes began to walk around the hall, stopping to bow reverently to one another. Then, after the third circle, they returned to their posts, bowed again to the master and, in one fluid motion, threw off their black cloaks to leave only pure white robes. According to Sufi lore, this is a symbolic departure from their shrouds, leaving their worldly existence behind. They stood in the gesture called an *alif*:

both arms crossed so that each hand rests upon its opposite shoulder.

Now, as the musicians began to play, the whirling began. Unfolding their arms, the dervishes held their right hands upwards towards Allah, their left tilted to the earth. What followed was essentially a spinning dance, but with one foot anchored to the ground like an axis. The right foot propels the rest of the body around this central point, the dancer spinning anti-clockwise in tightly controlled movements.

And as they whirled, heads gently tilted, eyes closed, a palpable awe passed through us. They moved with such grace, the hems of their skirts flowing out like water, that they seemed to have moved beyond human form. This was the *sema* – meaning 'hearing' – and it has evolved within the Mevlevi order into complex forms and symbolic details. But watching it, one sees beyond the ritual to the simple human act of spinning, as the earth does, or as a child may hold out its hands and whirl across a summer field. There's something elemental about it, something of the act which takes us immediately beyond 'mind' into pure existence.

Minutes passed, or was it much more? Rarely has any sight uplifted or transported me as much as the sight of these dervishes whirling through space. They moved round the room like a carousel, each dervish locked within the silence of his own orbit. Afterwards, I thought of the reason humans dance at all: to resist gravity, to free themselves of worldly problems, to lose themselves. Certainly, as the attendant had said, this could scarcely be called performance. It felt more like prayer or meditation, and these men ethereal forms, moving through emptiness.

As the whirling stopped, we heard more chanting from above, this time the *fatiha*, the first *sura* of the Koran. All the dervishes bent to kiss the floor. Then the master began another prayer to Mevlana, and finally, all at once, the dervishes chanted '*Hu*', all the names of God in one, a low trembling noise.

As they filed out of the room, we were left alone again. The city rushed back.

The train left at 7.20pm. There was just time to make the ferry for Haydarpasa, the train station on the Asian side of the Bosporus. Over the handrail I watched the city passing through the gloom, smelled diesel oil smoking on the ferry chimney. Beside me, a gypsy woman of incredible girth munched grey meat from waxed paper. I heard a dance beat ring once from a distant phone, gulls crying, the harsh static of the boat driver's CB radio.

In the station I found an old-fashioned restaurant, bought hoummous, a large piece of flat bread, some olives and fried aubergine. The proprietor had the ghoulish face of a mortuary attendant and soft hands bedecked with a ring the size of a plum. He packed the provisions carefully for me and added a baklava for good measure. Behind him, moustachioed dock workers drank glasses of clear raki at the day's end.

Thus supplied, I boarded the train with five minutes to spare, and lay down in the blissful confines of my own cabin. Far from the rickety locomotive I might have expected for travel to Anatolia, this was the latest in sleek modern trains. I had two bunks to choose from, a washbasin, curtains to draw back across the windows. I lay back on the lower bunk. The train eased out of the station as if it were running on oiled tracks. The city receded into memory.

Konya: Birthplace of Rumi

Less well known than Rumi in the West, but certainly a sublime mystical poet in his own right, was a man called Bahauddin Valad, Rumi's father. By the time of his son's birth in 1207, Bahauddin was famous throughout the Islamic world, often by his sobriquet 'The Sultan of Mystical Knowing'. But by 1212, Bahauddin's renown was beginning to cause him problems. When the King of Balkh became convinced that the mystic wished to usurp his power, it is said he sent Bahauddin the keys to his crown. Out of respect, Bahauddin took his family into exile. Their journey would take many years, leading them through Baghdad, Mecca and Damascus, but finally, by invitation of the pious Sultan of Rum, the family came to rest in Konya.

Stepping from the train into the sharp, grey light, I arrived in two cities simultaneously. In Rumi's time, the city was the capital of the Seljuk empire, a liberal, highly creative hub of spiritual and artistic thought. Today, it's the most conservative town in modern Turkey: sleepy, producing cement, carpets and fertiliser, home town of Necmeddin Erbakan, the nation's most famous hard-line Islamic politician, and indeed one of the places where he found his strongest support.

Nevertheless, I was glad to be here. As I had wished, this was another world from Istanbul: a self-enclosed world, existing by its own logic. In a small café, snug with the heat of its log oven, I ordered *çey* (tea) and was offered a glass of spicy beet juice on the house. It flowed like blood from a clay-coloured jug, and left the teeth crimson. The taste was of earth and soil.

From my table, I found a perfect place to scrutinise the city. Through smeared glass, I saw huddled figures pacing towards the mosques with intent. A young woman carrying firewood tied with strips of plastic bag, twisted to create a makeshift twine. Boys with a football. A pear tree covered in white blossom.

'You are here for Mevlana?' asked the café proprietor, a grizzly of a man wearing half-moon glasses.

I said that I was. Few tourists would come to Konya for any other reason, I surmised.

'Our greatest son,' he muttered fondly. 'People come from all over the world to this place. My grandfather fought in the War of Independence – against the Greeks, you know. He took a copy of Mevlana with him to the front.'

'What happened to the book?' I asked excitedly. 'Do you still have it?'

The man shook his head. 'My father lost it! His own father had kept the book safe through the Battle of Afyonkarahisar-Eskişehir. My father was a merchant seaman – he had his bag stolen in Algeria and the book was inside. Such carelessness!'

In the afternoon I walked to the mausoleum. Spring was breaking the back of winter and an effervescent light lit up the white marble. Here Sultan 'Ala' al-Din Kayqubad, a Seljuk sultan, offered his rose garden as a fitting place to bury the great mystic Bahauddin. When Rumi himself died in 1273, he was entombed beside his father, and a mausoleum covered in exquisite turquoise faience was erected over his grave. Above the threshold, a Persian inscription reads:

> This station is the Mecca of all dervishes
> What is lacking in them is here completed
> Whoever came here unfulfilled
> Was here made whole.

After I passed through a turnstile, I strolled into a marble-paved courtyard, flanked to the left by seventeen dervish cells covered with small domes. In the middle of the space, there was a fountain built by Yavuz Sultan Selim, where the dervishes could wash before prayers. Once, it must have been a little like an ashram, I mused to myself: a place of learning, community and work. Now it was like museums everywhere: smelling of age and forgotten rituals, like a snuffed-out candle. Turnstiles clattered behind me as more pilgrims paid their dues.

At the entrance itself, I stepped through doors inlaid with Seljuk motifs and Persian text. Inside, the room was elevated, the air temperate. There was soft light from candelabras; oil lamps; chandeliers; the walls decorated with rare and precious Ottoman calligraphies. In the adjoining room, housing the tomb itself, I found myself surrounded by Muslim pilgrims. A tour bus that had driven overland from Iran had disgorged fifty theology students who were visiting the sacred sites of Turkey. They were in their early twenties but looked younger, clutching Korans, plastic briefcases, pads of note-paper. They wore the cheap black suits of missionaries.

'Are you Sufis?' I asked one of them, an earnest young man with bad skin. 'We are Muslims,' he said brusquely. 'Are *you* a Muslim?'

'No.'

'Then why are you here?'

'Mevlana said "Come everyone," did he not?' I pointed out. 'Does one have to be Muslim to hear his words?'

'Come everyone to *Islam*, he meant.' The boy shouldered rudely past me to kneel down before Rumi's tomb. Behind a panel of silver latticework, draped in a black silk shroud, rose the sarcophagi of Rumi and his father, and above them, stone versions of the Sufi fez, similar to those I'd seen in Eyup cemetery, symbolising the death of the ego.

I moved away, a little offended by such a curt reply. And yet such a response was a timely reminder of how very differently Rumi is perceived in parts of the Muslim world. While for Western liberals, Rumi's poetry, whirling practices and seemingly broad-minded world-view make him a kind of poster child for liberal Islam, others consider this very far from the truth. Some scholars, much in the manner of the Iranian theology student, try to draw semantic lines around Rumi, emphasising his total faith in Islam and his meaninglessness outside that context. One can't help but see the irony in this – or its refutation of everything that Rumi was trying to teach.

Some Islamic modernists go further still, rejecting Rumi altogether. Their principal complaint, it seems, is in Rumi's assertion of absolute unity with God – called *Wahdat-ul-wujood* in Sufism. From the earliest origins of Sufi mysticism, this notion has caused problems. That anyone should claim absolute unity with God smacks of heresy, a lack of humility. In times gone by, many Sufis were put to death for such statements, such as Husayn ibn Mansur al-Hallaj, also known as al-Hallaj (the wool-carder), who was beheaded in Baghdad for having uttered '*Ana 'l haqq*' – I am the Truth.

I stepped outside, sooner than I had expected. I hadn't found the peace or the sense of fulfilment I'd hoped the tomb would bring. It was the middle of the afternoon and the streets were almost empty. I wanted to walk for a time to stretch my legs. Strolling down the main street I found only shops selling religious paraphernalia: prayer beads, holy books, dried bunches of *miswak* – the twigs of the *Salvadora persica* tree with which it is said that the prophet Mohammed used to brush his teeth. In the public gardens, an old man fed pigeons from a paper bag; bees moved among the early flowers.

Dejected, I moved restlessly through the town. There were carpet shops everywhere, selling flat woven kilims the like of which would once have adorned the tents of nomads, simple huts, the grandest of Sultanate palaces all across the Ottoman world. Both Ibn Battuta and Marco Polo came through Konya, the latter referring to its carpets as 'the most thin and beautiful' he had ever seen.

'Come in, come in,' entreated the proprietors. 'Lovely carpets. Wonderful kilims. Exquisite sisims.'

After an hour of wandering, I accepted. The carpet shop was an ancient building, exotically piled with inestimable carpets, its walls hung with them, only a bare strip of ceiling, from which an uncovered bulb cast a trembling light, free of their overwhelming presence. I'd accepted because it was about to rain and because the merchant in question was something of an exception: I put him at no more than six. He wore a tiny waistcoat, and the first fez I'd seen in Anatolia.

'Anyone here?'

Just then the father appeared. He had bright umber eyes, a tight skullcap pulled over a short brow, and an enormously ugly face, redeemed by a laissez-faire smile.

'Ah. Welcome, welcome. I see the boss has caught your attention.'

The tiny child, still grinning inanely at his own success, was repeating his entreaty like a kind of mantra. 'Carpets, carpets, carpets, lovely carpets.'

'That's enough now,' said the man. He switched to

Turkish and the child ran scurrying to some inner sanctum. He turned to me. 'How is his English? Very good, no?'

'Very good. He'll sell the hind leg off a donkey one of these days.'

The man roared. 'A donkey's leg, you say! Well, that would be something. Now, have a seat. What kind of carpet will you take?'

I confessed that, if the truth be absolutely known, I didn't want one at all. I gestured to the clouds beyond the door lintel.

'Ah well. That is honest. You take shelter, yes. I can understand this. We will have coffee, and then, perhaps, you will change your mind about that carpet. If you think my son has talent, well, I am the teacher.'

We ventured into the interior of the shop. He gestured to a pile of about twenty carpets, which made an appealing-looking seat.

'I am not just a trader,' he explained, dropping some of his mercantile bluster. 'But something of a scholar. I have written a history of traditional Seljuk carpets.'

'Are these Seljuk?' I asked, pointing to the ones I was sitting on.

He shook his head. 'Those are of Ottoman design. Original Seljuk carpets are incredibly rare. Only a handful left in the world. But we believe those are the methods which the Ottomans learned from and copied. They were the pioneers.'

I asked if his book was available in English.

Hakan, as he now introduced himself, shook his head mournfully. 'Only in Turkish, my friend. Very few copies available. Small readership.'

Could he tell me more about Seljuk culture?

Hakan looked pleased. 'Certainly, my friend. What a pleasure! The Seljuks were a fascinating people. They came from somewhere north of the Caspian sea, a branch of Oghuz Turks. Their empire stretched from here to the Hindu Kush, and from central Asia to the Persian gulf. Until the beginning of the eleventh century, they controlled Jerusalem, if you can believe it.'

'Were they tolerant?'

'They were like modern liberals!' roared Hakan. 'Other faiths like Christians were allowed to go about their business. Poets and scholars found patronage. New types of architecture began to be used. Caravanserais spread out along the Silk Road.'

'And they were tolerant of Sufis?'

He held a finger aloft. 'For them the Sufi was a highly evolved man, a great man. It was a Seljuk sultan, you know, who invited Bahauddin to bring his family here.'

The coffee arrived. A pretty young woman wearing a paisley scarf laid down a silver tray. Turkish coffee steamed in its *cezve* – the long-handled copper pot used to make the traditional brew. She looked timidly at the ground, then retreated quickly from sight.

'You will try this coffee,' said Hakan. 'My wife makes the best.'

Certainly, it was delicious, medium sweet, brewed so that the grounds rested on the bottom. (One sure sign of a poor cup of Turkish coffee is to get a mouthful of grounds in the first sip.)

The caffeine was working on Hakan like engine oil. He picked up speed, his arms flew about in florid gestures. 'I will tell you my theory of the Turkish carpet,' he began. 'It's a perfect metaphor for the people themselves.'

'How so?'

'Woven of many threads,' he began. 'A fusion of many different geographical regions. On one hand practical, but on another tending towards luxury, aspiring towards fine detail and even the metaphysical.'

'A carpet can be metaphysical?'

'Do Muslims not pray four times a day on a carpet?' said Hakan, his voice rising. 'In the Koran, carpets are mentioned in the description of Paradise. "Rich carpets, all spread out!" it says. And, there are the motifs.' Hakan laid down his cup and moved to one side of the room. He leafed through several small carpets until he found the one he was looking for. It depicted a lantern of sorts, set into a niche.

'The light of God,' he explained. 'Shining from the wall of his house, a mosque.'

'And what of the new carpets?' I asked. 'I've seen many synthetic ones, using chemical dyes, artificial fibres, machine-made.'

Hakan's eyes gleamed. 'You are an old-fashioned man,' he said. 'A fine quality. And it is true that the new carpets, like the country, are becoming modern too quickly. We are in too much of a hurry to forget the past.'

I told Hakan a little of my journey, and my wish to understand the world of the Sufis. He was easy to talk to and I found myself becoming as loquacious as him. Not even Atatürk, I conjectured, could rid a country of a thousand or more years of history. Soon, whether in ten years or a hundred, Turkey would *have* to allow the Sufis to practise again. They were not, like the fez, the symbol of a past allied purely to religious tradition. They were a symbol of man's capacity to smash tradition for something purer, something beyond linguistic definition. Even as I finished Hakan was nodding.

'You are correct, my friend. Rarely am I hearing such words. But,' his voice lowered stealthily, 'I should warn you to be careful of speaking these opinions too often in Konya. There are those who will, as I do, find them pertinent. But others do not wish our country to liberalise. They seek a return to the total control of orthodox Islam. You know, quite recently, some local politicians tried to enforce the segregation of men and women on the buses. Can you *imagine* if such a bill had passed! They would have us return to the dark ages.'

'What of Sufis?' I asked. 'Is it still possible to find them?'

Hakan looked surprised. 'I am a Sufi,' he said. 'What of it?'

'But what of the laws? Could you not be arrested?'

He seemed to find this hilarious. 'Arrested? I think not. We are peaceful men. We harm no one. Where is the problem with this?'

'So you belong to a *tekke*?'

'Certainly.'

'And you practise whirling?'

'Of course! This is what Mevlana taught.'

I sat back, bemused. Clearly, there were differences of opinion on the matter.

'So I could visit your *tekke*?' I enquired delicately.

He tugged his beard. 'It may be. But I would have to ask permission. This is not, you might say, a usual request. But I don't see why not. Did not Mevlana himself say "Come everyone"?'

Meeting Hakan and his family turned out to be the very key I needed to unlock the gates of the city. They were that family I've met time and time again across the world: happy to open their arms to a stranger, generous to a fault, expecting nothing in return. Returning the following day, I was ushered through the side door of the shop into a warm kitchen, and saw a vinyl-covered table, a blue bowl of walnuts, an Ottoman carpet hanging from the wall. If their possessions were few, their pride was immense. In preparation for my visit, Hakan's wife, Nursel, had got up early to make cheese *borek* – a filo pastry filled with pungent feta cheese and spring greens. The rich smell of it hung in the air. While I sat at the kitchen table, where their son was drawing ocean liners on a length of brown paper, I felt that sense of contentment which always comes when one eats in the house of a local. Here is where real life happens.

After his second slice of *borek*, Hakan fetched his most treasured possession. It was a nineteenth-century Koran bound in red hide. It had been in his family for 150 years, he told me. His great-great-grandfather, a calligrapher of some repute, had spent almost twenty years copying it.

He slid it reverently across the worn surface of the table. Below me I saw a maze of intricate loops and whorls, dots and flares. I was too nervous to touch it.

'The true calligrapher uses a pen cut from a reed,' said Hakan. 'That is best.'

'Like the *ney*?' I asked, referring to the reed used for the flutes favoured by Rumi.

'Exactly! Then the reed is buried for several years in the earth until its colour changes. The masters know *precisely* when the time is right to dig up their pens.'

'And the ink?'

Hakan drew closer, eyes sparkling. He was like an alchemist imparting secrets. 'Soot is ground to a powder so fine it is like flour, and then mixed with water. That is the ink. The paper is dyed with tea, then coated with egg whites. At last, it is ready to receive the word of God. This, my friend, is a *true* Koran. They say that the more pious the one who copies it, the greater its quality.'

'I wish I could understand it,' I said, carefully turning one of the old pages. 'Or see beyond the calligraphy.'

'Even *when* you understand Arabic it is difficult,' admitted Hakan. 'Rumi himself compared the Koran to a bride.

"Although you pull the veil away from her face, she will not show herself to you," he said.'

'Then what is the trick?'

A chuckle. 'Stop pulling!'

That afternoon Hakan talked of Rumi. Although I had read much of the poet's work, I knew little of his life. But as the afternoon lengthened, a steady stream of coffee cups coming and receding before us like tides, I heard a great many of the stories and legends which remain. First I had seen Hakan as a carpet seller, secondly as a family man. But as evening drew near, I began to see him as a fine example of the Sufi I had hoped to meet: eloquent, well versed in calligraphy, poetry and music. I felt sure Dr Kilic would have liked him.

'By the time of his father's death, Mevlana was already a great scholar,' said Hakan. 'At twenty-four, he was known throughout the country for his learning. But at that stage he was not a mystic! He was just a man. Until, one day, something happened which would change everything. Mevlana met Shams.'

'Who was Shams?' I asked.

Hakan's face broke into the contented smile of storytellers everywhere who have received the very question they've been trying to provoke.

'Shams Tabrizi was a mystic, a wandering dervish. He simply moved from town to town, immersed in his love of God. For him, God was not to be found in books but in life. Shams was a divine presence, and it was he who awakened in Mevlana the sudden realisation of the *true* path to God. He was Mevlana's master, his friend. Before, Mevlana was – in a manner of speaking – *sober*. He was a scholar, a quiet man. But after meeting Shams, Mevlana was drunk! He found himself intoxicated by God. And he began to write poems spontaneously, because his intoxication was too great to be contained. It spilled out of him.

'So began the greatest friendship of Rumi's life. But Mevlana's students were not happy about this elderly dervish who was taking up all of their master's time. After several years, their threats to Shams became so violent that he left. Some stories, in fact, recount that he was murdered. And from this deep loss, this sense of being cut off, literally, from God, Rumi wrote some of his best poems.'

Later that week, with the permission for my visit to the *tekke* granted, Hakan and I walked the dark streets of Konya. Dusk had fallen and with it the promise of summer receded for another few weeks. I pulled my jacket more tightly around me, my breath streaming like frost in the air. Certainly, I felt a little nervous. From its earliest origins, Sufism has had something of mystery about it, something secret and hidden. Bahauddin and Rumi lived in times similar to our own in many ways, with wars and strife raging about them, and the fundamentalists clinging more and more staunchly to their doctrines. They, like the Sufis before and after them, rejected conventional beliefs. God is in our hearts, they claimed. He is not in the mosque or the madrasa or in the pages of books. He is within us.

That was the heresy for which they had long been pushed underground. Later, with Atatürk, their crime seemed not straying from doctrine, but speaking of faith at all. For as long as human beings have professed beliefs, I reflected, there have been others holding their own more important. It seemed the very mind set, trapped in right or wrong, that the Sufis were trying to move beyond. Idries Shah wrote:

> Cross and the churches, from end to end
> I surveyed; He was not on the cross.
> I went to the idol temple, to the ancient pagoda,

No trace was visible there.
I bent the reins of search to the Ka'ba.
He was not in the resort of old and young.
I gazed into my own heart,
There I saw Him, He was nowhere else.

The *tekke*, when we came to it, was an unassuming building at the end of an unassuming street. From outside it looked like an office building from the last century: municipal, its masonry patched haphazardly with concrete. Inside the door, a substantial pile of shoes testified to the gathering within, at least a hundred pairs, I noted: shabby trainers, mud-caked loafers, effete Ottoman slippers.

A low-ceilinged corridor, calligraphy on the walls. Then we were in a large room. Men were sitting on prayer mats and brightly coloured cushions, many of them smoking. A chandelier above us was missing several of its bulbs; it gave off a sober golden light. The place had an air of happy decrepitude, not entirely dissimilar to a Turkish social club I'd once visited in the East End of London. It was, in fact, a *tariqat*, a school of Sufism, and these men *murīdīn* – meaning literally 'desirous' of the knowledge and love of God.

Before Atatürk's time, *tariqats*, with their long-established *silsilah* (lineages), had enormous political power in Turkey, especially those of the Mevlevi, the followers of Rumi. This was an élite *tariqat*, which numbered senior bureaucrats and even sultans among its members; the early Ottoman rulers and princes wore the woollen Mevlevi (*Hurasani*) cap, while the reforming Selim III (1789–1808) was an enthusiastic member and patron of the order.

We sat down at the edge of the room, Hakan's friends greeting us both warmly. Tea was fetched, cigarette packets proffered from all angles. English was tentatively employed;

we talked of Rumi, of course, and they seemed pleased and gently moved that someone should share in their love of the ancient dervish.

Like an ashram that many Hindu men may visit annually or merely in times of difficulty, this place, I felt, had a function as a place of refuge, a neutral zone which gave perspective on the vicissitudes of life without. In Islam, there are no monks or monasteries: the Prophet himself lived *in* the world, worked and had a family. His emphasis was on the need to be 'in the world but not of it'. These *tekkes*, too, provided order and a framework for the transmission of the great gems of cultural life: transcendent chants, literature, the Persian language. Once they also provided refuge for travellers, medical services, food for the poor, mediation for family or tribal disputes.

After an hour of tea drinking, the atmosphere changed abruptly, the laughter dwindled and we stood up for prayers. Knowing neither the prayers nor the bows and prostrations, this was difficult for me but I followed as best as I could. Something about it moved me, and I recollected a first yoga class taken years past: the solace of moving in unison with other people, sounds of chanting, homage to something higher than ourselves.

The prayers went on for a long time; by the time the final vowel sounded I was on the verge of some kind of insurrection. My knees felt weak, my throat was hoarse and my back ached from all the prostrations. If nothing else, I mused insubordinately, the Muslim prayers are a punishing callisthenics regimen.

At last, the prayers finished. 'Now the *zikr* will begin,' whispered the man next to me. 'Musicians will come in now.'

Zikr is the principal Sufi practice. It means 'remembrance' and its liturgy differs vastly across different Sufi orders. For some, *zikr* is recitation of holy texts, in others chanting, music, meditation. In the *dargah* of Hazrat Nizammudin in Delhi, the *zikr* comes in the form of *qawwali* music. Here amongst the Mevlevi (as well as others like the Qadiri and Rifai), it comes as whirling, but all, it seems evident, function as a method of inducing trance, an altered state of consciousness not entirely dissimilar, perhaps, from what William James discovered in his laboratory.

Clad in black and wearing their tall fez, the musicians lined up solemnly on one side of the room. I tried to make out the instruments: a pear-shaped lute held vertically on the knees), a *tanbur* (long-necked lute with frets), an *ûd* (short-necked, fretless, plucked lute) and a *kudüm* (a pair of small kettledrums). There was also a *kanun*, a type of zither, and of course the *ney*, the reed flute once played by Rumi himself.

From here, things proceeded much as they had done in the Galata Mevlevihanesi in Istanbul. But with Hakan beside me, the rituals became a little more comprehensible. First, there was a recitation of *Ya Hazreti Mevlana* – meaning 'presence of our master'. In Istanbul, I had taken this to refer to Rumi, but in fact, explained Hakan, it was the Holy Prophet. After this opening the *ney* sounded, and though I had been struck by its sound before, here it seemed to take on a palpable shimmer of longing and regret. Perhaps it was the acoustics of the room, or the circumstances of my being here. But from the moment of its first trembling note it sent shivers down my spine, as if I were hearing the voice of a child, lost in a dark wood, crying out. It spoke to that longing deep within me, which had first impelled me on this journey, a longing for connection and return.

The dervishes walked round in a circle three times, bowing to each other, then to the dervish master.

'They are recognising in each other the divine spark,' whispered Hakan.

Finally, there came a recitation from the Holy Koran: 'Whichever way you turn, there is the face of God,' Hakan translated.

The whirling began. The atmosphere in the room was absolutely still. It was as if those who weren't dancing were completely frozen; nothing moved except the central space, where spectral figures, apparently between worlds, moved in graceful arcs. For a moment I half closed my eyes. I could see skeins of ghosts, white blurs, gliding through space. Their dance has been practised over many years, and yet it seemed artless, as natural as a leaf falling.

'Everything on this earth revolves,' whispered Hakan. 'Electrons, protons, atoms. The blood in our own bodies. The Sufi does not whirl himself into unconsciousness, but into *consciousness*! He is moving with the earth, with all things in nature. He is aligning himself with the revolutions of all beings.'

This thought stayed with me for hours afterwards, days and weeks. I thought of how children are fascinated by roundabouts, spinning tops, merry-go-rounds. I watched footage of the earth spinning on its axis, planets orbiting each other. To see the whirling dervishes is to sense these things, to move towards them. It's a simple aligning of energies, a moving with the flow of things. But in this very simplicity there comes the power of mountains.

Within half an hour, the ceremony was over, and I was walking back through the deserted streets. Hakan had offered me a lift but, despite the cold, I wanted air around me, the space to breathe. One by one the Sufis, with much hand-shaking and good wishes, vanished in their rusty vehicles, and the streets reverted to night sounds: a far-off dog's bark, the wind in tall trees. Behind us, the lights in the *tekke* went out, and a chain was drawn across the door.

What I had seen had moved me deeply, and yet it was also very clear that, in itself, there was nothing particularly esoteric about it. There's a romance about Sufism, fanned by the secrecy, the sense of it being underground, that it's easy to get lost in. Beyond that, however, there is merely a group, like the *sadhus* in India, determined to move beyond the surface of things, to inhabit a more satisfying level of reality.

The philosopher Colin Wilson speaks of our normal waking consciousness as a 'robot', a creature which goes through the motions of life with only occasional glimpses of the intelligence within. For the Sufis, that 'intelligence' is God, and in their rituals they find ways to reconnect with it, to stay alive to it. Rumi's poetry is so important precisely *because* of its ability to convey the essence of that experience, the sheer exuberance of connectedness.

On that walk back through the sleeping streets of Konya, I could feel every breath, every air particle, moving in and out of my lungs. I was completely conscious of every stride, every sound, beads of cold dew on the tulips, cloud formations spread across the sky. Inwardly, I could even feel myself spinning, atoms churning, moving ever closer towards the truth.

Yet another thread had tied itself off. What seemed essential from here on was that it was time to cease *observing* these mystical practices and to take part in them myself. I had gone as far, on an intellectual level, as perhaps I could. If the Sufis had taught me anything it was to begin to see with the heart: a metaphor that I took to be about entering into life with those faculties which lay beyond the mind. If higher consciousness, or *sunyata*, or even God – to use a word which still rested uneasily with me – were the goal, then the mind could be of little use from this point on.

In the final part of my quest, I would turn to shamanism, that most ancient magico-religious phenomenon in which the individual learns to enter trance states and gain direct experience of expanded states of consciousness. It would be a journey that, once and for all, would transform my notions of 'reality'. On the far side I would emerge anew.

The Way of the Shaman

Millennia before Christ, Buddha or Mohammed ever walked the earth, humans were already engaged in elaborate sacred rituals. Perhaps as many as 25,000 years ago, during Palaeolithic times, the hunting cultures of Siberia and Central Asia coined a word, *saman*, defined as a technique of ecstasy. From this came the word 'shaman', meaning religious leader, priest or healer, but more specifically describing someone with the ability to enter trance states in order to gather knowledge in the non-human realms.

At this point in my quest, the subject of shamanism had come up too often to ignore. The oracles I had seen in Ladakh were a direct link with a shamanic tradition predating Tibetan Buddhism, while Mata-ji was also enacting methods passed down from a shamanic past. Even Sufism, according to some scholars, springs from a belief system far older than Islam itself, one which believed in healing, ecstasy, the preparation of charms.

Shamanism, then, is the mother of all religions. But what made it so particularly relevant to my own journey was in its emphasis on 'spirit worlds' – other realms of consciousness in which the shaman can meet and 'master' spirits. Several years before, I might have baulked at the word 'spirits', for its connotations of the supernatural. But now, I saw things differently. Western science traces our ailments to the body: a virus, faulty wiring or bacteria, behind our problems. For a Ladakhi oracle, a spirit may be responsible, for a Sufi *pir* there may be a djinn. Each group gives the problem a name, and for each group that problem becomes real and visceral, something which may be killed with antibiotics, or driven away by a more powerful awareness than its own.

What I had come to believe was not that one answer was right and the others outdated superstition, but that *all* were right. No one who has ever experienced a serious migraine can fail to see how someone might interpret that seemingly malevolent pain as 'other' than oneself, give it a name perhaps, see it as an invading force to be driven away. Part of the task of anthropology, and simply being a traveller in the world, is to learn how these other interpretations can also have validity, not just how they work within a cultural framework but how they are 'true'.

What is also true on the level of healing is that many of the shamanic methods *work*. This, too, is not merely lucky coincidence, as some scientists suggest, but an aspect of a healing system that incorporates far more than the merely physical: it includes energy fields, mind states, awareness of the surrounding biosphere. Shamans spend years in the most arduous training in order to explore and penetrate layers of consciousness. They are the masters of expanded awareness, with infinitely subtler, more penetrating understanding than our own.

For the flower power generation, already turned on by Kerouac and LSD, the term 'shaman' arrived first in the books of Carlos Castaneda. Castaneda was a Peruvian-born American author who wrote a series of books that describe his purported training under the tutelage of a Yaqui shaman named Don Juan. His books sold more than eight million copies and their effect on popular culture was enormous. *Time* magazine would later call him 'the godfather of the New Age', a fitting moniker for someone who brought, for the first time, the shamanic world-view into popular culture. I read the books myself at university, but only on the level of psychedelically inspired adventure stories rather than anything which might have a bearing on my own life. Picking them up again a decade later, I read them as if for the first time. They were about changing the ways one perceived reality and about some of the primary techniques which shamans had invented to do so.

For readers of the Don Juan books, a strange new universe unfolds. The mysterious shaman leads Castaneda through a peculiar series of teachings and initiations in order to train him as a 'sorcerer'. He learns how to turn off his inner dialogue completely, control and interact with his dreams, to behave in a manner Don Juan labels 'impeccability'. On occasion he imbibes powerful hallucinogenic plants, and at the end of Castaneda's fourth book, both shaman and student deliberately cross over into another plane of existence.

History doesn't relate whether Don Juan really existed or not, or whether Castaneda conjured the entire oeuvre from his imagination. But what is certainly true is that much of the teaching and world-view evoked by Carlos Castaneda is concurrent with that of shamanism. William James' discoveries about consciousness in the nineteenth century were predated by probably twenty or thirty *thousand* years by indigenous peoples, who used plant substances, drumming and dance to leave their rational consciousness behind.

Unsurprisingly, perhaps, given the general revivals of mysticism that are under way, interest in shamanism has exploded in recent years. Even as deforestation and development are forcing indigenous peoples to the cities, scores of Western seekers visit Central and South America in the hope of finding raw spiritual knowledge. Implicit in this search is the notion that shamans are the repositories of a deeper spiritual wisdom than our own, possessing techniques that can radically improve the quality of our lives.

My own first forays in shamanism – embarrassingly trite, in retrospect – revolved around the picking of some magic mushrooms from a farmer's field on the edge of Dartmoor. A friend of mine had returned from Guatemala, where he'd seen mushroom motifs on the ruins of Mayan temples. With these mushrooms, he pronounced, we'd see the future, receive healing, possibly commune with God.

But while these were all likely uses to which the ancient civilisations had put the psilocybin mushrooms, all I received were a few tremulous colour visions and the mother of all stomachaches. We felt spectacularly let down, not least by the copious vomiting which followed. For many years after, I avoided hallucinogens entirely, considering their advocates little more than pleasure-seeking wastrels, far outside any respectable spiritual quest. But more than this, I feared the directions my mind might take me. Long spells of depression left me conservative as regards the substances I subjected myself to, for fear of losing control completely.

When I visited Peru, shamanism reappeared in my life in a way which made me reconsider all this. In South America for some journalism work, I visited the great Tambopata Madidi wilderness on the Peru–Bolivia border, an area two thirds the size of Costa Rica. After my article was finished, I stayed on for a while, keen to explore the jungle. This was a fierce, unruly place, further outside my experience than anywhere I'd ever been. Here intricately coloured beetles landed on one's hand. Spiders the size of soup plates shimmered from aerial webs. The 'numinous' was everywhere, compounded by the knowledge of so many dangers, from plant and animal alike, which bustled and swarmed beneath every leaf. I found it fascinating to imagine what kind of spiritual relationship to the world had evolved here, as opposed to, say, Ladakh, whose ecology was so comparatively barren and empty.

To help me navigate this labyrinth, I engaged the services of a local guide, Juan, who became my friend and confidant for a few weeks. Together, we travelled the Amazon in a metal *peque peque* boat, staying in village shacks, jungle lodges, tents. Juan had grown up in the rainforest and knew his environment from the inside out. For him, nothing existed interdependently of anything else, and the jungle was alive, not merely with flora and fauna, but with spirits. He'd received his knowledge, he said, from his father: a shaman and teacher of plant medicine who'd taken him into the jungle from the moment he could walk, to hunt, pick fruits and medicinal herbs and learn the old stories.

'My father is an Ayahuascero,' explained Juan. 'People from all over the Oriente region come to call on him, and to receive the wisdom of the ayahuasca vine.'

Something stirred in my memory. Several years before I'd met a traveller in India who waxed lyrical about the ayahuasca vine, saying it had changed his life. William Burroughs, too, had written about it in *The Yage Letters*, in which he recounts his search for a near-mythical hallucinogenic plant. For Burroughs, who hoped the plant might be a possible cure for his long-term heroin addiction, yage was to be 'the final fix'.

'What is this ayahuasca vine?' I asked. We were motoring gently along the eastern shore of the great river, in the hope of spotting capybara, a barrel–shaped rodent: something like a giant guinea pig. Above us, the clouds had parted for the first time in days, and all seemed right with the world.

'In Quechua, ayahuasca means "vine of the soul",' said Juan, gruffly. He was a short, weathered man who liked to chew tobacco. He kept his gaze fixed on the river, alert to the movement of currents. 'It shows us the spirit realms.'

'Why do you take it?'

'To learn things. To make problems go away. There are many reasons.'

Juan seemed uncharacteristically surly. Was this an area of knowledge he preferred not to discuss with Westerners, I asked. Were there prohibitions against sharing the secrets of the vine?

Juan lowered the revs of the boat, and the canoe slowed a little against the gurgling current. 'It is not that,' he explained. 'In fact, many gringos come here now to drink the medicine. For some shamans, it is big business. It is merely that this knowledge is sacred. To say what the ayahuasca can do, or what it means to drink, is for a shaman to say. You must ask my father.'

Juan's reverence for the ayahuasca vine says much about the relationship of indigenous people with the world around them. They consider plants to be living teachers, with a spirit and a personality of their own. Some of the plants teach by bringing visions or strong dreams, others – like trees – bring the student virtues which they display themselves, such as fortitude, or resistance to strong weather. Although the shaman/pupil relationship is important in some tribes, the knowledge itself comes from nature, and the shaman merely offers the tools to receive it. In a non-literate culture there's an obvious logic to this, but it also poses difficult questions for science. How can a plant teach us something? Or is it merely that to ingest certain plants forces us to perceive the world differently?

Curious to know more, I asked Juan if I could meet his father. He seemed pleased by the request, and said that we would be literally passing his village the following day. The subsequent morning we left at first light. Before us, the Amazon, a river with a total flow greater than the next ten largest rivers in the world combined, moved along in a brackish chop. On either side of the channel, the jungle offered a claustrophobic embrace. Monkeys chattered, technicolour birds fled the treetops, a heron stabbed a wriggling fish on its spear-like beak.

Slow progress that day. Roiling clouds which, at noon, opened violently. Sitting beneath a plastic tarpaulin, Juan and I stopped to watch flaming spikes of lightning hit the water. The river seemed to boil as the rain struck its surface. In the jungle beyond I imagined birds tucking heads beneath their wings, rodents seeking burrows, butterflies hovering, disconsolately, beneath banana leaves. We seemed in the grip of primordial forces and, for the duration of the storm, I found myself considering that this feeling – of being entirely at the mercy of the natural world – was the birthright of everyone born in the jungle. It was the starting point for trying to understand the shamanism that had originated here.

Beneath the rattle of the heavy rain, we ate our sandwiches – processed cheese between limp white bread – and drunk *yerba mate* from a thermos. *Mate* was, strictly speaking, an Argentinian drink, but Juan had acquired a taste for it from his brother, currently working on a stock farm in the pampas of Córdoba. The rain shot the tarpaulin so stridently there was no point in attempting conversation, so for a time we simply watched this menacing rainstorm, and tucked our jackets more tightly against the wet. Within an hour it had eased enough to allow us back on the river. After the storm, the silence was limitless.

Downstream, we came across gold prospectors, shrivelled, hungry-looking men working by the river's edge. A powerful diesel motor, belching soot into the air, propelled a hammer crusher which broke down rocks from the river.

'Very bad for the river,' muttered Juan, staring at them with disgust. 'They wash the ore with mercury and then flush it away in the river. It kills animals and fish. Eventually, it will probably kill those men too.'

'How much gold do they find?'

'For the ones that do it by hand, maybe three or four dollars per day. With that machine, thirty, forty dollars. Small amounts. It's enough to survive.'

By four o clock, we reached his father's village. At the water's edge a group of small children were splashing about, no adults in sight. A grinning boy of about six swam up to the edge of our boat and pulled himself up with scrawny arms.

'*Holá*, Pablito,' hailed Juan, patting him on the head. 'My sister's child,' he explained. 'Very naughty one!'

A short slope led upwards to a muddy track, at which the usual ramshackle dwellings of South American village life began, shacks made of hand-cut planks, corrugated metal, strips of plastic filling the gaps. There were rangy, long-necked chickens in the dirt, as well as tiny black-haired pigs uttering ferocious snorts. A fishing net hung from a tree to dry and, in a streak of brilliant turquoise, a bird crossed our line of sight. It was a paradise tanager, said Juan. It had a throat of violet and a pale-green hood.

This was one of the very few villages along this stretch of river, Juan told me. Further into the jungle there were uncontacted tribes, about whom little was known. On the other side was Puerto Maldonado, the capital of the Madre de Dios region, and an important town in the brazil nut trade.

'Those who leave the village go there,' said Juan. 'They work in logging, brazil nuts, or some in tourism like me. Puerto Maldonado's full of drugs, prostitution and missionaries. These missionaries come here,' he grinned, 'to teach us jungle people about the existence of God. But as you will see when you meet my father, ours is a different God from the one they offer.'

The village was scarcely more than ten houses. From some of them, smiling people offered waves to Juan, from others came the drifting smoke of cooking meat, mewling babies, silence. These people lived gruelling lives – that much was evident in their faces – but there was community here, proximity to nature, laughter. I realised, too, how reliant these people were on traditional healers like Juan's father, so far from any city or hospital. Pushed up against the jungle, they had evolved to take what they needed from its grasp. It provided food, building materials and medicine, as well as an entire system of belief.

A few weeks earlier, I'd seen great swathes of clear-cut land, like Tolkien's vision of Mordor, on the edge of the rainforest. Here, more than anywhere in the world, the impact of material progress was tangible; one could measure it in feet and inches, smell the brush burn in the air. All of us in the 'developed' world knew about this, read about it sorrowfully over our Sunday newspapers, and yet to *see* it was to move from knowledge to experience. These were the very trenches that lay between the two worlds.

Similarly, the conflict between Western missionaries and the indigenous world-view speaks volumes, not only about First World arrogance, but about the rational versus the enchanted. A typical sixteenth-century account by Spanish navigator Gonzalo Fernandez de Oviedo described 'revered' old men, who used tobacco to 'worship the devil'. Later visitors would not believe that the shamans were communicating with anyone at all, putting their rituals down to trickery or 'hocus-pocus'. Even amongst anthropologists it took until the twentieth century before ideas about shamanism began to change. Romanian historian of religion Mircea Eliade was amongst the first to contend that, at the heart of all religions, was an experience of the sacred. In this, he claimed 'shamanism is the religious experience par excellence'.

On the far side of the village, Juan's father came out to meet us. He was eighty-nine and looked sixty, with long silver hair, nut-brown skin and a great quietness about him. His teeth were few, but other than that he appeared to be in radiant health.

Shaking his hand, I found myself in the shadow of a mountain. To look into most people's eyes is to find questions there, projections and needs that colour our responses. But here there was only attention, perhaps even a certain levity. After he had said hello, he went straight back to what he had been doing, which was sweeping the floor of the hut and feeding a small fire with wood. Our arrival hadn't surprised him at all.

'There was a ceremony last night,' explained Juan, after some words with his father. 'Some people came from Puerto Maldonado to take the vine.' He broke some brazil nuts with a hammer, and handed me some.

'Can I see the plant?' I asked.

Juan asked his father, who assented and we followed the old shaman to the edge of the jungle. 'It grows everywhere,' he said, in a high musical voice. 'I only have to go a few feet and it is there. It is there to help us.'

I knelt down beside a fairly average-looking sprawl of vivid green leaves. Later I would learn its Latin name, *Banisteriopsis caapi*, and that it's a jungle vine of the family Malpighiaceae.

'There are many different colours,' said the shaman. '*Cielo* or the sky plant is a mild ayahuasca. Then there is *trueno* or thunder for the stronger experience. Then there is black, white and red. All offer different experiences. She is the mother of all plants. But she does not awake unless she is mixed with another.'

We walked on into the jungle, leaving the village behind, a hot buzz of flies about my face. Within a few minutes we had reached another humble-looking plant, which he called 'chacruna'. A relative of the coffee family, *Pschotria viridis*, it provides a potent source of dimethyltryptamine or DMT. To ingest chacruna by itself, however, is to feel nothing. The human stomach easily breaks it down into harmless compounds. When combined with ayahuasca vine, on the other hand, the DMT reaches the brain stem intact. And in that experience, as I would eventually discover some months later, nothing can ever be the same again.

'This is the most powerful drug I have ever experienced,' William Burroughs wrote in an unpublished article he sent to Allen Ginsberg in 1956. 'Yage is not like anything else. It produces the most complete derangement of the senses.'

We had a few more hours before we had to return to the river. I wasn't to drink the vine that day, but I wanted to learn as much about it as possible. There was something in the old man's manner that seemed to radiate authority. Like Amrabati, the *sadhu* who had spent years with his hand tied about his head, the shaman exuded the strength of one who has moved through fire and survived. He had nothing to prove, no questions to ask. He was, perhaps, the most entirely 'present' individual I had ever met. Time in India had made me attentive to the qualities that deep practice brought.

Over Nescafé in cracked glasses, I learned a little. Endless insects swarmed in the damp heat about our faces. The old man's frankness surprised me, actually. Afterwards, Juan told me that Westerners had been to speak to the old man before, and he considered it perfectly acceptable to discuss his life with us. 'If the planet is to survive,' Juan translated, 'then my father believes as many people as possible should drink ayahuasca. It is a medicine for what is happening now, against the ego, against chopping down trees, against war.'

If all that seemed a heavy burden of expectation to lay before a humble plant, I was certainly interested to hear more. Clearly, as with the yogic practices of India, Buddhist meditation and Sufi *zikr*, shamanism provides a framework by which to move beyond conventional understandings of reality. Perhaps it was *this* that the old man spoke of. If we could learn to disidentify with cumbersome ego structures and become comfortable in the visionary realms, could it not be possible that we would return fundamentally changed, more awake, better human beings?

'When one drinks the medicine,' said the old man, facing Juan and me from his rickety chair, 'one comes to learn that what one considers reality and non-reality is completely false.' Hints of a grin. 'Even one drink can show us the futility of the way in which we have been living. Sometimes people come here with big drug problems – cocaine, heroin – and they give up after one dose of ayahuasca. Can any other plant do this?'

'Why did you call ayahuasca the *mother* of all plants?' I asked him.

'Because she is the mother teacher. Drinking ayahuasca we learned, thousands of years past, about the jungle. She told us what we could eat, what we could plant, which herbs and barks are good for disease. She told us which plants we could mix her with to take us into the spirit world. Even now, when there is something I want to know, the mother tells me. She is the gateway to that realm where all questions are answered.'

The notion of ayahuasca as the mother plant is common amongst all the Amazonian and Andean tribes who consider it sacred. And although it's hard to imagine how a plant might offer such specific knowledge to its user, it can't be denied either that the likelihood of ever accidentally mixing *Banisteriopsis caapi* and *Pschotria viridis* in the midst of the richest, most diverse ecosystem on the planet is extraordinarily remote, hundreds of thousands to one at best. Certainly, it could be coincidence, but is the other answer so impossible?

Later I would read an extraordinary article by a Jewish academic, Benny Shannon, printed in the *Guardian*, in which he hypothesises that many of the visionary experiences reported in the Old Testament might be put down to the use of psychoactive plants. He even hints that the Tree of Knowledge itself may refer to such a plant. And while, predictably, Israeli radio stations and chat rooms flew into overdrive in the aftermath of his article, with accusations of 'heresy' flying about, the notion may be entirely plausible. We know that many ancient civilisations (South American, Indian, Australian, African, Chinese, to name a few) evolved cosmological theories directly influenced by narcotic plants. Is it so impossible that ours too owes something to the power of nature?

'During my training I went into the jungle on my own for several years,' the shaman continued. 'I built a small shelter of leaves and bark, and a fire to brew my ayahuasca on. I drank it every other day, as well as many other sacred plants.

I ate only what I hunted or picked from trees. I learned to master sorcery, to speak with the spirits of animals, I learned the magic songs, the *icaros*. When I returned, I was a shaman.'

His account was a few sentences at best, and yet it seemed to hint at a training of almost unfathomable difficulty. Why would anyone put themselves through such an ordeal?

'But what does that mean?' I asked. 'To be a shaman.'

The old shaman looked me directly in the eyes for the first time. They were empty, like a fire that has burned itself out. 'It means we can travel to the other worlds,' he said. 'To the magic worlds – at will. We understand the language which is spoken there. And that we can help others make the same journey, if they have the courage to try.'

Back in London, the experiences of the jungle quickly faded. The almost impossible vitality and effervescence of the Amazonian ecosystem was replaced by a neutral, slightly heavy feeling. The material plane of existence held forceful sway here, and the consensual logic was that 'this' was reality: these red buses, tax return forms, career ladders. Tapping 'ayahuasca' into Google, however, provides immediate perspective: this is not exclusively the case. Just as the Eastern religions have their Western converts and high priests, a huge shamanic subculture exists throughout North America and Europe. Scores of people, it seems, spend their time obtaining rare South American cacti and plant materials with serious spiritual intent.

All of this, plainly, was part of the great process of re-enchantment that I'd been exploring from the start. And yet suddenly it seemed that 're-enchantment' was an unsatisfactory term after all. What was going on was not some return to an Edenic innocence, or to a pre-industrial unity. It was something entirely novel: the beginnings of a new world order, perhaps, or a new epoch in human evolution. Like the children of the 1960s, not content with the behavioural patterns and ideologies of their parents, a new generation was seeking these experiences not merely out of some outdated desire for kicks, but to conquer and supersede the limitations of our normal mind states.

I had once called this feeling 'magic', but the journey thus far had deepened that notion. Magic was but a facet of the state touched upon by the mystics from every tradition, and which William James called 'the universal saintliness, the same in all religions'. It was what the nineteenth-century psychiatrist Richard Maurice Bucke called 'cosmic consciousness' after he found himself – subsequent to an evening discussing poetry with his friends – 'wrapped as it were by a flame-coloured cloud'. It was the stillness and exultation that characterised all life's peak experiences, in which one is simply 'being' rather than 'becoming', suddenly at one with the Absolute.

If I had already been exploring unconventional ideas, this new suspicion made me more uncomfortable still. Was I in danger of becoming one of those madmen on the outer fringes of society, espousing outlandish ideas with little or no basis in reality? For many scientists even the notion of a collective consciousness is absurd. That human beings, like schools of fish, should share a cognitive aware-ness of some kind, even if that awareness lies beyond our line of sight, is an idea spoken of by mystics but beyond that unproven.

But if one held that all the different schools of mysti-cism were moving towards the same thing, and counted the millions of men and women, to varying degrees, who were a part of that process, it wasn't so far-fetched after all. For the philosopher Jean Gebser, whose work has been increasingly considered seminal since his death in 1973, such a process was well under way. Gebser believed that the stress and chaos in Europe from 1914 to 1945 were the symptoms of a structure of consciousness that had run its course. In his masterpiece *The Ever Present Origin* Gebser hypothesised that a new form of human consciousness (integral consciousness) was in the process of emergence.

In any case, it was time to try the Vine of the Souls for myself. Amongst my old yoga crowd in London, several had already drunk the brew, and it proved easy enough to book myself into a ceremony. In two weeks I would fly to Barcelona, drive to a secret location and meet an Ecuadorian shaman who would guide me through the experience.

Steve, an Iyengar yogi of many years, lent me books on the subject and hand-wrote a list of foods it was preferable to avoid for a week before drinking.

'When you first drink, you'll probably vomit a great deal,' he explained. 'The medicine cleans you out, physically and emotionally. Indians called it *la purga*. So before you put yourself through such an experience, you can lighten the load by eating as purely as possible. No onions, garlic or chilli – eat what the Indians call a sattvic diet. And then, depending on which school of shamanism you're following: no vinegar or fermented foods, nothing too acidic, no coffee or alcohol. And no sex.'

'Sex?'

'Sexual energy is the same primal stuff that you need to work with ayahuasca,' said Steve. 'But traditionally, the shamans say the plant is jealous if it knows you've been with another. Failing to respect it can make it angry.' He laughed. 'And *believe* me, you don't want to do that.'

So what exactly *would* happen when I drunk this potent hallucinogenic brew? Interestingly, it is the chacruna rather than the ayahuasca which appears to contain the active ingredient. Chacruna contains the indole alkaloid DMT, a powerful entheogenic compound, already present in the human brain in small amounts. By ingesting a quantity of DMT, the user experiences intense visions, or by another reckoning gains access to the shamanic reality. Some people I spoke with said they'd met alien beings, spoken with the gods or found themselves plunged into specific moments of their own history. Somehow, unlike the earlier claims of my psilocybin mushroom buddy, I believed them.

Steve, a serious man not liable to wild claims, said he went further in one ayahuasca experience than in ten years of yoga. 'I'm not knocking yoga,' he added. 'It's another powerful tool. But comparatively speaking, it's the middle path. It works slowly, over years of patient practice. Ayahuasca is the fiery path. It's the fast track to enlightenment. Sometimes it can be truly hellish. But always you come out cleansed, feeling like you've just shifted some stuff that's been holding you back for years.'

Despite all this advice, my mood seemed to worsen in the week before the ceremony. I got flu and found myself in bed, staring at the ceiling, my whole body in revolt. More than anything in the world, I didn't want to go through with this experience. Why thrust a sharp stick into an already angry hornets' nest? What if I lost my mind completely? Or spun off into some psychic hell realm from which no one would be able to pull me back? These days I never smoked marijuana and drank far less than I had, merely for fear of rocking an already fragile mind. Devoid of anything to compare it with, I imagined a complete psychological meltdown, the snapping of some vital pathway.

Whether I was actually ill, or merely vehemently trying to escape the coming experience, I never found out. But pulling myself out of bed in the pre-dawn for my flight to

Barcelona was one of the most gruelling experiences of my life. My limbs moved like lead. My brow gave off an icy sweat. I was terrified, with every fibre of my being, of what was to come.

Barcelona: *La Purga*

At Barcelona airport I met Agata, a Chilean woman living in Spain, who was organising the retreat. She was seven months pregnant, full of vitality, and with a reassuring matter of factness about the experience to come.

'You are still a little sick,' she said, as we sped through the drizzle. We were leaving Girona and, on either side, commuters flocked home through the suburbs. 'But even on a purely physical level the ayahuasca will help you. It is a total medicine. You'll see.'

When I told her about the strict diet I'd been on, culminating in a total fast for the last twenty-four hours, she laughed melodiously. 'Certain foods are best to avoid, sure. But you need some energy too. We'd better stop and get you something. You'll need your strength for tonight.'

As the light bled from the sky, we pulled off the motorway and on to the empty, pastoral lanes of Catalonia. It was October and the sunflowers drooped limply in the fields. There were vineyards, rich woodland, a shepherd with a stick reminding us of an older world still hanging on. As the 1970s Volvo lit the lanes with its feeble headlights, I seemed to enter a state of calm acceptance. Like a man heading for the noose, I resolved to meet my fate with a smile.

It was ironic, I thought, too, that after several years in India and elsewhere, searching for this esoteric knowledge, the mountain, so to speak, had come to me. Shamans who would once have lived solely amongst their communities in the Amazonian and Andean regions of South America were now being invited to bring their knowledge abroad. How many other gatherings like this one, I wondered, were happening even now?

How the shamans brought their plants with them, though, was another matter. Ayahuasca's legal status remains ambiguous at best. By American law, the plants themselves are not illegal, but a plant brew which contains DMT is. France classifies both plants as controlled substances. A Brazilian church called Santo Daime, for whom ayahuasca is a holy sacrament, has been challenging this notion in many countries around the world on the basis of religious freedom. At the time of writing, several legal cases remain open, with a US trial date set for 2009. The outcome of this, I suspect, is unlikely to be a good one for the Ayahuasceros, and yet, of course, the practice will continue. The modern world seems unlikely, just yet, to accept the imbibing of hallucinogenic plants as a valid tool for spiritual experience.

At the neck of a small valley stood the farmhouse which would be our home for the next few days. Its owners, explained Agata, rented out the space for yoga retreats, five rhythms dancing and occasionally shamanic workshops such as ours. Spain's rural economy, like many in Europe, has faced massive decline in recent years and it seemed fitting that certain of its inhabitants should seek to fill the gaps like this. A traditional *finca*, it had whitewashed walls, a red-tiled roof and two mongrel puppies that yapped at our arrival.

At the house Agata showed me to a large, low-lit room, with a woodburning stove in one corner. Fifteen or twenty sleeping mats had already been laid out, and those who had arrived were arranging their sleeping bags, pillows and blankets for the night ahead.

I claimed one, lay down and watched the people arriving. Catalans mostly, but there was one girl from Austria and a lawyer from Bern. All of us from different walks of life, some hippies, some business people, all of us with different clothes and aspirations. None of us, in any case, were the people we thought we were. As we would soon discover, the structures we put our faith in were as ephemeral as straw.

The shaman arrived at about 8 p.m. He was an Ecuadorian, a Shuar tribesman from the foothills of the Andes, with feathered white hair which hung down across his back. Physically he was a small man, with a lean bone structure and unobtrusive clothes. He looked around the room thoughtfully before seating himself behind the altar. He took a series of objects from his bag.

First impressions are always difficult, but my immediate sense was that he shared with Juan's father a hard-earned equanimity. For the Shuar, the shaman is an *uwishin* – meaning 'one who knows the secrets'. Their journey towards knowledge involves astonishing hardship and deprivation, a mental training we can only dream of.

Even though he was fifty-two years old, he was still considered an apprentice compared to some of the elder *uwishin* of the tribe, Agata told me. Amongst the Shuar, there were several in their late eighties who had reached a stage at which it was believed they knew all the secrets of existence. They held the power to heal or practise sorcery, and their spirit powers allowed them to control *tsentsak* – invisible magical darts that could cause good or harm.

But for now his manner seemed entirely urbane and relaxed. He introduced himself, bade us welcome and encouraged each person in turn to share with the group what they hoped to achieve that night.

'Intention is important,' he said, looking each of us in turn in the eye. 'By speaking your intention aloud, the Mother will hear you. You must gather your focus for the night ahead.'

A young woman at the far end of the room began. The light was dim now, and the warmth from the iron grate comforting against the autumn night. Outside a wind was picking up and the ancient walls seemed to sigh.

'I'm here to heal the relationship with my mother,' she began. 'We've always resented each other, for a reason neither of us fully understands. I ask Mother Ayahuasca to help me get through to her, and to heal the years of unhappiness which lie between us.'

The shaman nodded, then gestured for the next person to speak. In this way we continued, a diverse range of needs and expectations ringing out in the room. Many of these people, it turned out, had drunk the brew twenty or thirty times, some of them having spent time in South America drinking intensively. What was becoming clear, too, was that it's a plant whose effects can be as practical as they are spiritual. Many of these people wanted help with their day-to-day lives, as much as any lofty merging with the universe.

When it came to my turn I spoke nervously, unsure exactly of any intention other than to break through some barrier which had been making me unhappy for a long time.

'I ask the Mother for knowledge,' I began. 'Sometimes I feel like I'm outside of life, peering through a keyhole. I'm looking for a way in.'

When the last person had spoken, the shaman extinguished the final light. Pulling some hot coals from the fire with tongs, he dropped them on to an iron platter before the altar, and began sprinkling herbs on them. They sizzled and popped, and the room filled with an acrid, although not unpleasant, odour.

'Now I pass round tobacco juice,' he said, in his thick accent. 'Place half or one teaspoon of the liquid in your hand and snort it up each nostril. It prepares you to receive the ayahuasca.'

Two jam jars of this black liquid began moving in opposite directions. Each person, I noticed, reacted to their dose by clutching their nose as if they'd been burned. For the Shuar, like many other tribes, *mapacho* (tobacco) is a useful and important sacred plant. They drink it, smoke it, or snort it, sometimes on its own, or in combination with other shamanic plants.

In conjunction with ayahuasca, it has the capacity to open up one's consciousness to the visionary realms, and I tried to bear this in mind as I snorted what felt like a jet of battery acid into each nostril, my nasal cartilage on fire.

At last it was time to drink. As the shaman took out two large plastic bottles of thick black liquid from his bag, I watched a bubble of fear rise up in the pit of my stomach, then burst with an almost audible pop. Was I really about to drink of the tree of knowledge, and if so was I strong enough to bear the truths it contained within it? With almost a trace of amusement, I wondered if these might be my last few moments amongst the 'sane' – whoever they were – before I crossed the River Styx, never to return.

The room was dark. I was conscious only of a body on either side of me on a sleeping mat, and directly in front of me, the shaman, hunched over a single candle flame. Each person in turn left their place to stand before him, and as the girl to my right lay down I realised that the time for reflection was past. It was time to step forward.

A shot glass of bitter black liquid. Not as unpleasant as I'd feared, certainly not the revolting poison that many yage accounts seem to note. Tastes of the earth, traces of tree bark and sap. After I'd drunk I accepted a pinch of herbs which I sprinkled over the coals in offering to the spirits. Then I returned to my mat, lay down and waited for what was to come.

Half an hour passed before I felt anything change. Time spent waiting, breathing, listening to the noises around me. I was lying still in the darkness, sometimes sitting back against the wall. Opening my eyes I saw a rapid shimmer of colour pass across my irises. I closed them, feeling my heart beating faster now, my breath quickening.

Again a flash of colour. I closed my eyes and there it was again. Like flecks of multicoloured paint flicked against a screen, which ran down slowly, then disappeared.

On the other side of the room, the shaman began to play a Jew's harp. It gave off a droning noise at a constant pitch, but with overtones that shifted as he moved his mouth, stirring up the room's air.

I was following my breath again. According to the shaman's advice, it was preferable to use the breath as an anchor, a way of keeping grounded in the body, lest the flood of hallucination sweep one away entirely. As the colours began to multiply and gather strength like fireflies, I could see what he meant. By watching the breath stream, one could observe the visions as a witness, rather than let them take control. It was similar, perhaps, to the way Sufis remain entirely present during their whirling, rather than give in to the trance. Although they whirl until their cognitive minds dissolve, their left feet remain firm, maintaining contact with the world.

The colours changed, began to form recognisable patterns.

I was looking at a grid like that on a primitive computer screen: blue squares, lines and crosses. *This is incredible,* I thought lucidly. Then it shifted. The grid tilted to reveal another grid beneath it. The same happened again and beneath the second grid I saw thousands, infinite grids. Which of them was real? Were *any* of them real? On one side of the grid the word 'time' appeared, and on the other axis the word 'space'. Then the whole thing began to dissolve. What was left beyond space and time? Endless worlds, parallel universes, webs of unimaginable complexity. I blinked confusedly, already spinning down through the looking glass.

Putting down the harp, the shaman began to rattle. Made from a gourd or calabash filled with quartz stones, the rattle creates the distinctive music of the shamanic soundscape, and is also one of the most visible tools of the 'witch doctor'. I'd seen rattles many times, usually in anthropological photographs or museums, but not until this moment did I understand them.

Sssh Sssh Sssh came the rattle.

I opened my eyes.

Sssh Sssh Sssh

It was as if something had moved the room, displacing the air. This was not *sound*, so much as a physical presence which brushed through one's consciousness, rustling the very fabric of reality. Sound was no longer a concept but a material fact. Suddenly, the rattle seemed an invention of genius, its true value only realised in the other worlds. Every particle was alive!

Sssh Sssh Sssh

The blue grid of lines stopped moving, then slid apart, like the backdrop of a theatre set dragged away. It was as if my brain was taunting me with one reality, then another, switching them back and forth at lightning speed. I was struck forcefully by the feeling that neither world was more 'real' than the other. Both were films projected against a blank wall. Outside the ayahuasca realms, one of them held firm sway. But here, the ayahuasca world seemed just as valid. It was, in fact, far more precisely detailed than the other, its colour spectrum and soundscapes infinitely richer.

The shaman began to sing. *Icaros* are on one level sacred chants, but on another plaintive cries intended for the ears of jungle spirits. They're believed to have magical properties: the ability to effect energy fields and to heal disease. Lying on my back, my eyes tightly closed, I received the gift of the *icaros* like a life raft. It was like a rope held out in churning waters, and I reached out to hold on to it, allowed it to keep me afloat.

Visions overlaid and replaced each other at a speed beyond understanding. I seemed to be travelling to cyber realms, through fantastical worlds made up of DNA strands and star dust.

At one stage I focused in on a library. On a desk was a book with my name on it and as I recognised that fact the camera pulled upwards to reveal a shelf with a thousand other books on it, then further upwards to reveal a library of several thousand shelves. Upwards again and I was looking down at thousands of libraries, each of them containing infinite numbers of books. This continued until we pulled into clouds, the world below obscured.

Even as the vision passed I felt my heart wrench, and then there was acceptance. Giving up any sense of personal importance was the very first hurdle, and once over it, my own place in the world seemed as irrelevant as a falling leaf in a forest of falling leaves. We were mere atomic particles floating in the void. Nothing that I'd understood to 'matter' had any credence here.

To my right someone began to vomit. Before the ceremony all of us had been given plastic bags and I could hear someone rustling theirs now, retching with a force and energy that was partly hideous, partly liberating. The sound made me suddenly aware of my own body again and I snapped back to following my breath, aware of having been lost in the 'mind' for some time. How much time had passed? Several hours, seconds, days? The concept of time becomes redundant under yage, a fact particularly recalled by those whose experiences have been unpleasant. Trapped in the face of visions one would rather not see, seemingly outside the fabric of time, the experience can seem close to hell.

The next day dawned cold and clear. We got up slowly, sharing our experiences, some euphoric, others more philosophical. For the first few hours my brain was foggy. I moved in a dream to the kitchen, made a cup of mint tea, then went to sit outside on an old dry stone wall, with the rolling Catalonian fields stretching away. Everything about me was silent.

I felt several things. Relief to be intact, firstly. I was here, no more unbalanced than before. I felt good, actually, for having challenged myself to push the boundaries of reality a little further. But there was something else too: a sense of great humility. Of the four or five hours of visions, the one of the library remained. In the world of ego and personality such a vision would have been painful: reductive, somehow, of who I thought I was. But in the ayahuasca world that lesson came to me as a blessing. How liberating not to have to *be* anything! How freeing to realise that *recognition* was irrelevant, that *time* as I had understood it was irrelevant. It was like realising that an onion was not the skin or the individual layers, all of which could be peeled away. It was something beyond all of that, something formless and eternal.

The day passed quietly, in reflection on what had passed, but also with a sense of mental preparation for what was to come when we drank again that evening. Behind my thoughts, the ayahuasca world still flickered on the edges of this one. It loomed, like the memory of Narnia, which, once they had returned, the four Pevensie children began to doubt they had ever visited. Was it mere hallucination? Or, as the shamans believed, a spirit world, a parallel reality to this one, which those bold enough could return from enriched?

By six that evening we were in our places again. The shaman, who had been singing until dawn that morning, appeared as energised and present as before. He sat cross-legged, his dark eyes scanning the room with intensity.

'So we are here once again,' he said, smiling genially. 'And, as those of you who have drunk before will know, the first night is merely a preparation for the one to come.'

Nervous laughter through the room.

'Last night you began to open yourselves to the spirit world,' he continued. 'But tonight we must go further. We must use the knowledge we gathered last night to go deeper, to remain more focused on the breath. For those of you who wish, you may drink a second glass, or even a third. Tonight, we will see the spirits together.'

I drank again: the same faintly musty taste of bark and regeneration. I lay on my back under my sleeping bag, with crackling wood in the grate, aware of the bodies sprawled out on either side of me, each person falling back into the netherworlds of consciousness. In front, the shaman began his rattling again and, as the now familiar colour flashes took hold, I felt the ayahuasca world nudging against this.

This continued for some time, perhaps an hour. For some reason I seemed less inclined to welcome the visions this evening. As soon as they took hold I opened my eyes, or felt around in a panic for the plastic bag in case I needed to vomit. Inwardly, I could feel the pressure of the visions begin to build, like a river in spate pressing against a dam, and I lay on my back and let it fill me, my fists gently closed. When the shaman tapped me gently, I saw another glass in front of me, and I took it, swallowed it in a single gulp, then lay down again.

Before I knew it I was falling back through space, down a rabbit hole with neither beginning nor end, surrounded alternately by colours and darkness. After some time, I made out a white light in the distance. I could see figures moving within it and as I drew closer, I could see a small boy, perhaps ten years old, lying in a hospital bed. He seemed familiar, and the woman peering over his bed also someone I'd seen before. White sheets, an IV, yellow liquid passing from a nose drip.

A moment later I was observing the scene no more, I *was* the scene. The small body on the bed was me, and the woman my mother. Back in 1984, only eight years old, I'd suffered a burst appendix and been rushed to intensive care. It was an experience I'd almost never thought of since it happened. My memories of it were faint at best, yet here I was, with the clinical scents of the hospital room, the tubes and lights, and my mother's face – twenty years younger – peering over me with that fierce protectiveness I knew so well.

As I looked out through the eyes of the child I'd once been, I felt an awareness I could never have had at the time. It was the strangest feeling: to be observing my younger self, and yet also to *be* my younger self again, to feel what I once felt, but with an adult consciousness now sorting through things which I couldn't process at the time.

Fear was what I felt most. I could feel the profound terror of a boy, seriously ill, who didn't really understand what had happened to him. A burning pain in the stomach, throbbing fiercely, combined with a sense of pure helplessness. I was a small animal, alone in the woods, stuck in pure fright. It was absolutely primal.

The vision began to shift again. Moving through the years that followed, like a photograph album blown from page to page at lightning speed, I retained the consciousness of the small boy I'd been, but saw, too, how that feeling of pain and helplessness had never really left me. In everything I'd done since, every decision, interaction and relationship, I'd held on to it, carried the weight of that fear like an unhealed wound festering below the surface.

The pain seemed to be getting worse. It started where my appendix had once been, spread out across my abdomen, up my chest, filling my entire body. I was clutching my side, moaning gently, the pain pulling me under. Was this remembered pain, or pain as I was feeling it now? For a time that could have been minutes or hours I lay there in this limbo, struggling for breath.

Just when I thought I was at my limit, I began to vomit. Vomiting is one of the hardest experiences for the novice of ayahuasca to come to grips with. One of the great social stigmas, it seems to reduce us to the animal realm, causing feelings of embarrassment like almost no other human experience.

But when one is *doing* it, no such awareness exists. Like a dog that's chewed grass then slinks off into the woods to purge itself, I began to retch. I was purging out the pain that had lain dormant in me for more than twenty years. I was purging out childishness and pure fear. In a flash I saw myself in some jungle clearing, surrounded by other young men, engaged in some primal coming of age ritual. I was shrugging off childish things and becoming an adult. I could feel strength pouring down on me, filling me, so that I fought back the urge to let out some primal roar.

Coming to, I felt someone take away the plastic bag in my hands and replace it with a clean one. Something truly malevolent had passed out of me; I could feel it moving away from me in the room like some dark radioactive substance. Now that I'd vomited I could feel myself leaving the ayahuasca realms, coming back into the room where all these different people fought their battles, and yet now I wished to stay. I was filled with bliss, with lightness. Like a man who's carried stones upon his back without realising it, I was free of some terrible burden, feather-light. Everything would be different from here on.

Sleep beckoned. I felt its pull, yearned to fall back into it. But I could hear a voice, a persistent whisper. Opening my eyes I saw Agata standing over me.

'Come,' she said. 'It is time for the sweat lodge. Come with me.'

To one side of the house was a tepee, a conical tent made of canvas stretched over tall sapling poles. Moving slowly, and with my stomach still burning from the ayahuasca, I followed the others through the darkness. Dawn was not yet upon us, and it was absolutely quiet out here; our breath was streaming. Beside the tepee a bonfire roared, and the yellow light warped and shifted under the influence of the drug. Beneath my feet the grass was soft and layered with rime.

I stripped down to my underwear, stepped inside the tent. We sat in two concentric circles, women on one side, men on the other. In the middle of the tent was a hole into which enormous glowing basalt rocks were being carefully placed. I saw the shaman's face as he dropped the glowing stones from a pair of blacksmith's tongs. Suffused with an unearthly glow, his eyes were wild and lit up with ayahuasca, and yet he was also entirely 'here', monitoring each and every person in the room, his consciousness everywhere and nowhere at the same time.

Within minutes the temperature in the sweat or 'medicine' lodge was unbearable. The canvas door was now closed, and about twenty of us were sealed within this small structure. I'd experienced saunas before, and even a sweat lodge of sorts, but this was incomparably hotter. I felt that if the temperature moved merely one degree hotter, my very skin would peel off.

'This heat is medicine,' announced the shaman. 'When you think you can't take any more, surrender. When your mind begins to break, surrender. If you want to cry out, cry out. *Feel* the medicine purifying you.'

He began to sing again, and to the sound of *icaros* I drifted back into the ayahuasca realms, then back into this one, both of them united by a sense of heat that was more than any human could bear. On the other side of the tent a girl wailed and screamed, and then more screams joined hers, screams of pain, screams of surrender. Sweat poured from us in torrents, rivers of sweat, the skin sloughing away.

Next some nettle branches were passed around, and although in a normal situation this might have been the straw that broke the camel's back, I accepted one and used it to rub my skin, the prickling opening up the physical body still further, releasing memories, stored experience, all the unresolved minutiae of life. Some burst into hysterical laughing, from the other side of madness – and I found myself joining in. The laughter of the insane, of those who had passed caring.

More stones were added to the fire. Visions appeared and passed away. Against my back I could feel the canvas of the tepee and for a blissful moment I imagined ripping through the entire tent, breaking my way out to the other side. I could feel the strength of bears welling up in me.

'Surrender,' came the shaman's voice. 'There is only *this* moment.'

Perhaps a half an hour passed. The limits of all of our endurances were passed a hundred times, a thousand. Time lost all meaning, and so it was simply not possible to rationalise this place as a hell realm, some purgatory we were forced to endure. We were simply here, trapped in the moment. Death would have been the most blissful release.

And then at last – dreamlike, ethereal – the door opened. Outside a pale, almost mauve light told me dawn had broken. Very slowly, crawling on hands and knees, we moved towards that ecstatically cool portal, hardly daring to dream of what it might feel like. Ten people were ahead of me, five.

I hardly remember what came next. One minute I was on my hands and knees, drenched in sweat, the next I was lying face down on the grass, sobbing great lungfuls of air. Released from some primordial womb, I felt as new and empty as any six-pound baby.

Opening my eyes, I saw the green fields swathed in mist. Steam was pouring off our bodies, and I simply gave into the moment at last, weeping like a child. I couldn't stop.

Over the weeks that followed this ayahuasca retreat, I seemed to grow into a new lease of life. Something profound had healed in me; I left Barcelona bursting with vitality, several feet taller. Even on a purely physical level, the drug had worked with a potency greater than any holistic detox or vitamin regime imaginable. I felt, at last, as if I had broken through the firmament.

But more than this side effect, a greater shift had taken place within my consciousness. Certain workings of the mind had been revealed, glimpses of another world that still danced beyond the line of sight. I thought again of *soma*, the sacramental drink of the Rig Veda, and of the eleusinian mysteries of ancient Greece. Part of the Demeter cult, these annual initiation ceremonies, which lasted for two millennia, were believed to unite the participant with the gods through the use of a sacred drink, *kykeon*.

How can these plant substances, used in every culture, broaden our fields of perception? Certainly, the notion that drug use is merely an escape is absurd for anyone who has drunk ayahuasca. No one would subject themselves to such a forceful smashing of the ego for the sake of mere distraction. To drink the liquid is to be engaged in a conscious process of discovery and investigation. What is real? What lies beyond? What secrets lie beyond our cognitive horizons that can raise our quality of life, make us better human beings?

For me, the participatory nature of the ayahuasca experience made it life-changing, while most of the other things I'd witnessed were merely interesting, cause for reflection. Ayahuasca took me *into* the spirit world that the oracles knew, it showed me the intricate constructions of ego upon which I'd based my dreams and aspirations. At the beginning of my quest I'd read of Maya, the veil of illusion which the Buddhist and Hindu scriptures say trap human beings in separateness. In a single dose of ayahuasca this was no longer an idea, but a lived reality. There *were* illusory structures keeping us in ignorance. They were the structures our world was built on: a world of short-term pleasure, of celebrity and the need for outside affirmation of who we were.

It seemed I'd come the full circle: from innocence to experience. The true 'enlightenment' – permanent immersion in that world beyond the veil – eluded me yet. But I knew now what it was, and it loomed in my sights at every moment, as the true goal of human existence, the *meaning* I'd been trying to find from the beginning.

Festival of the Flying Monks

Far above us, on the crumbling parapet of Matho monastery, I saw the first of Ladakh's two most powerful oracles stumble drunkenly to the edge. Then the other joined him, prompting a wail of terror from the crowd. The oracles were wearing long black wigs which spilled down their backs, their eyes blindfolded with black cloth. One of them held a sword in his hand and he was slashing the air with it, causing the High Lamas to rush backwards to safety.

I felt my breath draw in. If Norbu's sister had exuded great power, then these oracles were of a different order entirely. It was like looking upon a bear, or some creature that could simply crush one into a pulp. It wasn't their physical appearance, though, that created this impression. It was the power which coursed through them. More than anything I'd seen, these men seemed possessed of a supernatural energy of some kind, and I found myself scarcely able to look upon them, as they ran madly from one end of the parapet to the other, emitting high-pitched shrieking noises, seemingly unafraid of falling. The pink-cheeked little girl next to me buried her face in her mother's skirt.

Khedup had his hand over his mouth. 'See the drawings on their stomachs. This is how they are seeing.'

Peering closer, I saw what he meant. As they veered from the edge of the parapet again, it was possible to make out on the oracles' stomachs elaborately painted drawings, not dissimilar to the ferocious *chom* masks of a Tibetan deity: two white eyes, with brows of orange fire, and between the two, a third eye, the point of spiritual illumination. The rest of the monks' torsos were painted coal-black, so that it indeed seemed that some malevolent face was peering out at us as the monks ran up and down the parapet of the monastery, ranting at the crowd below.

Was it really possible that they were seeing through these painted eyes rather than their own, I wondered. Clearly, *one* wrong footing on that ledge and they would fall to an immediate death on the flagstones below. At one end of the parapet was a gap and I watched, dumbstruck, as one of the oracles merely leaped over it, almost as if he were flying.

'Did you see that!' said Khedup. 'They have nine layers of cloth on their faces, and yet they can jump like that! This is too exciting!'

They disappeared from view for a moment, and I realised I was breathing heavily. What *were* these creatures? It was easy to see why the villagers were so terrified. One could see, occasionally, the monks beneath, struggling to retain control of the spirits. Cynically, I wondered if they *could* actually see through the strips of cloth after all. The alternative – even after all I'd seen – was difficult to contemplate.

'They are coming down!' said Khedup, clutching the stone so tightly his hands were white. 'Here they are!'

In the next moment the oracles burst out into the courtyard below, prompting a wail of panic from the crowd. As one of them sprang forward I could see the sabre glinting in his hand, and a section of the crowd struggled desperately backwards, trampling those not quick enough to move out of the way.

The second oracle joined him now and together they ran up and down, leaping about with effortless bounds, gnashing their teeth and filling the air with their mysterious speech. One of them stuck his tongue out and proceeded to slice the sword along it. The crowd roared! Then the other took up a great vessel full of *chang* – a beer made from fermented barley – and began to drain the entire thing, droplets catching the light as they spilled from the corners of his mouth. It was like watching two lions that had escaped the Colosseum. Everywhere they went, the crowd fell into panic.

Suddenly, as quickly as they had arrived, the oracles disappeared from view again, back through the doors of the *dukhang*, or central hall. I caught a final glimpse of them – a blur of matted hair and wild energy – as a group of monks appeared to usher them away. In their wake the heavy doors of the inner sanctum shut swiftly. We wouldn't see them again today.

Three days earlier I'd flown from Delhi to witness this greatest of the Ladakhi winter festivals. My old friend Norbu had sent me an email suggesting that if I felt what I'd seen during the summer was interesting, then this Matho festival couldn't be missed. 'Oracles will receive the Rong-Tsan Kar-Mar,' he wrote, 'who are amongst the most ancient, powerful deities we have. They meditate in a hidden cave for three months before the day of the festival.'

And so I'd come for one more look at the oracles, still one of the most perplexing things I'd seen on this long journey. Stepping out at Leh airport, I found a serene town frozen in the amber of intense cold. At minus ten, the icicles had formed symmetrical daggers on the low branches of the apricot trees. But the blue light, which I remembered so well from summer, was as clear and magnificent as ever.

Certainly, I was glad I'd come. To visit Ladakh in winter,

witness the majesty of a great religious festival and take in the details of this pristine mountain culture, was an immense privilege. And yet once the oracles had been and gone, I felt no closer to understanding the whole thing than I had before. If anything, this was an even more theatrical – less participatory – experience than my audience with Norbu's sister, six months before.

I put my disappointment to Khedup, the young monk who'd been patiently explaining the day's events to me. What was the point of these oracles, I asked him. After almost two days of waiting, we'd seen them for less than five minutes before they vanished again. Was it mere spectacle, I wondered. Or did they really help the Ladakhi people in some way?

'The goal of all Buddhists,' explained Khedup diplomatically, 'is to remove suffering and become happy. Rong-Tsan Kar-Mar deities help us achieve this. They are able to see things which normal human beings cannot. Inside, just now, they are making a prediction about the year to come. Whether the harvest will be good or bad.'

'It seemed over in a flash,' I said. 'But at least they weren't wearing the red ribbon which would signify bad news.'

Khedup patted me on the back consolingly. 'But you have other means of gathering information, yes,' he said. 'You have all kinds of technologies, the internet. You can even fly across the world to find out your answers.' He grinned. 'These Rong-Tsan Kar-Mar came here for the Ladakhi people, because this place is so wild and cold, with a small population. As the story goes, Dorje Palzang, who founded Matho monastery, brought them with him from eastern Tibet, luring them with sacrificial cakes. In Ladakh the deities settled here, where they can still be called upon for help.'

There was a certain logic to what Khedup said and finally

I accepted the festival for what it was, banishing that need for concrete answers from which, several years into my journey, I was still not entirely free. When the prediction came from the oracles – apparently the harvest would be plentiful that year – the villagers seemed palpably relieved, and in that this highly esoteric tradition displayed an obvious logic.

Looking back over the last few years, I reflected on a range of experiences, all of which had given me some insight into the range of practices by which humans attempt to penetrate the veils of consciousness. Some, like these Buddhist oracles, remained virtually inexplicable. Others, like the meditative and shamanistic practices intended to break down the power of the human ego, seemed more comprehensible, part of our great human struggle for transcendence.

At the great Mela festival, I'd met Ram and his motley brotherhood of *Naga sadhus*. Perpetual wanderers, they were probably camped out in some tranquil forest glade even now, packing themselves another chillum pipe and preparing to meet Shiva once again. Despite the encroaching materialism that was changing the face of India, the *sadhus* remain essentially unchanged from the forest ascetics written of in the Vedic texts. In their quest for *moksha* – total liberation from the wheel of *samsara* – I found them wholly admirable.

Then there was the witch woman – the *sadhvi* who'd read my palm in the old fort. And Mata-ji, the village shaman whose mediation between the human and divine realms allowed her to berate the gods themselves. In times of global fanaticism, it seemed entirely to India's credit that such a range of religious traditions should be thriving side by side. A great hero of mine, the Italian journalist and writer Tiziano Terzani, spent his last years in India, and concluded that India represents 'our last hope for a truly spiritual society on earth'.

This theory may be tested severely as the world's largest democracy meets the social and ecological challenges of the twenty-first century, but I feel hopeful. The sacred – even according to its most non-theistic definition – is everywhere in the former lands of Hindustan.

Facing equal challenges – as the mullahs struggle to retain power over the hearts and minds of men – will be Turkey, midway between Europe and the East in so many ways. The worldwide resurgence of interest in Sufism, however, may eventually pressure the government into allowing the dervishes to whirl again and its people to find God in whatever way they wish. And as Rumi's poems appear in new translations, reaching a wider audience across the globe, his unique message may help more and more to see the unity that lies behind all traditions: the still voice that lies at the centre of the turning world.

Finally, my experience of drinking ayahuasca – ancient soul medicine of the shamans – has left a strange imprint on my consciousness, the ramifications of which are still unfolding day by day. As a plant with a genuine power to benefit humanity, it remains the most potent I've discovered, although I accept that the experience may not be for everyone. After a journey witnessing so many others find their own way through the veil, it was simply overwhelming to break through myself at last, as if I'd finally begun to understand where my search was leading after all.

That veil, ultimately, is human consciousness itself, our last frontier. While the human mind is undoubtedly capable of great ingenuity and invention, it is also a beast that – with increasing frequency if one believes the statistics – seems to be turning upon its handlers. With the World Health Organisation predicting that depression will be society's worst problem by 2020, the way we think and relate to the world around us is clearly a major concern. Evidently, the proper functioning of the human mind also affects a far wider sphere than merely ourselves. In our inability to think beyond personal gain, we may have destroyed the biosphere which supports our own existence.

All of which raises significant questions about the human species at this point in our evolution. If the human being is the greatest example of Darwin's evolutionary chain, then we are about to be put to the ultimate test: can we change our habits fast enough to survive? Evidently, some sort of dynamic shift will be necessary, and not merely one of patterns of consumption, if humanity is to flourish into the twenty-second century.

In the hopes of many, it will be science that ushers in this new era of peaceful and harmonious existence with the earth: cleaner, more efficient fuels; the end of disease; the means to grow crops on less or perhaps no land at all. In the hopes of the scientists, greater knowledge of the physical world will lessen the human struggle, thereby promoting peaceful coexistence and some progressive development towards an ordered world.

But another possibility also exists, an idea that sees the shift happening 'internally', *within* human consciousness itself. By this reckoning it is the mystics, and the great traditions they uphold, which yield the possibility to save us from ourselves. According to this school of thought, some of the religions have been attempting just this for thousands of years: offering systematic techniques for moving beyond ego-based thought patterns, for disarming the 'self' which entices us towards such self-destructive behaviour. Far from being some impenetrable Oriental sage, the Buddha was merely the quintessential student of the human mind. 'Are you a god?' asked several men to him, shortly after his enlightenment. 'No,' replied the Buddha. 'I am awake.'

If there is a drawback, however, to the paths laid out by the Buddha and others, it is that they are immensely difficult. Conquering the ego is an almighty feat and, in this, the notion that all of us, somehow, will become enlightened in time to save the planet seems unlikely. During my journey, however, one idea began to cross my radar, overheard again and again in backpacker cafés, in ashrams and yoga *shalas*, and even once on the Piccadilly line as I travelled to King's Cross. In alternative circles, the year 2012 is widely considered to be a year of great significance: the ancient Mayans, it seems, whose lunar calendar demonstrated exceptional accuracy, believed it would mark the end of a 26,000 year cycle, after which humanity would cross the threshold of a new and more harmonious age.

Even after some of the things I'd experienced, the idea struck me as far-fetched. The fin-de-siècle doomsday merchants who'd been proven wrong in 2000 now had a new date to circle in their calendars, a point of change that eradicated the need for any personal responsibility. And yet, simultaneously, I couldn't quite discount it. Quite evidently, humanity is at a turning point. Without a marked shift of some kind, we will simply destroy the biospheric support system that gives us succour and follow the other species to extinction. Our relentless need to 'consume' will usher in our own downfall. Like the tribes on Easter Island who, in their insatiable drive to build new idols, chopped down the trees which sustained them, we will be the victims of our own folly.

The 2012 idea, therefore, represents a much-needed ray of hope, and for that reason alone it's worth considering. As much as humanity has made a mess of the planet, signs of a new awakening are everywhere. Earth-centred religions are on the rise, and the resurgence of interest in the mystical suggests that many of us, collectively, are feeling our way towards new ways of living. Yoga *shalas* occupy key positions on high streets, natural farming methods are returning to the mainstream and Oprah Winfrey, of all people, has championed the teachings of modern mystic Eckhart Tolle, making him a household name in the United States.

Could it be then that 2012 is already with us? If the ancients *were* in touch with some divinatory system that allowed them to predict grand planetary shifts in the future, perhaps they saw a point – *this* point – at which humanity would *have* to change if it were to survive. Far more likely than some sudden cosmic flash of light, they foresaw an era in which values would begin to shift, at which we would finally begin to practise habits of behaviour which benefit the many, rather than the few.

2012, then, is possibly already under way. Now back in London during one of the worst economic crises in living memory, I see the evidence daily. Banks are folding, house prices falling, unemployment at stratospheric levels. One half of society, it seems, is anxiously waiting for things to return to 'normal', so we can all carry on as happily as we did before. But another portion of society, I believe, is noticing the fork in the road where history has landed us. To take this road less travelled will entail a complete re-evaluation of the goals our culture encourages us to strive for. It will entail a conscious prioritising of the 'inner' rather than the 'outer' in our lives. It will entail immersing ourselves in the sacred again.

As for my own journey, well, it continues day by day. And perhaps, at last, that old restlessness is setting down. My central focus these days is on living in the present, and on the days when I manage to do that the numinous looms closely, glinting with the unknowable wonder of things. More and more I'm trying to encourage those activities in my life which *allow* for this state of being, and in that I've come back to beekeeping, and I find a new understanding of the stillness I once sensed in that ancient art.

Walking past a pet shop not long ago, I realised there was one final piece of the jigsaw still missing. I noticed two green parakeets through the glass, and I saw them trapped within a tiny cage, their once iridescent plumage now dulled through long confinement. Smiling to myself, I remembered how the Ladakhi oracle had once instructed me to find two such birds and free them. How could I have forgotten? Or perhaps, through some strange prescience, it was exactly these birds she had spoken of. Parakeets were now surviving happily in the English climate, I'd recently read, as one small benefit of global warming.

I went inside, and without a second thought, handed over the money for the two birds and their small metal cage. Then I walked to the nearest park, my heart pounding a little, and opened the tiny clasp that kept the door fastened. I looked about me, at this small well-tended square in north London, and for a moment felt myself in Ladakh again, Victorian houses replaced by jagged mountains.

The two birds peered through the open door. For a second they hesitated, not quite believing how far the horizon could extend. A second later, in a green blur of feathers, they were bounding upwards into the sky.

Further Reading

Abrams, David. *The Spell of the Sensuous: Perception and Language in a More-Than-Human-World.* Pantheon Books, 1996.

Brunton, Paul. *A Search in Secret India.* Weiser Books, 1985.

Bucke, Richard Maurice. *Cosmic Consciousness: a Study in the Evolution of the Human Mind.* Book Jungle, 2007.

Cohen, S. S. *Guru Ramana: Memories and Notes.* Sri Ramanasramam Press, 2006.

Crick, Francis. *The Astonishing Hypothesis: the Scientific Search for the Soul.* Charles Scribner's Sons, 1994.

Dawkins, Richard. *The God Delusion.* Houghton Mifflin Harcourt, 2006.

Devereux, Paul. *The Long Trip: the Prehistory of Psychedelia.* Penguin, 1997.

Easterbrook, Greg. *A Moment on the Earth: the Coming Age of Environmental Optimism.* Viking, 1995.

Eliade, Mircea. *Shamanism: Archaic Techniques of Ecstasy.* Princeton University Press, 2004.

Friedlander, Shems. *Rumi and the Whirling Dervishes.* Parabola Books, 2003.

Gebser, Jean. *The Ever Present Origin.* Ohio University Press, 1985.

Housden, Roger. *Travels Through Sacred India.* Thorsons, 1996.

James, William. *The Varieties of Religious Experience: a Study in Human Nature*. Modern Library, 1994.

Kakar, Sudhir. *Shamans, Mystics and Doctors: a Psychological Inquiry into India and its Healing Traditions*. University of Chicago Press, 1991.

Kipling, Rudyard. *Plain Tales from the Hills*. Penguin, 1991.

Kraepelin, Emile. *Readings in Cultural Psychiatry*. Continuum, 2000.

Lachman, Gary and Wilson, Colin. *A Secret History of Consciousness*. Lindisfarne Press, 2003.

Leavitt, John. *Poetry and Prophecy: the Anthropology of Inspiration*. University of Michigan Press, 1997.

McKenna, Terence. *Food of the Gods: the Search for the Original Tree of Knowledge*. Bantam, 1993.

Maugham, W. Somerset. *The Razor's Edge*. Vintage, 2003.

Mehra, Jagdish. *Albert Einstein's Relations with Belgium: Including the Correspondence between Einstein and Queen Elisabeth of the Belgians, 1929 to 1955*. 1988.

Narby, Jeremy and Francis Huxley, eds. *Shamans through Time: 500 Years on the Path to Knowledge*. Tarcher, 2004.

Nebesky-Wojkowitz, René de. *Oracles and Demons of Tibet: the Cult and Iconography of the Tibetan Protective*. Oriental Book Store, 1990.

O'Brien, John Maxwell. *Alexander the Great: the Invisible Enemy*. Routledge, 1992.

O'Flaherty, W. D. 'The Post-Vedic History of the Soma Plant', in Robert Gordon Wasson, ed. *Soma: Divine Mushroom of Immortality*. 1968.

Oliver, Mary. 'Cold Poem', *American Primitive*. Little, Brown and Co., 1983.

de Purucker, G. *Fountain Source of Occultism*. Theosophical University Press, 1974.

Rumi, Mavlana Jalal-al-Din. *The Book of Love: Poems of Ecstasy and Longing*, translated Coleman Barks. HarperCollins, 2005.

Rumi, Mavlana Jalal-al-Din. *The Essential Rumi*, translated Coleman Barks. HarperCollins, 2009.

Russell, Jeffrey Burton and Douglas W. Lumsden. *A History of Medieval Christianity: Prophecy and Order*. Peter Lang, 2000.

Shah, Idries. *The Way of the Sufi*. Penguin, 1991.

Singh, Khushwant. *Delhi: a Novel*. Penguin, 2000.

Tagore, Rabindranath. *On the Edges of Time*. Greenwood Press, 1978.

Terzani, Tiziano. *Un altro giro di giostra*. Longanesi, 2004.

Twain, Mark. *Following the Equator*. Dover Publications, 1989.

Wilbert, Johannes. *Tobacco and Shamanism in South America*. Yale University Press, 1993.

Wilson, Colin. *Mysteries*. Hodder and Stoughton, 1980.

Acknowledgements

Many thanks to Peter Straus and Jennifer Hewson at RCW. To Helen Garnons Williams and Erica Jarnes at Bloomsbury for their brilliant editing and support. To Rosemary Davidson for picking up on the idea in the first place. To the Arts Council and the Royal Society of Literature for their invaluable funding. To the numerous kind people who helped me in India, Turkey and South America: Phil and Juliet at the incomparable Yoga Magic, my home away from home; Yogi Ajay Menon and family in Varanasi; all at the Oriental Guesthouse in Ladakh; Katie Silcox; Simon Hayes of Senderos and Kate Rupal; Prabir Ghosh and Sumitra in Calcutta; Dr Mahmud Erol Kilic; and many others . . . In the UK to my family for their unflagging patience and support, to George Festing likewise. A humble Namaste and a big hug to my wife Lucy for everything else and beyond.

A NOTE ON THE TYPE

The text of this book is set in Bembo. This type was first used in 1495 by the Venetian printer Aldus Manutius for Cardinal Bembo's *De Aetna*, and was cut for Manutius by Francesco Griffo. It was one of the types used by Claude Garamond (1480–1561) as a model for his Romain de L'Université, and so it was the forerunner of what became standard European type for the following two centuries. Its modern form follows the original types and was designed for Monotype in 1929.